D&AD50

50 YEARS OF EXCELLENCE IN DESIGN AND ADVERTISING AND THE PEOPLE THAT MADE IT HAPPEN

TASCHEN

Contents

Page 72

Page 78

Page 84

Page 90

Page 96

Page 132

Page 138

Page 144

Page 150

Page 156

Page 192

Page 198

Page 204

Page 210

Page 216

Page 252

Page 258

Page 264

Page 270

Page 276

Page 312

Page 318

Page 324

Page 330

Page 336

Preface

Anthony Simonds-Gooding

This fascinating book takes the reader through the first 50 years of D&AD, as seen through the eyes of each year's President and other luminaries.

For five decades, D&AD has relentlessly championed enduring ideas, wonderfully expressed – always charming, intelligent and witty, always showing respect to the consumer, building empathy and bringing a smile to the face.

It has always been determined to stand out from the crowd, unlike all those who seem to want to sound and look just like everyone else. Such people seek "creativity with precedence". In other words, they are comfortable only if someone else has done it already. This approach is often described as "low risk", while D&AD's unique approaches are described as "high risk". Bizarre.

My hope for the next decade is that D&AD's beliefs and values take an increasing hold in the marketplace.

Businessmen will begin to see more readily that any product advantages they enjoy from the low-risk approach are short-lived, and that only one product can be the cheapest (and often profitless). The most sustainable competitive advantage for a brand is its deep-rooted empathy with the consumer. This is something that cannot be easily or quickly copied.

I feel confident that if any of the contributors to this book had been let loose on a client's business, then they would have been delighted.

The icing on D&AD's cake is that it is a registered charity, which reinvests its money – some millions of pounds over the years – into student education. This ensures that the talent tank remains topped up, so that following generations can continue to fly the flag of creative excellence.

Enjoy the read. Viva D&AD!

Vorwort

Anthony Simonds-Gooding

Lassen Sie sich von diesem faszinierenden Buch durch die ersten 50 Jahre des D&AD geleiten. Betrachten Sie diesen Zeitraum aus Perspektive der Präsidenten der jeweiligen Jahre und anderer Koryphäen.

Seit fünf Jahrzehnten setzt sich D&AD beharrlich für bleibende, wunderschön umgesetzte Ideen ein – die stets charmant, intelligent und witzig sind, stets respektvoll gegenüber dem Konsumenten, für Empathie sorgen und ein Lächeln ins Gesicht zaubern.

Der D&AD war immer fest entschlossen, sich von der Masse abzuheben – nicht so wie der Rest, der einfach nur aussehen und klingen will wie alle anderen auch. Solche Leute trachten nach einer „Kreativität mit Vorrangregeln". Anders gesagt fühlen sie sich nur dann wohl, wenn bereits ein anderer die Sache vor ihnen gemacht hat. Häufig nennt man diesen Ansatz „risikoarm", während die einzigartigen Ansätze des D&AD als „hoch riskant" beschrieben werden. Bizarr.

Meine Hoffnung für das nächste Jahrzehnt ist, dass sich die Überzeugungen und Werte des D&AD in steigendem Maße auf dem Markt durchsetzen werden. Geschäftsleute werden immer mehr erkennen, dass alle mit diesem Ansatz des geringen Risikos erzielten Produktvorteile nur kurzlebig sind und dass nur ein Produkt das billigste sein kann (und oft genug keinen Profit bringt). Der wahrhaft nachhaltige Wettbewerbsvorteil einer Marke ist die tief verwurzelte Empathie des Konsumenten. So etwas kann man nicht mal eben auf die Schnelle kopieren.

Ich bin überzeugt, wenn man irgendeinen Beiträger aus diesem Buch auf einen solchen Klienten losgelassen hätte – er wäre begeistert gewesen!

Das Sahnehäubchen bei D&AD ist, dass es sich um eine eingetragene Wohltätigkeitsorganisation handelt, die ihre Einnahmen wiederum in die Ausbildung investiert – und im Laufe der Jahre sind mittlerweile mehrere Millionen britische Pfund ausgeschüttet worden. So bleibt sichergestellt, dass die Talentreserven stets gefüllt sind, damit auch spätere Generationen die Fahne kreativer Höchstleistungen hochhalten können.

Genießen Sie die Lektüre! Viva D&AD!

Préface

Anthony Simonds-Gooding

Ce live fascinant emmène le lecteur à la découverte des 50 premières années de D&AD, vues à travers les yeux du président de chaque année, et d'autres illustres personnalités.

Pendant cinq décennies, D&AD n'a jamais cessé de défendre des idées qui ont depuis pris racine, en les exprimant toujours avec charme, intelligence et humour, dans le respect du consommateur, dans un esprit d'empathie et avec l'envie de faire sourire.

D&AD a toujours voulu se démarquer de la foule, contrairement à ceux qui semblent vouloir ressembler à tout le monde. Ces derniers sont adeptes de la créativité qui a déjà des précédents. C'est-à-dire qu'ils ne se sentent à l'aise que si quelqu'un d'autre à déjà fait ce qu'ils font. Cette approche est souvent considérée comme comportant un «faible risque», alors que les approches uniques de D&AD sont accusées d'être à «haut risque». Comme c'est étrange.

Pour la prochaine décennie, j'espère que les convictions et les valeurs de D&AD feront encore plus de chemin. Les hommes d'affaires commenceront à se rendre compte que tous les avantages qu'ils obtiennent grâce à cette approche à faible risque ne fonctionnent que sur le court terme, et qu'il n'y a qu'un seul produit qui puisse être le moins cher (et souvent aussi, le moins rentable). Pour une marque, l'avantage concurrentiel le plus durable est une empathie profonde avec le consommateur. Ce n'est pas quelque chose que l'on peut copier facilement ou rapidement.

Je suis certain que si n'importe lequel des créatifs qui apparaissent dans cet ouvrage avait reçu carte blanche sur le projet d'un client, ce client aurait été ravi du résultat.

La cerise sur le gâteau de D&AD, c'est qu'il s'agit d'une organisation à but non lucratif, qui réinvestit son argent (plusieurs millions de livres sterling au cours des années) dans l'éducation des étudiants. Cela garantit que les réserves de talent restent toujours pleines, afin que les générations suivantes puissent continuer à défendre les couleurs de l'excellence créative.

Bonne lecture. Vive D&AD !

Introduction

Tim Lindsay

CEO of D&AD (2011–present)

I was fortunate enough to join D&AD at a great time: the run-up to our 50th anniversary. I've always loved our organisation, because it has glamour and charisma. Part of that comes of course from D&AD's origins in the creative, social and cultural revolution of the early 60s; from those brave, young, iconoclastic individuals who, fed up with the constrictions of the establishment, started their own association to showcase their work and stimulate excellence in their field.

With this book, we wanted to create something that captured the important moments, celebrated the important work and added up to a joyful history of the first 50 years of D&AD.

Of course, we continue to look forward, and have exciting plans to make D&AD an even greater force for creative excellence and education in the world. Sometimes, however, it's important to also look back – to remember who we were and why, and to make sure that we live up to the legacy.

Tim O'Kennedy

CEO of D&AD (2009–2011)

I joined D&AD in the summer of 2009. Anthony Simonds-Gooding, at that time Chairman, asked me, "Tim, why do you want to do this?", as if to imply that I would be slightly mad to do so. I heard myself say, "Because it's D&AD," and that really was the truth. Throughout my career, the Pencil has been held by all around me as an acknowledgement of brilliance like no other.

In 2009, it wasn't all rosy: the recession had bitten. Revenues were falling, and there was a steady bass-beat of dissent. Had we become too "international"? Had we fallen out of love with design? Were we really serious about education?

The thing that struck me hardest when I joined was the lack of swagger: that vital sense that we were special, that the world needed us and that if we acted with integrity, intelligence and confidence, the world would come with us. Perhaps more than anything else, that sense of confidence was what I tried to instil.

I had amazing experiences in my brief time there, such as singlehandedly pitching to 22 different design and advertising agencies in São Paulo in just four and a half days. (I boarded the aircraft home on all fours.)

Having an unnamed Creative Director of a major western agency in Beijing actually rip a Black Pencil from my fingers so that he could have his photo taken with it.

Presenting, with the hilarious Sanky, the 2011 Awards night – the first time we had declined to use a professional, and the first time we did the Student and Professional Awards together. I will never forget the expressions on the faces of those creative students who won Pencils.

It was also enjoyable to hand over a record-equalling two Black Pencils to my erstwhile colleagues at Wieden+Kennedy for their astonishing work on Old Spice.

The thing that will always continue to amaze me, however, is the extent of D&AD's influence around the world, considering its actual size. It is a testament to the original idea, to be sure, but also to the hard work of those 40 or so very dedicated individuals whom I had the pleasure of working with.

David Kester

CEO of D&AD (1993–2003)

I was appointed in 1993 aged 28, a mere stripling. So many things happened over my decade in the role, but here is a selection of the lesser-known headlines:

Giant Yellow Pencil Drops From Sky and Destroys Café Royal. The year was 1994, and we led D&AD out of the Grosvenor and on to a sit-down ceremony at the Odeon, Leicester Square, to be followed by a party at the Café Royal. All did not go to plan. It poured with rain. The back-up plan – an army of students lining the route with yellow umbrellas – vanished into McDonald's. When guests arrived at the Café Royal, the party concept of a giant Pencil dropping from outer space was mistaken for a real incident.

Capitalism Goes on Trial in Home of British Synod. In 2001 we staged a conference called 'SuperHumanism'. The backdrop was the explosion of the internet and the anti-capitalism riots, while the event itself came on the eve of the Enron scandal. We gathered 500 industry leaders at Church House, Westminster; the star attraction was a standoff between top Nike adman Dan Wieden and 'No Logo' author Naomi Klein. Everyone expected an all-American bust-up, but in British style they both agreed to disagree.

Tony Kaye Steals D&AD Show at Saatchi Gallery. The year was 1995, and we staged the D&AD exhibition in the Saatchi Gallery. Billy Mawhinney came up with a cracking title, 'The Cream of British Design & Advertising', and gave us a Damien Hirst cow in a tank of Boddingtons as the poster. Hirst's dealer, Jay Jopling, threatened court action. Then Tony Kaye, who always has beef with the art world, paid two actors to occupy the car park and improvise the infamous incident between Hugh Grant and Divine. He also paid a homeless man to sit in the gallery as a work of art. There was a lot of media coverage but not quite in the way we had in mind.

Sacrilegious Annual Causes D&AD Walk-out. Graham Fink caused trouble with his idea for the Annual to be a giant bible with a cross made of Pencils on the front. However, when he discovered that the D&AD Awards Director was a devout Christian and might resign, Graham replaced it with the Tony Kaye cover.

Designer Sleeps Through Judging. Peter Souter was President in 2002, when we decided to do all the judging in Brighton. All the greats were there, from John Hegarty to Jarvis Cocker: 200 in total. Well, 199 to be precise. For one famous US typographer, it was all too much. Despite the Awards Director repeatedly banging on his hotel door, he snoozed his way through the judging.

I am delighted to have contributed towards 20 per cent of D&AD's half-century.

Einleitung

Tim Lindsay

CEO des D&AD (2011 bis heute)

Ich hatte das ganz große Glück, in einer spannenden Phase zum D&AD zu kommen: während der Vorbereitungen auf unser 50-jähriges Jubiläum. Schon immer habe ich unsere Organisation wegen ihres Glamours und Charismas geliebt. Ein Teil davon stammt natürlich aus den Wurzeln des D&AD in der kreativen, sozialen und kulturellen Revolution der frühen 60er-Jahre – von jenen mutigen, jungen, bilderstürmerischen Menschen, die es satt hatten, vom Establishment eingeschränkt zu werden, und darum eine eigene Vereinigung gründeten. Dort wollten sie ihre Werke publik machen und für exzellente Arbeit in dieser Branche sorgen.

Mit diesem Buch möchten wir die bedeutendsten Momente festhalten, die wichtigen und besonderen Werke feiern und die erfreuliche Geschichte der ersten 50 Jahre des D&AD zusammentragen.

Natürlich richten wir weiterhin unseren Blick nach vorne und hegen spannende Pläne, um D&AD in der ganzen Welt zu einer noch mächtigeren Kraft für kreative Höchstleistungen und Fortbildung zu machen. Doch manchmal ist es auch wichtig, Rückschau zu halten – sich zu erinnern, wer wir sind und woher wir kommen, und darauf zu achten, dass wir uns unseres Erbes auch würdig erweisen.

Tim O'Kennedy

CEO des D&AD (2009 bis 2011)

Im Sommer des Jahres 2009 kam ich zum D&AD. Damals hatte Anthony Simonds-Gooding den Vorsitz und er fragte mich: „Tim, warum willst du dir das antun?" Es hörte sich an, als müsse ich wohl ein bisschen verrückt sein, mir so etwas vorzunehmen. Ich gab zurück: „Weil's der D&AD ist." Und das war wirklich die ganze Wahrheit. Seit Anfang meiner Karriere hielten alle in meiner Umgebung den Pencil als einzigartige Bestätigung für Brillanz hoch.

2009 sah es insgesamt nicht so rosig aus: Die Rezession hatte voll zugeschlagen. Der Umsatz sank und es gab einen konstanten Unterton der Unstimmigkeiten. Waren wir zu „international" geworden? Hatten wir die Liebe zum Design verloren? Nahmen wir die Ausbildung wirklich ernst?

Was mich am härtesten traf, als ich zum D&AD kam, war der Mangel an Großspurigkeit: jenes vitale Gefühl, dass wir etwas Besonderes sind und dass die Welt uns braucht. Wenn wir nur integer, intelligent und selbstbewusst handelten, dann würde uns die Welt schon folgen. Vielleicht war es mehr als alles andere gerade dieses Selbstbewusstsein, das ich einzuträufeln versuchte.

In meiner kurzen Zeit dort machte ich erstaunliche Erfahrungen, etwa als ich in São Paulo im Alleingang in nur viereinhalb Tagen die Pitches von 22 verschiedenen Design- und Werbeagenturen abwickelte. (Ins Flugzeug nach Hause konnte ich nur noch kriechen.)

Oder als mir in Beijing ein ungenannter Creative Director einer großen westlichen Agentur tatsächlich den Black Pencil aus den Händen riss, damit er sich damit fotografieren lassen konnte.

Oder wie ich 2011 mit dem unvergleichlich komischen Sanky die Awards präsentierte – das war das erste Mal, dass wir uns keinen Profi genommen hatten, und das erste Mal, dass die Verleihung der Student Awards und der Professional Awards gemeinsam stattfand. Ich werde niemals die Gesichter der jungen kreativen Studierenden vergessen, als sie ihre Pencils gewannen.

Es war mir auch ein Hochgenuss, meinen ehemaligen Kollegen von Wieden+Kennedy zwei Black Pencils für ihre hervorragende und erstaunliche Arbeit an Old Spice zu überreichen – das war rekordverdächtig.

Allerdings bin ich auch immer wieder sehr überrascht, in welchem Ausmaß der D&AD in der ganzen Welt Einfluss hat, wenn man dessen tatsächliche Größe berücksichtigt. Damit wird zum einen die ursprüngliche Idee bekräftigt, aber zum anderen auch die harte Arbeit der etwa 40 Personen gewürdigt, die sich intensiv engagierten und mit denen ich die Freude hatte, zusammenarbeiten zu dürfen.

David Kester

CEO des D&AD (1993 bis 2003)

Ernannt wurde ich 1993, gerade mal 28 Jahre alt und kaum mehr als ein Bürschchen. Während meiner Dekade in dieser Rolle geschahen so viele Dinge, und ein paar der weniger bekannten Schlagzeilen möchte ich hier in einer kleinen Auswahl vorstellen:

Gigantischer Yellow Pencil fällt vom Himmel und zerstört das Café Royal. Im Jahre 1994 hielten wir die Zeremonie des D&AD nicht im Grosvenor House ab, sondern verlegten sie auf die Sitzplätze des Odeon-Kinos am Leicester Square, und anschließend sollte im Café Royal Party sein. Nicht alles verlief nach Plan: Es schüttete wie aus Eimern. Unser Plan B – eine Armee Studenten, die die Route mit gelben Regenschirmen säumen sollten – verschwand bei McDonald's. Als die Gäste am Café Royal eintrafen, hielt man unser Partykonzept eines riesigen Pencils, der aus dem Weltall zur Erde herabstürzt, für einen realen Zwischenfall.

Kapitalismus steht im Haus der britischen Synode vor Gericht. 2001 hielten wir eine Konferenz zum Thema „Superhumanismus" ab. Hintergrund waren die explosive Entwicklung des Internets sowie antikapitalistische Unruhen, und während das Event stattfand, zeichnete sich der Enron-Skandal ab. Wir beriefen 500 Branchenführer ins Church House von Westminster. Die Hauptattraktion war das Unentschieden zwischen Dan Wieden, dem Top-Werbemann von Nike, und der „No Logo"-Autorin Naomi Klein. Alle erwarteten nach amerikanischer Art ein totales Zerwürfnis, aber sehr britisch kamen beide überein, nicht übereinkommen zu können.

Tony Kaye stiehlt dem D&AD in der Saatchi Gallery die Show. Es war das Jahr 1995, und wir richteten die D&AD-Ausstellung in der Saatchi Gallery aus.

Billy Mawhinney ließ sich den knackigen Titel „The Cream of British Design & Advertising" einfallen und stellte uns eine Kuh von Damien Hirst in einem Tank voller Boddingtons-Bier als Plakat vor. Jay Jopling, der Kunsthändler von Hirst, drohte gerichtliche Schritte an. Dann heuerte Tony Kaye, der sich liebend gern mit der Kunstwelt anlegt, zwei Schauspieler an, die auf dem Parkplatz den berühmten Zwischenfall mit Hugh Grant und Divine nachstellen sollten. Er bezahlte auch einen Obdachlosen dafür, sich als Kunstwerk in die Galerie zu setzen. Das brachte großes Medienecho, war aber nicht ganz das, was wir uns vorgestellt hatten.

Lästerliches Annual sorgt für Eklat beim D&AD. Graham Fink wollte das Cover des D&AD-Annuals als riesige Bibel mit einem Kreuz aus Pencils gestalten und sorgte mit seiner Idee mächtig für Ärger. Jedenfalls, als er merkte, dass die Direktorin der D&AD-Awards überzeugte Christin war und mit Rücktritt drohte, ersetzte er es durch ein Cover von Tony Kaye.

Designer verschläft Jurysitzung. Peter Souter war 2002 Präsident, als wir beschlossen, alle Beratungen der Jury in Brighton abzuhalten. All die großen Koryphäen waren da – von John Hegarty bis Jarvis Cocker: 200 insgesamt. Tja, genauer gesagt nur 199. Für einen berühmten Typografen aus den USA war es einfach zu viel. Obwohl der Awards Director wiederholt an seine Hoteltür wummerte, verschlief er die gesamte Jurysitzung.

Ich bin sehr erfreut, 20 Prozent zum halben Jahrhundert des D&AD beigetragen zu haben.

Introduction

Tim Lindsay

Directeur général de D&AD (depuis 2011)

J'ai eu la chance de rejoindre D&AD à un moment très particulier: la période qui a mené à notre 50e anniversaire. J'ai toujours aimé cette organisation, car elle allie glamour et charisme. Bien sûr, une partie de cela vient des origines de D&AD dans la révolution créative, sociale et culturelle du début des années 1960; de jeunes iconoclastes courageux qui, fatigués par l'étroitesse de l'establishment, ont créé leur propre association pour présenter leur travail à leur manière et stimuler l'excellence dans le secteur.

Avec ce livre, nous voulions capturer les moments importants, souligner l'envergure du travail réalisé, et récapituler dans la bonne humeur les 50 premières années de D&AD.

Bien évidemment, nous continuons à regarder vers l'avenir, et nous avons des projets très stimulants pour faire de D&AD un moteur encore plus puissant de l'excellence dans la créativité et l'éducation dans le monde entier. Mais il est parfois bon de regarder aussi vers le passé, pour se souvenir de qui nous étions et de ce qui nous a motivés, afin de veiller à ce que nous soyons à la hauteur de notre héritage.

Tim O'Kennedy

Directeur général de D&AD (2009–2011)

J'ai rejoint D&AD durant l'été 2009. Anthony Simonds-Gooding, président à l'époque, m'a demandé: «Tim, pourquoi veux-tu faire ça?», comme s'il voulait dire que j'étais un peu fou de m'embarquer là-dedans. Je me suis entendu répondre: «Parce que c'est D&AD», et c'était la vérité. Tout au long de ma carrière, j'ai vu autour de moi des gens porter le Pencil comme la reconnaissance d'une excellence sans pareil.

En 2009, tout n'était pas rose: la récession avait attaqué. Les recettes étaient en chute libre, et on entendait le bourdonnement constant de la dissidence. Étions-nous devenus trop «internationaux»? Avions-nous perdu notre amour du design? Étions-nous vraiment engagés dans l'éducation?

Ce qui m'a frappé le plus durement lorsque je suis arrivé, c'était le manque d'assurance: ce sentiment profond que nous représentions quelque chose de spécial, que le monde avait besoin de nous et que si nous agissions avec intégrité, intelligence et confiance, le monde viendrait à nous. Plus que toute autre chose, c'est sans doute ce sentiment d'assurance que j'ai essayé d'insuffler.

J'ai vécu des expériences incroyables pendant la courte période que j'ai passée ici, par exemple lorsque j'ai présenté nos projets à 22 agences de design et de publicité de São Paulo en seulement quatre jours et demi (lorsque je suis monté dans l'avion du retour, j'étais à genoux).

Ou encore lorsqu'un directeur de la création que je ne nommerai pas, qui travaillait dans une grande agence occidentale à Beijing, m'a littéralement arraché un Black Pencil des mains pour se faire prendre en photo avec.

J'ai présenté, avec l'inénarrable Sanky, la soirée de remise des prix de 2011. C'était la première fois que nous avions décidé de nous passer des services d'un professionnel, et la première fois que nous avons remis les prix des étudiants en même temps que les prix des professionnels. Je n'oublierai jamais les expressions sur les visages des étudiants lauréats.

J'ai aussi eu le plaisir de remettre deux Black Pencils (un record) à mes anciens collègues de Wieden+Kennedy pour l'extraordinaire campagne Old Spice.

Mais ce qui m'étonnera toujours, c'est l'étendue de l'influence de D&AD dans le monde, si l'on tient compte de la taille de l'organisation. C'est la preuve de l'efficacité de l'idée d'origine, mais aussi du travail acharné de la quarantaine de personnes dévouées avec lesquelles j'ai eu le plaisir de travailler.

David Kester

Directeur général de D&AD (1993–2003)

J'ai été nommé à ce poste en 1998, à l'âge de 28 ans, alors que je n'étais qu'un jeune gringalet. La décennie que j'y ai passée a été constellée d'événements, mais voici une sélection des gros titres que l'on ne connaît pas forcément :

Un Yellow Pencil géant tombe du ciel et détruit le Café Royal. En 1994, nous avions décidé de faire sortir D&AD du Grosvenor et d'organiser une cérémonie devant un public assis à l'Odeon de Leicester Square, suivie d'une soirée au Café Royal. Les péripéties se sont accumulées. Il a plu des trombes d'eau. Le plan de secours – une armée d'étudiants équipés de parapluies jaunes le long du chemin – avait disparu dans un McDonald's. Lorsque les invités sont arrivés au Café Royal, l'attraction de la soirée, un Pencil géant tombant de l'espace, leur a fait une peur bleue : ils ont pensé que c'était un vrai accident.

Le capitalisme sur le banc des accusés au siège du synode britannique. En 2001, nous avons organisé une conférence intitulée « SuperHumanism ». En toile de fond, il y avait l'explosion d'Internet et les émeutes anticapitalistes, tandis que la conférence elle-même a eu lieu à la veille du scandale d'Enron. Nous avons réuni 500 leaders du secteur à Church House, à Westminster. La grande attraction était la rencontre entre l'instigateur de la campagne de pub de Nike, Dan Wieden, et l'auteure de *No Logo*, Naomi Klein. Tout le monde s'attendait à un affrontement à l'américaine, mais eux ont décidé d'accepter leur désaccord avec une grande civilité, dans le plus pur style britannique.

Tony Kaye vole la vedette à D&AD à la Saatchi Gallery. En 1995, nous avons organisé l'exposition D&AD à la Saatchi Gallery. Billy Mawhinney trouva l'excellent titre « La crème du design et de la publicité britanniques », et pour l'affiche il nous donna une vache de Damien Hirst dans un réservoir de Boddingtons. Le marchand d'art de Hirst, Jay Jopling, nous menaça d'intenter un procès. Puis Tony Kaye, toujours en bisbille avec le monde de l'art, paya deux acteurs pour occuper le parking et improviser le fameux incident entre Hugh Grant et Divine. Il paya également un SDF pour qu'il reste assis dans la galerie et joue le rôle d'une œuvre d'art. Les médias ont beaucoup parlé de nous, mais pas forcément comme nous le voulions.

Un album annuel sacrilège provoque une démission chez D&AD. Graham Fink a causé un petit scandale avec son idée de faire de l'album annuel de D&AD une bible géante décorée d'une croix faite de deux Pencils. Lorsqu'il découvrit que la directrice des récompenses de D&AD était chrétienne pratiquante et qu'elle risquait de démissionner, Graham décida plutôt d'utiliser la couverture de Tony Kaye.

Un designer dort pendant les délibérations. Peter Souter était président en 2002. Il décida que toutes les délibérations auraient lieu à Brighton. Tous les grands étaient là, de John Hegarty à Jarvis Cocker : 200 au total. Enfin, 199, pour être précis. Un célèbre typographe américain n'a pas pu suivre le rythme. Le directeur des récompenses a eu beau frapper comme un diable à la porte de sa chambre d'hôtel, il n'arriva pas à se réveiller pour aller juger les projets soumis.

Je suis ravi d'avoir contribué à 20 pour cent du demi-siècle de D&AD.

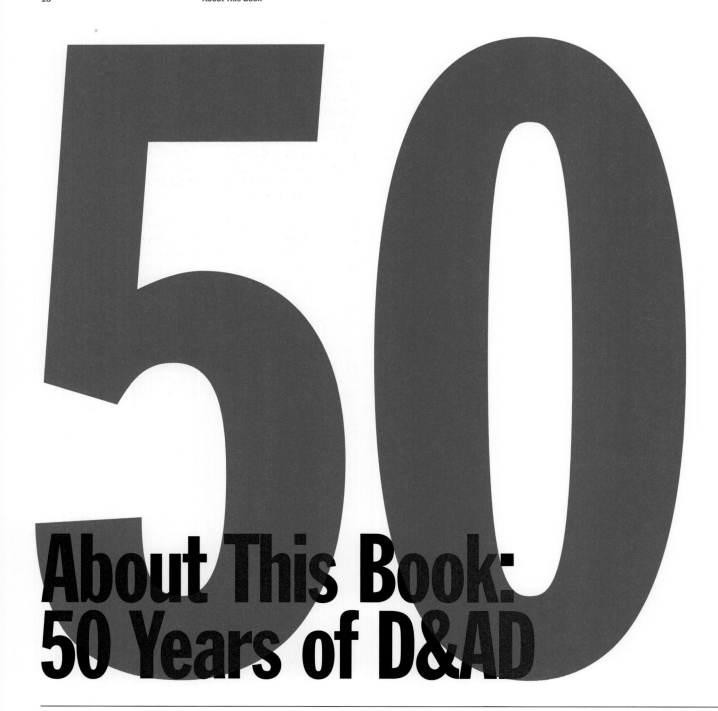

About This Book:
50 Years of D&AD

D&AD has been celebrating and nurturing outstanding work in design and advertising since 1962. It is a London-based educational charity that brings together the finest of the international creative community each year through its Awards, Annual, exhibition and education programme. Dedicated to celebrating creative communication, rewarding its practitioners and raising standards across the industry, D&AD has become a benchmark of quality and innovation both in the UK and globally.

D&AD's annual Awards have now been setting the gold standard for creative excellence for half a century, and have left an incredible legacy of five decades of the best and most innovative creative work, published in each year's Annual.

In this anniversary book, five pieces of work from each of the 50 Annuals have been personally selected and introduced by that year's President (or someone otherwise closely associated with that time). As such, these pages contain the very best of the best, and will serve as a source of creative inspiration for generations to come.

www.dandad.org

The Presidents

Since 1970, D&AD has elected a new President every year, drawn from different disciplines of its membership. The Presidents set their own agendas at the beginning of their terms, allowing them to focus on areas in which they would like to see D&AD expand or improve. Each year's President chooses someone to receive the President's Award in recognition of an outstanding contribution to creativity. Past recipients of the Award include Sir Alan Parker, Sir Jonathan Ive, Spike Jonze and Sir John Hegarty.

The Annuals

Also known as "the Book", the D&AD Annual has been published every year since 1963. It showcases the best of the year's creative work from around the world, providing an unrivalled source of creative inspiration. An authoritative archive of commercial creativity, the Annual's release is highly anticipated by industry and design fans. To get "In Book" is to have your work featured in the D&AD Annual.

The Yellow Pencil

A Yellow Pencil (formerly known as a Silver Award) is recognised the world over as a symbol of true creative achievement. In the early years, winners received an ebony pencil box containing a pencil with silver lettering. Designed by Marcello Minale, one of the founders of Minale Tattersfield, it was a thing of beauty but very delicate, so in 1966 Lou Klein designed the more durable Yellow Pencil. Yellow and Black Pencils are awarded in many different categories, from Spatial Design to Outdoor Advertising.

The Black Pencil

A Black Pencil (formerly known as a Gold Award) represents the best of the best. It is awarded for work that is truly groundbreaking. Black Pencils are particularly coveted because judges usually only give out just one or two each year – and sometimes none at all. A new benchmark was set at the turn of the century when an unprecedented double Black Pencil was awarded to Abbott Mead Vickers BBDO's 'Surfer' for Guinness. This was matched five years later by 'Grrr', by Wieden+ Kennedy London for Honda UK.

The White Pencil

Creative ideas persuade, motivate and mobilise people. At their most potent, they have the power to change the way people think and behave. The recently introduced White Pencil is a new initiative designed to harness that power. It is awarded to a creative idea with the potential to effect real and positive change in the world.

Evolution

Five decades of creative excellence

1962

D&AD is founded by a group of 30 London-based designers and art directors, including David Bailey, Terence Donovan and Alan Fletcher. Their objectives are to encourage the understanding and commissioning of good design and art direction, gain recognition for the industry and define and improve standards. The D&AD logo is designed by Colin Forbes.

1963

The first D&AD Awards are held, attracting approximately 3,500 submissions. The accompanying exhibition is seen by 25,000 people; many regret that no illustrated record is issued. The Committee of 1964 is accordingly charged with not only organising the exhibition, but also preparing the publication of a fully illustrated record of the show.

D&AD jury, led by John Pearce of Collett Dickenson Pearce.

 This year's award winners are to be found on pages 3, 34, 48, 59, 97, 101, 104, 107, 108, 110 and are marked with a

1964

The first D&AD Annual is published. J Walter Thompson kindly provides facilities for the Association's offices.

Winning ad for The Sunday Times.

Close up of an introductory page of the Annual. Winning work is only found on a few pages, indicated with the D&AD logo.

1965

New categories are introduced to the D&AD Awards, including Newspaper Features and Corporate Design. The exhibition tours the UK for the first time, sponsored by the Victoria & Albert Museum. The first D&AD Workshop is arranged; the educational programme will come to be run throughout the UK.

The coveted Gold Certificate.

D&AD Gold Medal Award of Distinctive Merit.

1966

D&AD's exhibition tours all over the world for the first time. The D&AD Yellow Pencil is designed by Lou Klein. "D&AD is not content to exhibit a mere cross-section of work each year. Its aims are more vigorous; to define and improve current graphic standards, to stimulate not to please" – Edward Booth-Clibborn, Chairman.

1967

The Association arranges a major exhibition in New York called 'It's Great! Britain', designed by Rodney Fitch. His Royal Highness The Prince Philip, Duke of Edinburgh, writes the catalogue introduction. Lord Snowdon attends, helping to actively promote British creatives in the United States.

Lord Snowdon, with Edward Booth-Clibborn, opening 'It's Great! Britain', the 1967 D&AD exhibition in New York. It runs from 27 November to 1 December and attracts over 4,600 visitors.

Jennie Lee, Minister for the Arts, opening the 1967 D&AD Show with Lord Snowdon.

The D&AD 67 Show being opened in Amsterdam on 25 October 1967 by the British Ambassador to the Netherlands, Sir Isham Peter Garran KCMG.

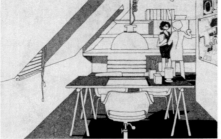

1968

D&AD moves to Nash House, along with the Institute of Contemporary Design, the Society of Industrial Artists and Designers, the Design and Industries Association and the Institute of Landscape Architects.

Bill Bernbach, guest speaker at the 1968 opening, talking to Dennis Hackett, Executive Chairman of D&AD, and Lord Perth.

An artist's impression of the new penthouse office.

1969

Copywriters are admitted to D&AD membership for the first time. D&AD elects specialist five-person juries, divided into speciality groups: Advertising, Print and Editorial Design, Art and Photography, and Film. Jury members include Charles Saatchi, John Salmon and John Webster.

1970

A D&AD exhibition designed by Rodney Fitch opens in Tokyo. D&AD holds its first ever auction of original advertising artwork (in conjunction with Sotheby's).

1971

The Awards are held at the Institute of Contemporary Art (ICA). Four Black Pencils are given.

1972

D&AD launches its Student Awards scheme, the brainchild of John Hegarty. The Sunday Times becomes the most Black Pencil-awarded client, with work done for it having won five of the trophies.

The Student Pencil in 2012.

1973

President Peter Mayle sets about actively promoting young designers to the industry. The annual exhibition is staged at the Design Centre, the headquarters of the Design Council.

1974

D&AD publishes the first edition of 'European Illustration'.
Deadline, D&AD's newsletter, is available free to
members. The first issue is dedicated to the work of
Seymour Chwast and designed by John Gorham.

Advertising and Copy jury comment on reviewed work.

1975

A Radio entry receives a D&AD Yellow Pencil for the first time.
In keeping with this, the D&AD Annual includes a "slim disk"
containing all of the Radio work selected for the exhibition.

Lord Elwyn Jones, the Lord Chancellor, is welcomed to the 1975 D&AD Show by President
David Abbott – with Richard Attenborough. In his opening speech, the Lord Chancellor says,
"I would like to congratulate the D&AD Association on the splendid work it is doing in promoting
British design to foreign countries."

Natale Netto, President of the São Paulo Advertising Association, with Edward Booth-Clibborn, Chairman
of D&AD, during the First International Advertising Congress, held in December in São Paulo, Brazil.

1976

D&AD introduces the President's Award, which recognises
outstanding contributions to design and art direction.
Colin Millward of Collett Dickenson Pearce is the Award's
inaugural recipient, selected by President Alan Parker.

Colin Millward, recipient of the first ever President's Award.

1976 Advertising jury.

1977

CDP sweeps the boards at the D&AD Awards, receiving
four Yellow Pencils and a Black Pencil in the Print category.

The Photographic jury reach for their buttons beneath the table
to cast a confidential vote.

The Editorial jury at great pains to conceal their verdicts from
the prying eye of the camera as they peruse the exhibits.

1978

D&AD President Michael Rand of The Sunday Times presents
the first ever D&AD Black Pencil for Radio to Tony Hertz for
his advertising work for EMI. Comedian John Cleese attends
to collect a Yellow Pencil for his radio campaign for Sony.

The D&AD 78 Show opens in Sydney in November, and is sponsored by John Clemenger. Seen here
with Edward Booth-Clibborn are some members of the newly formed Australian Writers and Art Directors
Club, based on the principle of D&AD.

The D&AD 78 Show opens in Belgium at the Royale Belge in November.

Television and Cinema Advertising jury – with Ridley Scott.

1979

For the first time ever, an exhibition of illustration work
is held in a Metro station in Paris. It is seen by as many
as 100,000 members of the general public each day.

First Student Awards, in collaboration with the Post Office – with David Abbott.

The D&AD Awards Dinner centrepiece. Designer: John Munday, CDP/Aspect. Director: Peter Stiles.

Opening of the D&AD exhibition at a Metro station in Paris.

1980

D&AD launches its first video showreel of moving image work. Designed to bridge the gap between college and professional life, the new Student Awards present students with commercially plausible briefs to tackle. Thirty-two years later, the 2012 briefs will be downloaded by over 50,000 people around the world and inserted into the HE curriculum.

Alan Parker, recipient of the 1980 D&AD President's Award.

1981

Martin Boase is elected as D&AD's first President with a business background. 1981 is a rich year for Black Pencils, with an unprecedented seven presented.

Television and Cinema Advertising jury.
Record Sleeves/Promotion jury.

1982

D&AD creates a specialised jury to judge Photography.

Ralph Steadman signing menus at the D&AD/Post Office Student Awards Scheme presentation lunch at the Park Lane hotel on 29 May 1982.
Poster Advertising jury.

1983

At 21, D&AD comes of age. The Annual Show is held at Harvey Nichols to introduce D&AD to the general public, and D&AD presents examples of work from the last 21 years in a small exhibition at the V&A.

D&AD celebrates its anniversary with a dinner at the Royal Albert Hall on 8 June. Entertainment includes the Pipes and Drums of the 10th Princess Mary's Own Gurkha Rifles, the Chelsea Symphony Orchestra, a one-man performance by John Wells, a film of 21 years of commercials from D&AD shows, Jeff Kutash and his Dancin' Machine and Darts.
David Bailey judging Photography.

1984

D&AD introduces Pop Videos to the Promo Video category. Judges this year include Malcolm McLaren. Pop Promos will continue to attract celebrity judges, such as Jarvis Cocker in 2002.

Promo Videos jury.
Direct Mail jury.

1985

Milton Glaser flies in from New York to present the D&AD/Post Office Student Awards Scheme. Already in its sixth year, the Student Awards highlight a long-running partnership between D&AD and Royal Mail.

Milton Glaser presents the 1985 Awards.
Press Advertising jury.
Direct Mail jury – with John Hegarty.

1986

The Advertising and Design categories are awarded at separate events, causing much controversy. Yellowhammer's anti-fur TV work for Greenpeace claims a Black Pencil.

Jury members.

1987

As D&AD celebrates its Silver Jubilee, the D&AD Annual is produced in colour for the first time. D&AD holds the UK/LA Exhibition of British Arts in Los Angeles.

Typography jury – with Neville Brody.
Television and Cinema Advertising jury.

1988

D&AD introduces the Product Design category to the Awards and opens its doors to international entries. The D&AD Awards Ceremony is transmitted simultaneously to New York, Amsterdam and Oslo.

Some of the first winners in Product Design.

1989

No Black Pencils are awarded. President John Hegarty announces: "Others may scatter Gold Awards as cheaply as confetti. D&AD treats it as a rarity to be cherished and sought after. Its members wouldn't have it any other way."

The Executive Committee for 1988 and 1989.

1990

D&AD moves to purpose-designed premises in Vauxhall.

The office in Graphite Square, Vauxhall.

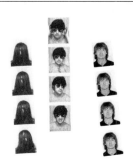   

1991

D&AD works with RECLAMA in Moscow to complete a unique student exchange scheme between the UK and the Soviet Union.

Pop Promo Videos jury.
TV and Cinema Advertising Craft jury.

1992

Anthony Simonds-Gooding becomes Chairman, marking a new era for D&AD and setting out the remit that will shape the organisation's future.

1993

D&AD launches the Festival of Excellence and a new education programme that includes Student Expo. The D&AD Annual Show tours South Africa, Hong Kong, Singapore, Kuala Lumpur, Australia, Japan and the USA, as well as the UK and mainland Europe.

Advertising jury.

Design jury.

1994

David Kester becomes CEO. The new team puts "new lead in the old pencil", to borrow a phrase from President Adrian Holmes. D&AD membership doubles and the education scheme is revitalised.

1995

Mary Lewis becomes D&AD's first female President. Ruby Wax presents the Awards, and D&AD's Festival of Excellence hits the headlines, sparking an "Is It Art?" debate. The Association launches 'The Copy Book', the first of its Mastercrafts series. Future instalments in the series will include 'The Graphics Book', 'The Product Book', 'The Commercials Book' and 'The Art Direction Book'.

'The Graphics Book'.

1996

D&AD launches www.dandad.org. A new judging system is introduced to allow more time for judges to discuss specialist work.

Press Advertising jury.

1997

D&AD introduces an interactive section into the Awards and produces a CD-ROM of the D&AD Annual. D&AD becomes secretariat for the Art Directors Club of Europe.

1998

The D&AD Awards Ceremony and Dinner is the biggest "sit down" event of its kind in the UK, with 2,500 guests. Featured speakers at the President's Lectures include Paul Smith and Michael Palin. D&AD launches a members' magazine, Ampersand.

Direct Marketing jury.
Corporate Branding jury.

1999

Fifty per cent of entries into the D&AD Awards are now international. The Workshop programme is further developed, resulting in over 1,000 registrations.

2000

At the D&AD Awards Dinner, two giant Yellow Pencils are stolen. An unheard of two Black Pencils are awarded for Guinness's 'Surfer', and the D&AD showreel is presented on DVD for the first time. The D&AD College Membership show, Student Expo, is renamed New Blood, and D&AD launches its Bloodbank website. By 2012 over 90,000 registered users of the site will be able to browse the portfolios of the next creative generation.

The 2000 D&AD Annual Show, curated by Jeremy Myerson and Kathryn Patten.

2001

Former D&AD President Richard Seymour convenes the Association's first international creative forum, 'SuperHumanism', at which creative superstars generate a powerful debate on corporate responsibility, creativity and design. D&AD is now investing £1.5million in education annually.

Judging Environmental Design.
Naomi Klein at the 'SuperHumanism' Conference.

2002

D&AD celebrates 40 years of Award-winning work with 'Rewind: 40 Years of Design and Advertising', a major exhibition at the V&A, and a book, published by Phaidon. The Awards Ceremony & Dinner becomes a 40th birthday party, complete with fireworks, fairground attractions, nightclub and gala dinner. Steve Jobs, CEO of Apple Computer, flies in to collect the company's fourth Black Pencil for Product Design.

'Rewind' at the V&A.

2003

More Yellow Pencils are won at the D&AD Awards than ever before, but the jury does not award a Black Pencil. Michael Johnson shakes things up by introducing the People's Pencil, an Award voted for by D&AD members, and a new Integrated Creativity category to reward collaboration and thinking across disciplines. He also introduces a series of President's Forums on difficult issues such as cultural diversity and creative education. Michael Hockney becomes CEO.

Awards Ceremony at Billingsgate.

2004

Entries are included for the first time from Bosnia-Herzegovina, Lithuania, Peru, Saudi Arabia and Slovakia. D&AD formalises its commitment to Excellence, Education and Enterprise, and holds the 17-day Congress event, which attracts over 10,000 visitors.

Judging.

2005

D&AD opts to emphasise its not-for-profit status.
The Annual is designed by Spin for President Dick Powell.

Steve Jobs speaking at the Awards Ceremony.
An impressive haul.
Dick Powell handing out Pencils.

2006

President Dick Powell presides for an extra ten months as D&AD aligns its programmes. Leo Burnett's website wins the first Black Pencil for a Digital entry.

D&AD Exhibition.
Judging the Student Awards.

2007

There are more Awards entries than ever before – a staggering 25,000 pieces of work from 58 nations, including Qatar and Bangladesh, both of which are submitting for the first time.

For the D&AD Flag Project, creatives from around the world send in photos showing their use of the D&AD flag. The images are printed in the D&AD Annual 2007.
Judges coming to an agreement.

2008

President Simon Waterfall leads D&AD in a year when there are 63 Yellow and six Black Pencils. "If you read this in 2008, you will remember the talent who did it under a silly haircut in Hoxton. If it's 2012, then the London Olympics are about to start, Great Britain is going for gold and no one will give a toss about design for a couple of months" – Simon Waterfall, President 2008.

Simon Waterfall in his custom-made Pencil outfit at the Awards Ceremony.
Sir John Hegarty and Rosie Arnold help promote the Awards by taking part in an ambient stunt in Soho.

2009

Peter Saville oversees design of the Annual, assisted by student Luke Sanders. A version is published by Taschen, making it available to the public all over the world. Tim O'Kennedy joins as CEO.

Awards Ceremony.
Audience at a President's Lecture by Neville Brody.

2010

"One of the many good things about being President of D&AD is that you get to choose who designs the Annual" – Paul Brazier, 2010 President. He chooses artist Bob and Roberta Smith. Dick Powell becomes Chairman.

Jimmy Carr presenting the Awards Ceremony.

Bob and Roberta Smith at the launch of the 2010 Annual.

2011

D&AD launches the Graduate Academy, a bridge between education and employment. The 2011 Annual is overseen by President Simon "Sanky" Sankarayya and Airside's Nat Hunter, and designed by Harry Pearce of Pentagram. It is the most environmentally sustainable ever produced. D&AD moves to brand new premises in Shoreditch.

D&AD publishes a refreshed edition of 'The Copy Book', in partnership with Taschen.

Sanky and Tim O'Kennedy presenting the Awards Ceremony.

2012

The first White Pencil, sponsored by Unilever, is awarded to recognise a creative idea that changes the world for the better. D&AD celebrates its half-century by giving a special award to eight companies, brands and individuals that have had outstanding success over its 50 years.

iPod Touches used by judges to record their votes.

Digital Design jury.

Pencils waiting to be handed out on Awards night.

> One of the many good things about being President of D&AD is that you get to choose who designs the Annual.

1963 Edward Booth-Clibborn

1964 Bob Gill

1965 Derek Birdsall

1966 Terence Conran

1967 David Puttnam

As Executive Chairman and President, Edward Booth-Clibborn was at the helm of D&AD for almost 30 years, during which it grew to become a beacon of creative excellence of worldwide repute. He is now a renowned publisher of illustrated books.

Bob Gill was the 'Gill' in Fletcher/Forbes/Gill, which eventually became Pentagram. He was a founding member of D&AD, and was elected into the New York Art Directors Club Hall of Fame. He received the D&AD President's Award in 1999.

Designer Derek Birdsall was a founding member, in 1958, of Birdsall Daulby Mayhew Wildbur Associates. He was also a founding member of D&AD and its first (Hon) Secretary. He was elected a Royal Designer for Industry in 1983.

Terence Conran remains one of the world's best-known designers, restaurateurs and retailers. He founded the Habitat chain of home furnishings stores in 1964, and has owned and operated over 50 restaurants. Today he is Chairman of the Conran Group. He received the President's Award in 1989.

David Puttnam spent 30 years as an independent producer of award-winning films. He retired from film production in 1998 to focus on his work in public policy. Puttnam was awarded a CBE in 1982 and a knighthood in 1995, and was appointed to the House of Lords in 1997. He was awarded a BAFTA Fellowship in 2006.

"D&AD is there to stimulate, not congratulate. That is the way to keep moving forward.

"Just by the nature of the people involved, we knew that D&AD was going to be different. We were all young, not very conventional and certainly not establishment types.

"There were no real graphic-design magazines in Britain at the time, and we felt something would be gained by the business if we put on an exhibition.

"One thing we were constantly told was that what we were doing – our revolution – was only relevant to our small and arty area of London. We didn't believe this.

"By 1967, the world itself was changing, and Britain seemed to be at the cutting edge of much of that change.

1968 Bob Brooks

1969 Michael Peters

1970 Brian Byfield

1971 Michael Wolff

1972 David Hillman

Bob Brooks was a founding member of D&AD. In 1967 he co-founded Brooks Baker Fulford, later known as BFCS. In 1977 he directed the BAFTA-nominated TV film 'The Knowledge', and in 1981, 'Tattoo'. He then returned to BFCS and continued directing until he retired in the late 90s. He received the D&AD President's Award in 1984.

Michael Peters OBE set up the design department for Collett Dickenson Pearce, and saw it win its first D&AD Pencil in the mid-60s. In 1970 he set up Michael Peters and Partners, and in 1992 he founded The Identica Partnership. He left Identica in 2007 and now works as a private consultant. He received the President's Award in 2009.

Brian Byfield was Art Director at McCann-Erickson and Grey, and Head of Art at Doyle Dane Bernbach. In the early 70s he formed his own agency. In 1978 he started Brian Byfield Films, for which he directed many award-winning commercials.

Michael Wolff was President of D&AD in 1971, and received the President's Award in 2003. He is a founder of Wolff Olins, still among the world's most iconic design companies. Now, as Michael Wolff and Company, he works with clients around the world both as a designer and creative advisor.

David Hillman became Art Director of Nova magazine in 1968, where he remained until 1975, winning scores of Pencils. In 1975, he designed a new French daily, Le Matin de Paris. In 2006, after 29 years as a Pentagram partner, he set up the eponymous Studio David Hillman.

"It was the final phase of print advertising before the onslaught of the television revolution, which exploded on the London scene just a few years later.

"Every ten years, D&AD changes. And it's now 40 years since that way we saw things.

"New advertising agencies and design groups were rattling the cages of the old guard.

"The excitement, exuberance and promise of the 60s still burned in 1971, but business, bean-counting and cautious processes were blunting the blades of creativity.

"The list of winners in the D&AD Annual 1972 is quite the roll call of today's industry heavyweights and icons.

1973 Chris Wilkins

1974 Alfredo Marcantonio

1975 David Abbott

1976 Alan Parker

1977 John Salmon

Copywriter Chris Wilkins's work for Guinness, written at J Walter Thompson, won D&AD TV Campaign of the Year. His 'Martians' commercial, written at Boase Massimi Pollitt for Cadbury's Smash, was named Ad of the Century in Campaign's millennium issue.

Alfredo Marcantonio was a Copywriter at French Gold Abbott and Collett Dickenson Pearce. He became Creative Director of Lowe Howard-Spink, and in 1987 joined WCRS. He later became Vice-Chairman of Abbott Mead Vickers BBDO London and Creative Vice-President of BBDO Milan. He now runs Marcantonio Plus Hobbs with Steve Hobbs.

In a career spanning 40 years, David Abbott worked in two agencies (Mather & Crowther and Doyle Dane Bernbach) and helped start two more (French Gold Abbott and Abbott Mead Vickers). He received the D&AD President's Award in 1986.

Sir Alan Parker CBE is a director, writer and producer. He was D&AD President in 1976 and received the President's Award in 1980. His films have won 19 BAFTA awards, ten Golden Globes and ten Oscars. He received a CBE in 1995 and a knighthood in 2002.

In 1967 John Salmon became Creative Group Supervisor at Collett Dickenson Pearce, under Colin Millward. Two years later, he was made Creative Director. He was President of D&AD in 1977, and received the President's Award in 1979.

"There was a hell of a lot of sex around in 1973.

"Following my two or three stints on the Executive Committee, some wag described me as 'the best President D&AD never had'.

"The great sweep of history is made up of the small brushstrokes of the everyday. By concentrating on the task in hand, we move things on.

"The UK borrowed from the IMF 'to avoid wholesale liquidation of the economy'. This went unheeded in the advertising creative community, where 'domestic liquidity' meant a couple of bottles of very good red at dinner.

"Promotion, riches and fame sometimes result from adopting an all-out pursuit of awards, but that isn't what D&AD set out to foster.

1978 Gerry Moira

1979 Andrew Cracknell

1980 Snowdon

1981 Martin Boase

1982 Steve Henry

Gerry Moira got his first proper copywriting job at Ogilvy & Mather, where he later became Creative Director, before becoming Executive Creative Director of the agency that became Publicis. He started his own agency, returned for a time to his old job at Publicis, and is now Creative Chairman at Euro RSCG.

Andrew Cracknell started as a Copywriter at Collett Dickenson Pearce in 1968. Via Pritchard Wood and Aalders Marchant Weinreich he became Creative Director at Kingsley Manton & Palmer, then moved to French Cruttendon Osborn. Agencies he has worked at since include Foote Cone & Belding, WCRS, Bates Dorland New York and Ammirati Puris Lintas.

Antony Armstrong-Jones, better known as Lord Snowdon, was D&AD President in 1980. He started taking photographs as a professional in 1951. Over the last 40 years, he has photographed everyone from Freddie Mercury of Queen to Her Majesty The Queen.

Martin Boase formed Boase Massimi Pollitt in 1968, and was President of D&AD in 1981. The agency joined Omnicom Group in 1989, and Boase chaired the Advertising Association for six years in the early 90s. Since retiring in the mid-90s, he has served on the boards of Emap and Taunton Cider and chaired Maiden Outdoor, Heal's and Herald Investment Trust.

Steve Henry was Founder and Creative Director of Howell Henry Chaldecott Lury, voted Campaign's Agency of the Decade in 2000. In 2009, he joined Albion as non-executive Creative Director. In 2011, Henry launched Decoded, a company that teaches anyone to "code in a day".

"By general consensus, and as evidenced by the Award jury photos in the Book, Britain was enduring its worst fashion crisis since the Middle Ages.

"What the 1979 Annual tells us is that we were a year of careful people doing careful work, very carefully.

"People sometimes frame photographs. I'm against all that. It's pretentious.

"It isn't particularly admirable, but one does focus on one's own craft. Broaden it out into others and it becomes less interesting, waters the thing down.

"Advertising back then was all about flair, arrogance, larking about.

1983 Tony Brignull

Tony Brignull spent most of his career at Collett Dickenson Pearce, and was President of D&AD in 1983. He also worked for Doyle Dane Bernbach and Abbott Mead Vickers and ran his own agency, Brignull Le Bas.

> " On reflection, the decision to hold the Awards dinner at the Royal Albert Hall was not the greatest of ideas. We had to sit on tip-up seats and eat airline meals on our laps.

1984 Rodney Fitch

Rodney Fitch CBE founded his design consultancy, Fitch, now owned by WPP, in 1972, and was President of D&AD in 1984. He left the consultancy at the end of 2009 and now works in higher education and as an independent advisor, consultant and non-executive to a broad portfolio of clients. He was awarded a CBE in 1990 for his influence on the British design industry.

> " The nation, hitherto choked politically and socially by Luddite lefties, was coming to its senses.

1985 Jeremy Myerson

Jeremy Myerson has been a writer, academic and activist in design and communication for more than 30 years. He was Founder/Editor of Design Week, which he launched in 1986. Today, he is Director and Chair of the Helen Hamlyn Centre for Design at the Royal College of Art.

> " The sharpest knives in the drawer left an overriding impression of a countercultural two fingers to the relentless promotion of a winner-takes-all approach.

1986 John McConnell

John McConnell was a Director of Pentagram for 31 years before he re-established McConnell Design in 2005. He received the D&AD President's Award in 1985, and was President the following year. He is a member of the Alliance Graphique Internationale, a Fellow of the Chartered Society of Designers and a Royal Designer for Industry.

> " It's fed into you to be creative – injected into you from when you go to art school. It's intelligence that is actually important; being clever is better.

1987 Jeremy Sinclair

Jeremy Sinclair joined CramerSaatchi in 1968. In 1970 he helped found Saatchi & Saatchi, and in 1995 he helped found M&C Saatchi. He was D&AD President in 1987.

> " Every agency was known by its initials – there were no Mothers or Nakeds or Red Brick Roads.

1988 Gert Dumbar

1989 John Hegarty

1990 Ron Brown

1991 Martin Lambie-Nairn

1992 Tim Delaney

Gert Dumbar established Studio Dumbar in 1977. With his team he has completed extensive corporate identity programmes for numerous major national and international clients. He was President of D&AD in 1988. Since 2003, Dumbar has taught at the Royal Academy of Art in The Hague.

Sir John Hegarty is Worldwide Creative Director and Founder of Bartle Bogle Hegarty. He was President of D&AD in 1989, and received the President's Award in 1994. He was awarded a knighthood by The Queen in 2007 in recognition of his services to the advertising and creative industries.

President of D&AD in 1990, Ron Brown joined Doyle Dane Bernbach as Senior Art Director in 1970. In 1972, he joined BBDO as Group Head, before moving to Young & Rubicam. He then returned to BBDO. He joined Abbott Mead Vickers when the agency was founded as a Director and Head of Art, in order to work with David Abbott. The partnership lasted 20 years.

Martin Lambie-Nairn formed his first design agency in 1976. He was D&AD President in 1991 and received the President's Award in 1997. He is recognised as one of the foremost designers of his generation in broadcast branding. He is a Royal Designer of Industry, a Fellow of the Royal Television Society and an Honorary Doctor of Art at the University of Lincoln.

Tim Delaney was D&AD President in 1992. He worked at Young & Rubicam and Boase Massimi Pollitt before joining BBDO, where he became Managing Director at 31. He founded Leagas Delaney in 1980 and received the D&AD President's Award in 1995. He remains a working copywriter.

> British designers are the only ones who really bring their sense of humour into the visual image.

> To borrow Churchill's famous quote on democracy, D&AD is the worst form of award scheme, apart from all the others that have been tried.

> The 1990 juries were as tough as ever.

> I gave my President's Award to Abram Games. During World War II he designed posters that became part of our culture and history.

> It was a tumultuous year compared to others... Secession was in the air.

1993 Aziz Cami

1994 Adrian Holmes

1995 Mary Lewis

1996 Graham Fink

1997 Mike Dempsey

Aziz Cami, President of D&AD in 1993, was one of the founding partners of The Partners, which has established a reputation within the design industry for creative and commercial excellence. He has over 40 years' experience in design and corporate branding.

After working his way through a number of agencies, Adrian Holmes became joint Creative Director of Lowe Howard-Spink in 1989, worldwide Chief Creative Officer at Lowe in 1999, and an Executive Creative Director at Young & Rubicam in 2005. He was President of D&AD in 1994, and is now back writing advertising for various clients and agencies in London.

Mary Lewis is Creative Director at Lewis Moberly, which she founded in 1984 with Robert Moberly. In 1995, she became the first female President of D&AD, and in 2001 she received the President's Award.

Graham Fink, President of D&AD in 1996, worked at Butler Dennis Garland, before moving to Collett Dickenson Pearce, WCRS, Saatchi & Saatchi and Gold Greenlees Trott. He founded thefinktank and The Art School, became Creative Director of M&C Saatchi, and is now Chief Creative Officer of Ogilvy China.

Mike Dempsey has been a graphic designer for over 40 years. During that time he worked in publishing for ten years, then founded the design consultancy CDT Design in 1979. He was D&AD President in 1997, and set up Studio Dempsey in 2008.

"The Festival of Excellence attracted a remarkable attendance of 4,000 people over seven days in May.

"Back in 1994, the term 'digital' had little if anything to do with our world; oh, how blissfully unaware we all were of Things to Come.

"Wonderbra's 'Hello Boys' set the tone of the year, politely cheeky and perfectly pitched... Guinness rode the crest of the wave, bravely, boldly and brilliantly.

"We had committed heresy and invited people from outside 'the business' to sit on juries. Not just any old people, either. Gilbert & George and Damien Hirst on Illustration. Martin Amis and Will Self for Copywriting.

"I bought my first D&AD Annual in 1964. A rather slim, humble, black and white affair. But it inspired the hell out of me and I was determined to be eventually included in its pages.

1998 Tim Mellors

1999 Richard Seymour

2000 Larry Barker

2001 David Stuart

2002 Peter Souter

Tim Mellors is based in New York and is Worldwide Creative Director of Grey Group. He has been a magazine journalist, a commercial film director and host of a TV series, and is a trained psychotherapist. He has been Creative Director at Publicis, Saatchi & Saatchi, Gold Greenlees Trott and his own agency, Mellors Reay, and was D&AD President in 1998.

Richard Seymour is co-Founder and Design Director of Seymourpowell, and was D&AD President in 1999. The consultancy has risen to the forefront of product and innovation design, with a string of world firsts among its achievements, including the first cordless kettle, the first pocket mobile phone and the first private spaceship. With Dick Powell, he received the President's Award in 1995.

Larry Barker, President of D&AD in 2000, started his advertising career at Aalders & Marchant, and went on to work at Boase Massimi Pollitt, after which there followed spells at Doyle Dane Bernbach, Abbott Mead Vickers and Bartle Bogle Hegarty. A move to Creative Directorship at WCRS preceded a return to BMP DDB, where he became Executive Creative Director. He now works full-time as a screenwriter.

David Stuart, President of D&AD in 2001, was a founding partner and Creative Director of The Partners. He has nearly 40 years' experience in both design and branding, and now advises companies on how best they can express themselves.

Peter Souter, President of D&AD in 2002, worked at Abbott Mead Vickers BBDO for nearly 20 years, and was Executive Creative Director for nearly ten of them. He left in 2009.

"Before you could make an internet film for the price of a sandwich, real directors were making real scripts that were as modern and cool as anything today.

"Nobody could possibly have imagined that, 13 years later, Apple would be the most valuable brand on the planet.

"Within seconds, the first shout of 'How did that get in?' would go up, closely followed by: 'Well, that never bloody ran.'

"Somehow the good-heartedness and generosity so often on display within our business abruptly goes missing when a client asks two or three creative businesses to come together.

"David Abbott wrote the first Economist poster... Eventually it became so universally loved and understood, we were able to run a poster where the logo wasn't even necessary.

2003 Michael Johnson

Designer/writer/thinker Michael Johnson runs johnson banks, a London-based design consultancy with a global reputation, and was President of D&AD in 2003. He writes for many design journals and lectures worldwide on branding, identity issues and design history.

> " There was no standout piece in the year – no 'Surfer', iMac or London Eye. Hence no Black Pencil.

2004 Nick Bell

Nick Bell, President of D&AD in 2004, started his career at Abbott Mead Vickers BBDO, before becoming Executive Creative Director of Leo Burnett, then JWT. He is now Global Creative Director at DDB.

> " Orange's 'Don't Let a Mobile Phone Ruin Your Movie' campaign by Mother was brave, and it was smart as hell on the client's side to buy a campaign that basically says, 'Don't use our product.'

2005 Dick Powell

Dick Powell, D&AD President in 2005, is co-Founder of design and innovation company Seymourpowell, which has produced some of the "milestone" products of the last two decades. He has sat on the boards of the Design Council and the Design Business Association and is now Chairman of the D&AD Executive. With Richard Seymour, he received the President's Award in 1995.

> " Nothing gets the creative adrenaline coursing through the veins more than a real dislike or hate for the way things are, married to an anarchic confidence that you can do it better.

2006 Dave Trott

Involved with D&AD since the 70s, and President in 2006, Dave Trott opened one of the most influential and anti-establishment agencies of the 1980s: Gold Greenlees Trott. He is now Executive Creative Director of CST The Gate. He received the D&AD President's Award in 2004.

> " It is advertising's job to amplify marketing's strategy. To be provocative, outrageous, stimulating.

2007 Tony Davidson

Tony Davidson, D&AD President in 2007, joined Boase Massimi Pollitt in 1985; it was here he first teamed up with Kim Papworth, his long-term creative partner. He later moved to Leagas Delaney and Bartle Bogle Hegarty, then joined Wieden+Kennedy London. He was made a Global Partner of Wieden+Kennedy in 2009.

> " The message is loud and clear: change or die, my friends.

2008 Simon Waterfall

2009 Garrick Hamm

2010 Paul Brazier

2011 Simon Sankarayya

2012 Rosie Arnold

Creative Director Simon Waterfall co-founded Deepend in 1994 and Poke in 2000, and more recently set up his new collaborative venture Fray, which aims to "defend creativity" above all else. He was D&AD President in 2008.

Garrick Hamm joined London-based brand design consultancy Williams and Murray in 1999 and is now Creative Partner at Williams Murray Hamm. He was President of D&AD in 2009. His film 'The Man Who Married Himself' won Best Comedy Award at the LA International Short Film Festival 2010.

Paul Brazier, D&AD President in 2010, started his career in advertising at Cogents, before moving to WCRS. He joined Abbott Meads Vickers in 1991, and is currently Executive Creative Director of Abbott Mead Vickers BBDO.

Sanky is a founding partner of interactive agency AllofUs, and was D&AD President in 2011. He teaches at the London College of Communication, Hyper Island in Sweden and Space Invaders in Copenhagen.

Rosie Arnold, 2012's D&AD President, has been at Bartle Bogle Hegarty since 1983, and in 2008 was appointed Deputy Executive Creative Director. She has been responsible for some of the agency's most iconic work.

" And then there was the seismic shift that destroyed markets, changed an industry and brought the world that much closer together: the iPhone was launched.

" We lost Patrick Swayze and Michael Jackson and the downturn in the world's economy continued to put fear into the hearts and minds of clients everywhere.

" The work filled the immense space. It felt like the warehouse scene in 'Raiders of the Lost Ark'. Row after row of possibilities... and somewhere in there, the Ark.

" Sometimes you have no real idea what's going to surface from the entries. I love it when you can see the idea from way across the room and it keeps getting better as you draw closer.

" It seems, going into the future, that not only is D&AD stronger than ever, but it is setting new standards of behavioural excellence too.

150
50 Years of D&AD

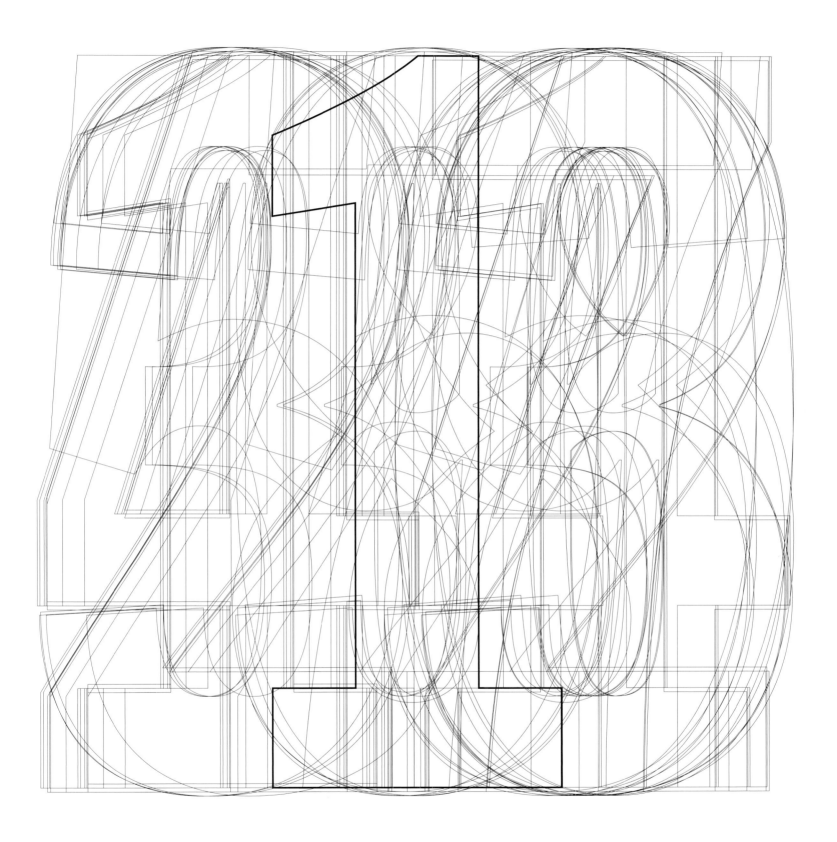

1963
Edward Booth-Clibborn

Photo James Mortimer

Edward Booth-Clibborn started his career
in advertising at J Walter Thompson
(JWT) in the late 1950s. In 1963 he
was elected Chairman of D&AD. Under
his almost 30-year leadership, D&AD
grew to become a beacon of creative
excellence of worldwide repute, with a
highly respected education programme
and an annual Book and exhibition.
He is now a renowned publisher of
illustrated books that range from major
art catalogues for museums around the
world to overviews of contemporary art,
graphics and subculture.

Design & Art Direction '63 The first annual
exhibition of the Designers & Art Directors
Association of London

1963 Annual

Annual Design Fletcher/Forbes/Gill

Title A... is for Apple
Client Apple & Pear Publicity Council
Agency Cammell-Hudson Associates

In 1963, ours was a young industry, keen to improve its creative standards. Our ambition, as set out in that first printed Annual, was "to demonstrate and gain acceptance of the part that imaginative design and art direction have to play in the context of modern society and to define and improve current graphic standards." In my opinion, these values are as important today as they were then. I used to say that D&AD is there to stimulate, not congratulate. That is the way to keep moving forward.

As an art director, I had work accepted in the first ever D&AD Awards in 1962 for advertisements for the British Butter Council, and this qualified me for membership. The first D&AD Awards were presented by Lord Snowdon at a luncheon at the Hilton Hotel in June 1963. There was no Annual for 1962, only a booklet – selling at six old pennies – listing the accepted work, designed by Fletcher/Forbes/Gill, which also designed the D&AD logo (the cover can be seen in the 1963 Annual on page 44). The 1963 jury on which I served selected the work

that appeared in the first printed Annual, and John Commander, Art Director of Balding & Mansell printers, was Chairman of the jury.

Later in 1963, at the D&AD AGM, Bob Brooks and Len Fulford put my name forward and I was duly elected Chairman. I was also a working Art Director at JWT at the time. The new job came with an old typewriter, a trestle table, an overdraft in the bank and the ever-helpful Janet Donovan as assistant. Since D&AD had no office, JWT kindly let us have the use of some of its space. We achieved many things with those few resources. The Books and the annual D&AD exhibition travelled all over the world promoting British creative talent, from Prague in Czechoslovakia to Jakarta, Indonesia. The 'It's Great! Britain' show, which was opened by Lord Snowdon in New York in 1967, went to Washington, Dallas and Detroit, showing the work of British advertising agencies, designers and film production companies. All these exhibitions gave D&AD and its members prestige and allowed their talents a showcase like never before.

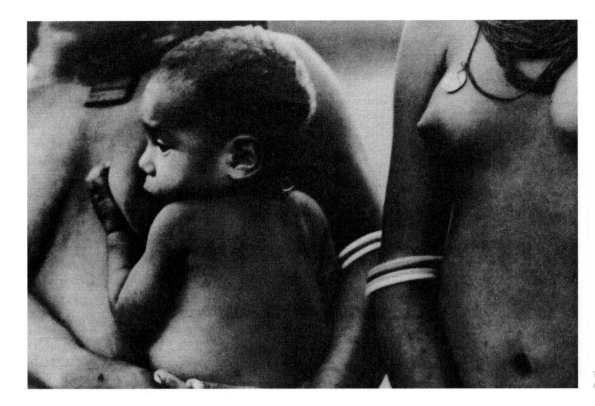

Title Town Magazine
Agency Cornmarket Press

In 1963, D&AD was the only body representing those working creatively in the new and constantly changing area of visual communication. In 1964 the Graphic Workshops started, in conjunction with the Royal College of Art; the first Education Committee's members were Bob Gill, Germano Facetti, Lou Klein and Brian Tattersfield. The education programme flourished, with many other illustrious names committing themselves to helping future generations and giving art students and schools the support of the industry.

An amusing story is that of the actual Pencils themselves. In 1964 Marcello Minale persuaded the Worshipful Company of Goldsmiths to sponsor and make the first Awards. Marcello designed the Gold Award as a pencil with gold lead in a mahogany pencil box; similarly, the Silver Awards had silver lead. Because they were so expensive to produce, the goldsmiths wouldn't do it again, so Lou Klein, who was on the Committee in 1965, came up with the wooden Pencil design that is now the highest of British creative accolades.

As for influential creative people from the early days, history tells the tale. People like Bob Brooks, Bob Gill, Alan Fletcher, Jock Kinneir and Derek Birdsall left powerful legacies. Colin Millward, the great Art Director for Collett Dickenson Pearce, was also important, as was Tony Palladino, Art Director at US agency Papert Koenig Lois. At that time, the Americans had an enormous influence and we looked to them to shake us up.

Lester Bookbinder, the photographer, was also significant, but for me, the Art Director Robert Brownjohn was the most outstanding, with a fresh and original approach that had a profound influence on us all. He went on to win the Black Pencil in 1965 for the titles of the Bond film 'Goldfinger'.

"
D&AD is there to stimulate, not congratulate. That is the way to keep moving forward.

The judged work of 1963 was published in D&AD 64. The three pieces of Award-winning work from that first printed Annual I would single out are: Robert Brownjohn's 'A is for Apple' film for the Apple & Pear Publicity Council; Spicers Paper, designed by Derek Birdsall and photographed by the late Robert Freeman; and Town Magazine, with Tom Wolsey as Art Director and John Bulmer as Photographer.

In many instances in my role as Chairman, I felt that important people were left out of Awards. In that first Book, I would have selected the work of Germano Facetti for his outstanding Penguin Books covers.

Looking back to those early days, those of us committed to D&AD played a key role in British ideas and our creative industries making the major contribution for which this country is now famous. I am proud and delighted to see D&AD reach 50. ●

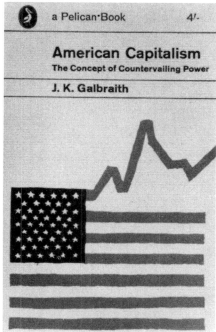
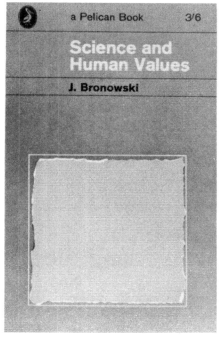

Title Book covers
Client Penguin Books
Art Director Germano Facetti
Designers George Daulby, Romek Marber

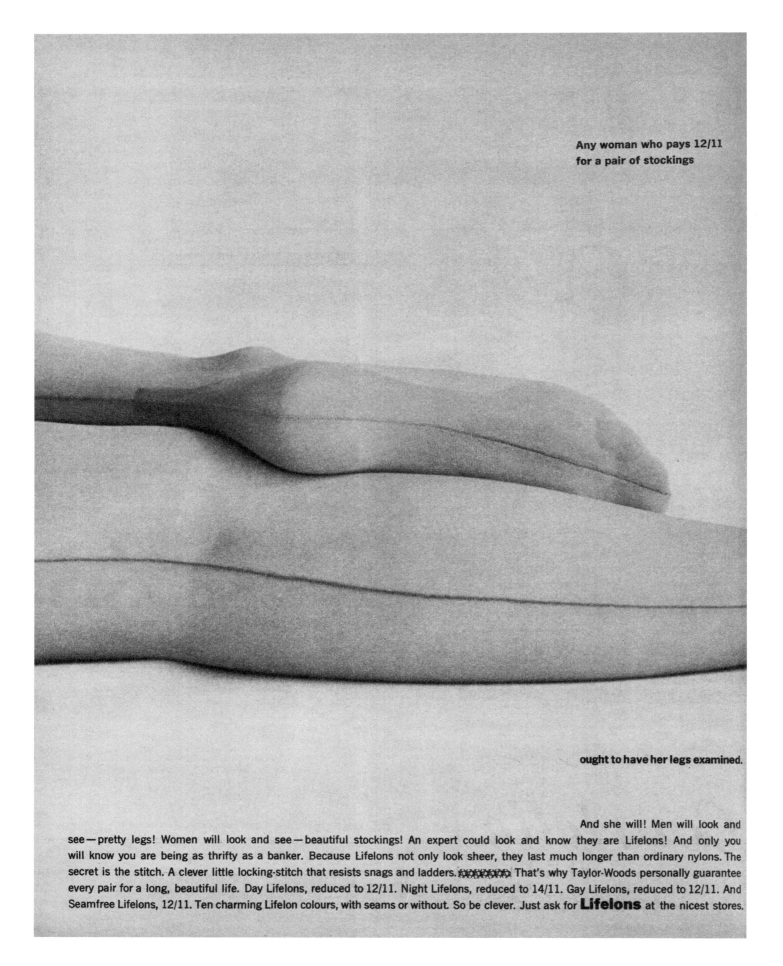

Any woman who pays 12/11
for a pair of stockings

ought to have her legs examined.

And she will! Men will look and
see — pretty legs! Women will look and see — beautiful stockings! An expert could look and know they are Lifelons! And only you
will know you are being as thrifty as a banker. Because Lifelons not only look sheer, they last much longer than ordinary nylons. The
secret is the stitch. A clever little locking-stitch that resists snags and ladders. ɪɪ That's why Taylor-Woods personally guarantee
every pair for a long, beautiful life. Day Lifelons, reduced to 12/11. Night Lifelons, reduced to 14/11. Gay Lifelons, reduced to 12/11. And
Seamfree Lifelons, 12/11. Ten charming Lifelon colours, with seams or without. So be clever. Just ask for **Lifelons** at the nicest stores.

Title Lifelon Stockings
Client Taylor-Woods
Agency McCann-Erickson

"Looking back to those early days, those of us committed to D&AD played a key role in British ideas and the creative industries making the major contribution for which this country is now famous.

Title Spicers Paper
Client Spicers
Agency T Booth Waddicor & Partners

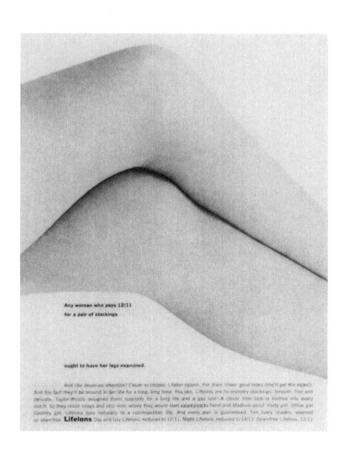

Any woman who pays 12/11
for a pair of stockings

ought to have her legs examined.

Title Lifelon Stockings
Client Taylor-Woods
Agency McCann-Erickson

1964
Bob Gill

Bob Gill is a designer, illustrator, writer, filmmaker and teacher. He was the Gill in Fletcher/Forbes/Gill, which eventually became Pentagram.

He was one of the founders of D&AD, and was elected into the New York Art Directors Club Hall of Fame. He has written a number of books about design and illustration. His latest is 'Bob Gill, so far.' He is now working and teaching in New York.

1964 Annual

Annual Design George Daulby; BDMW Associates
Cover Photography Len Fulford

Design & Art Direction '63 The first annual exhibition of the Designers & Art Directors Association of London at the London Hilton Hotel Park Lane W1 Open daily 10am to 7pm from Tuesday 11th June until 1pm Saturday 15th June Admission free

Title D&AD
Client Designers & Art Directors Association
Design Group Fletcher/Forbes/Gill

I guess the best way to begin is with Fletcher/Forbes/Gill, which started on April Fools' Day in 1962. I had come to the UK from New York, and realised that there was nothing to showcase what people were doing in advertising and design.

There was one organisation, the only organisation at that time that had anything to do with design, which was called the Society of Industrial Artists. It was very obviously a pre-war, stuffy organisation. When we started, because we were these Young Turks, they invited us to join. Fletcher, Forbes and I knew that these people were very conventional and boring, and that the SIA wasn't the right vehicle to really make magic happen. They were putting pressure on us to join so I suggested for the fun of it that a debate should happen, to expose them by showing that there was nothing there for young designers or young people in advertising, and that the subject of the debate should be: "The SIA is Full of Shit".

They didn't agree to this, so we compromised. The title became: "Why Join the SIA?" This did take place and a lot of designers came to it. Colin Forbes took the negative, and somebody from the SIA took the positive. In the end we were even more convinced that this thing wasn't worth anything, so I, Alan Fletcher, Forbes and a few other designers, including Derek Birdsall, decided to form D&AD.

Just by the nature of the people involved, we knew that D&AD was going to be different. We were all young, not very conventional and certainly not establishment types. There were a number of Americans involved, which also changed the colour of it in some way. We had exhibitions every year, which started very modestly of course. When I was on the 2012 jury two weeks ago, we had thousands of entries, so D&AD has really come a long way.

It was inevitable that D&AD would become more establishment. To bring in 200 jurors from all over the world and to publish these Annuals – it is a very big business today. However, it has done a lot for standards and for showing what's happening, no question about it. Previously the New York show was known to be the most prestigious exhibition of design and advertising, but it can no longer claim that.

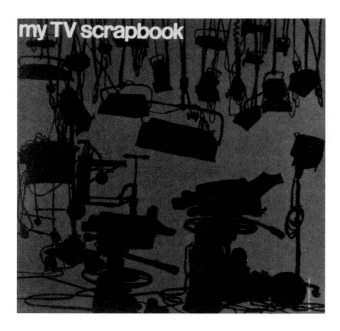

Title My TV Scrapbook
Client Spicers
Agency Waddicors & Clark Wilkinson

By 1964, D&AD had been going for a few years, and Fletcher/Forbes/Gill was very well represented in the exhibition. One of our strengths was our ability to solve problems as diverse as a leaflet of technical specifications for a building supply company, an advertising campaign for an international airline, posters for the BBC, two paper companies, D&AD's first exhibition and a picture book for children.

It would be very strange if the work was still absolutely contemporary – that would suggest something terrible – but I would say it was comparable when it comes to the ideas.

I have a resistance to joining things, so I don't have many memories of those years. Obviously I was on the jury from time to time because we were among the most important design offices, and there are pictures of me on the jury so I guess I was there. I don't have very specific memories, though. This is firstly because I've been out of London for a long time – I left in 1975. For people who are still in London, there's a natural memory of things that go from year to year. I left because some very interesting things came up for me in New York, and the swinging 60s were coming to an end. Also, the Tories were taking over, so the atmosphere was completely different. I wasn't very sorry to leave. ●

better Red than Dead

Swimming name-droppers are spoiled for choice in Israel. You can take the plunge in the Mediterranean (there are 117 miles of coastline dotted with popular, modern resorts such as Netanya, Ashkelon and Nahariya), the Sea of Galilee, or the Red Sea. People who will go to any lengths (or depths) to impress the neighbours, will at least try a tentative toe in the Dead Sea, rich in minerals and the lowest spot on earth. Non-swimmers, too, will enjoy Israel. History paused there, the Bible began there. You can ruminate over ruins, refresh yourself in an up-to-the-minute hotel. There is nothing historic about Israel's hotels; they have grown with the tourist industry and new ones are completed every year. Israel, too, has not left all the excitement to history, she is building something worth seeing herself. And she is not too engrossed to be gay. This series of advertisements in the Observer will tell you more about it. You can jump the gun by seeing your travel agent or writing for information to **ISRAEL GOVERNMENT TOURIST OFFICE** 59 St. James's Street, London SW1. HYD 2431 El Al luxurious Boeings will get you to Israel in four and a half hours. You can go at any time. Israel is an all-year resort. A two-week *sunshine-plus* holiday costs from 95 gns - including hotel accommodation and El Al jet flight.

EL AL
ISRAEL AIRLINES

Title Better Red Than Dead
Client El Al Israel Airlines / Israel Government Tourist Office
Agency John Collings & Partners / Progress Advertising

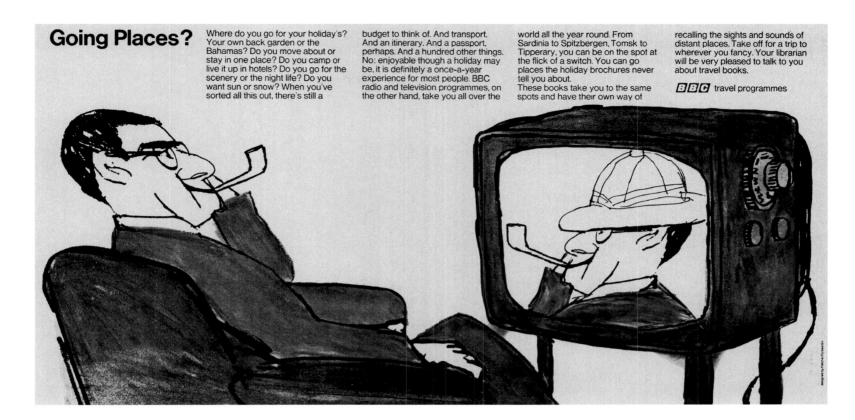

Going Places?

Where do you go for your holiday's? Your own back garden or the Bahamas? Do you move about or stay in one place? Do you camp or live it up in hotels? Do you go for the scenery or the night life? Do you want sun or snow? When you've sorted all this out, there's still a budget to think of. And transport. And an itinerary. And a passport, perhaps. And a hundred other things. No: enjoyable though a holiday may be, it is definitely a once-a-year experience for most people. BBC radio and television programmes, on the other hand, take you all over the world all the year round. From Sardinia to Spitzbergen, Tomsk to Tipperary, you can be on the spot at the flick of a switch. You can go places the holiday brochures never tell you about.

These books take you to the same spots and have their own way of recalling the sights and sounds of distant places. Take off for a trip to wherever you fancy. Your librarian will be very pleased to talk to you about travel books.

BBC travel programmes

Title Going Places?
Client BBC Schools Library
Agency BBC

What Colour Is Your World? by Bob Gill

Title What Colour is Your World?
Client Anthony Blond
Agency Fletcher/Forbes/Gill

"I suggested for the fun of it that a debate should happen to expose the Society of Industrial Artists and show that there was nothing there for young designers or young people in advertising, and that the subject of the debate should be: 'The SIA is Full of Shit'.

International Press Advertising
An exhibition at Reed House, 82 Piccadilly, London W1
10am - 5pm, Mondays - Fridays, 23 August - 10 October
The first of a series prepared for the Reed Paper Group
by Walter Herdeg, Editor of Graphis magazine

Title International Press Advertising
Client Reed Paper Group
Design Group Fletcher/Forbes/Gill

Title Nippon Design Center
Client Reed Paper Group
Design Group Fletcher/Forbes/Gill

Title Reed Paper in Action
Client Reed Paper Group
Design Group Fletcher/Forbes/Gill

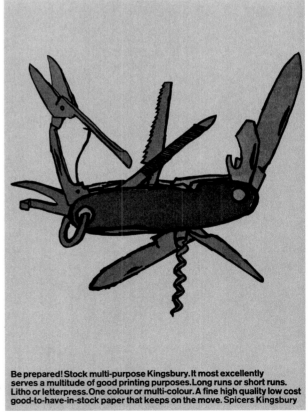

Title Asbestolux
Client Cape Building Products
Agency Taylor Wishardt

Title Kingsbury
Client Spicers
Agency Waddicors & Clark Wilkinson

1965
Derek Birdsall

Derek Birdsall was a founder member, in 1958, of Birdsall Daulby Mayhew Wildbur (BDMW) Associates. He was also a founder member of D&AD and its first (Hon) Secretary, while John Commander was first Chairman. He has designed many covers for Penguin Books, as well as Pirelli calendars, a book for Monty Python, the first issues of The Independent Magazine and The Sunday Telegraph Magazine and advertising for Balding & Mansell and Lotus Cars. He has been a consultant designer to Mobil Corporation, IBM Europe, Penguin Education and HRH The Prince of Wales's School of Architecture. He was elected a Royal Designer for Industry in 1983, became an Honorary Fellow of the Royal College of Art in 1986, and won the Prince Philip Designers Prize in 2005.

1965 Annual

Annual Design **Peter Wildbur; BDMW Associates**

I was a bit of a young lion, the youngest of the whole gang, I think. We were thought to be the best designers and illustrators in London. There weren't really any magazines about graphic design in Britain at the time, and we felt that something would be gained by the business in Britain and disseminating our work abroad if we put on an exhibition. In doing so, we got together with Fletcher/Forbes/Gill and various other design groups and decided to form D&AD.

The first exhibition was at the London Hilton in Park Lane, and Lord Snowdon, by then quite a successful photographer, opened it for us. I remember him coming in followed by a horde of photographers, clicking away. Finally he turned around and said, "I think that's enough, don't you?" The doors were shut and he turned around and asked if anyone had a cigarette. In those days, royalty didn't smoke in public – well, they still don't. One of my favourite recent memories is of going to a design dinner at Buckingham Palace in 2011. I was beginning to look a bit apprehensive when a friend who was standing next to me said, "Derek wants a cigarette." Within seconds, a flunky (there's no other word for it) tapped on my shoulder and said, "I've put an ashtray on the mantelpiece behind you, sir." I said, "Dear love of God, that's amazing," and my friend replied, "Well,

Lizzie does smoke." You can smoke in somebody's house, ergo you can smoke in Buckingham Palace.

One thing I remember vividly from the first couple of years was a session with Germano Facetti on the jury. It was quite a harsh jury, and everything we'd seen for the previous 20 minutes had been, "Out. Out. Out." Suddenly there was a big vote in for a series of spreads from a magazine with tits and arses all over it. Germano jumped to his feet and said, "F***ing tits and f***ing arses, that's all we're getting in today!" and stormed out. He was quite right.

We started D&AD with the idea of being mainly designers, with art direction and good advertising design being a part of it. But within two years the advertising guys took over. This happened partly because the advertising agencies were encouraged to give donations in terms of cash or awards, and of course the agencies paid for all their entry fees. Us little freelance designers had to pay our own entry fees. You can't expect young designers from the north of England, which is where I'm from, to stump up these prodigious sums of money. I stopped sending stuff in to D&AD easily 30 years ago. My kind of work, books mainly, hardly ever got a look in. We did talk for a while of starting a designers-only club but it never happened.

Title Bo Peep nursery furniture
Client D Meredew
Agency Planning Unit

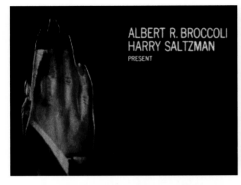

Title Goldfinger titles
Production Company Dart Films

And then of course there were these bloody lavish dinners, all funded by the advertising agencies. I happen to be what they call a Royal Designer for Industry, and I railed and railed a few years ago against having black-tie dinners. I said, "I didn't spend most of my life learning to be a designer so that I have to wear a bloody bow-tie to dinner." So they dropped the rule. I've never been to a dinner since anyway. Pretentious nonsense.

I remember that very first exhibition at the Hilton. We paired off to put the exhibits up, and I was with Bob Gill. Would you believe we used panel pins? It was so primitive in those days. We came to a book jacket I had done for Penguin Books called 'Chosen Words', and I held it up while Bob put the pins in. He looked at me and said, "Jesus, this is great." He shouted over a partition to Colin Forbes, who was pinning with Alan Fletcher, "Colin! This jacket for 'Chosen Words', did we do it?" And Colin said, if you'll forgive my French, "No, you f***ing idiot. Derek did it."

In those days and for some years afterwards, the designs represented in the book were very, very good. Some of it as good as anything that's done today. It was a great era for design in Switzerland, America and Britain. When I think of that time, I think of the work of Tom Wolsey, who was such an amazing Art Director. Also, the work of Collett Dickenson Pearce, the ad agency. They were very bright guys. Colin Millward, too, who was their Creative Director. They had a big series of ads for Acrilan, which was a new miracle fabric. Those ads were the highpoint of that year. Fletcher/Forbes/Gill was doing very good work at the time, as was BDMW Associates, I like to think, which was my group. ●

"There were no real graphic-design magazines in Britain at the time. We felt that something would be gained by the business in Britain and disseminating our work abroad if we put on an exhibition.

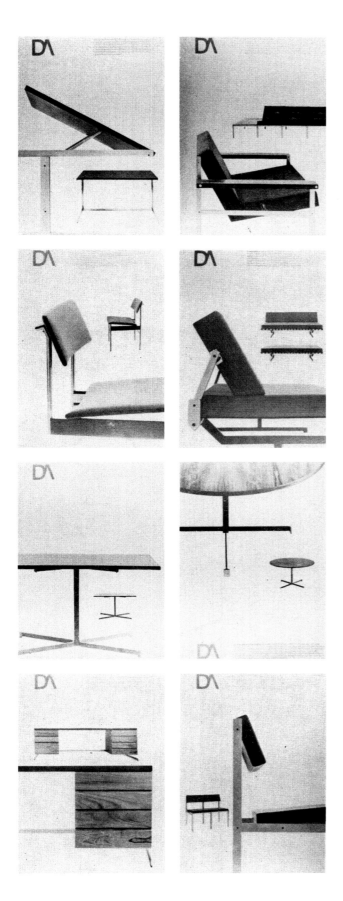

Title Brasilia chair
Client Design Associates
Agency BDMW Associates

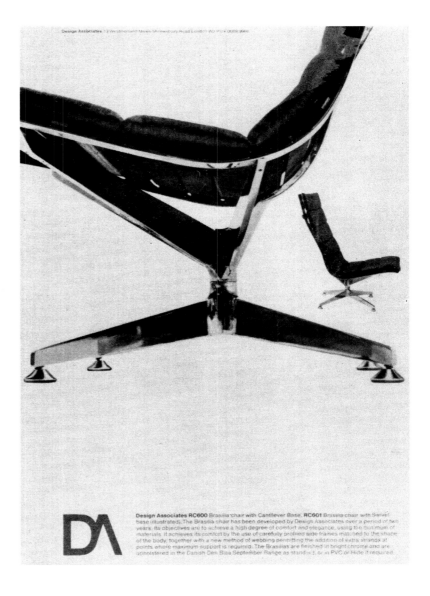

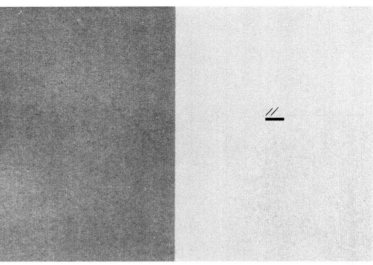

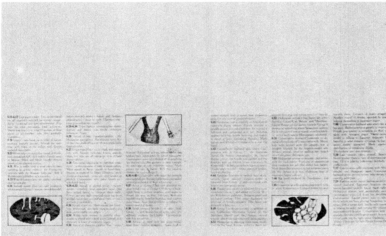

introduction

Many years ago I used to know a man named Pussy Bennett who was one of the country's leading fur-coat thieves. His technique was relatively simple; he spotted a fur-coat he fancied and followed the wearer home. Then he spent several days watching the house, getting an idea of the numbers and movements of the household. (He told me that women with very good fur-coats are widows who live in apartment buildings with one maid to look after them.) Pussy Bennett waited until the owner of the fur-coat went out—not of course wearing the coat—and left only the maid at home. He then arrived on the doorstep with a crate of Pol Roger champagne which he said was a gift from Lord Glasgow. He made up any name, for the maids were usually foreign and Lord was the important part, they all understood that Lord part. He then was admitted to the house to uncrate and dust and in-spect the bottles. When he left the house he made sure that he didn't leave any dust or pieces of packing from the crate and he even took the crate, inside which—given average luck —was the fur-coat.

Pussy said that anyone could gain entrance to anywhere if they were offering a crate of expensive drink as a gift. Quite apart from its potential as a catalyst for crime, drink has always been surrounded with mystical connotations. This has encour-aged some wine-sages to build drinking into such a ritual of nonsense that people are actually afraid of ordering wine in a restaurant. Surely it's astonishing that an honest man willing to pay—about double its value—for a bottle of wine in a restaurant should find reading a wine-list a frightening exper-ience. When Euripedes said, 'Wine as a terrible foe, hard to wrestle with,' it's my opinion he meant the wine-list or perhaps

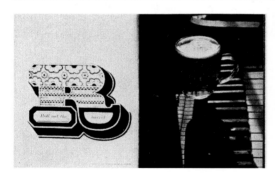

Drinks *pl.* 1. Liquids swallowed for assuaging thirst or taken into the system for nourishment. 2. Draughts or potions. 3. Intoxicating alcoholic beverages. **Man** *n.* 1. the male human being. 2. An adult male eminently endowed with manly qualities. 3. A person of distinction, position, importance or note. **Ship** *n.* (regarded as feminine, woman; she, her.) Vessel. **-ship** 1. Added to denote the state or condition of being so and so. 2. Skill in certain capacity.

Title Drinks~Man~Ship
Publisher Haymarket Press
Designer Derek Birdsall

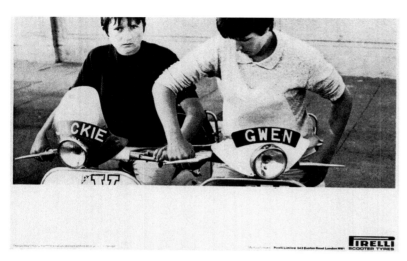

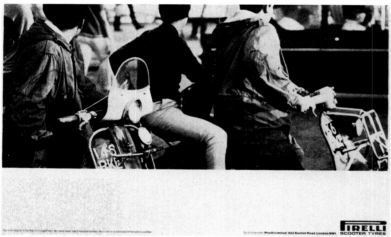

"

We started D&AD with the idea of being mainly designers, with art direction and good advertising design being a part of it. But within two years the advertising guys took over.

Title Pirelli scooter tyres
Client Pirelli
Agency Dorland Advertising

Title Hope Takes Many Shapes
Client British Petroleum
Agency Service Advertising

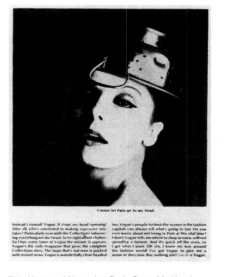

Title Where Do Travel Agents Go in Winter?
Client El Al Israel Airlines
Agency John Collings & Partners

Title Martell Brandy – Are You a Great Lover?
Client Matthew Clark & Sons
Agency Charles Hobson & Grey

Title Vogue – I Never Let Paris Go to My Head
Client Condé Nast Publications
Agency Collett Dickenson Pearce

1966
Terence Conran

Born in 1931, Terence Conran remains one of the world's best-known designers, restaurateurs and retailers.

His first design job was working for the influential architect Dennis Lennon on the 1951 Festival of Britain. Just over a decade later, he founded the Habitat chain of home furnishings stores, which revolutionised the UK high street by bringing intelligent, modern design within reach of the general public.

From The Soup Kitchen in 1953 to his latest projects, Boundary and Lutyens, Terence has owned and operated over 50 restaurants.

Today he is Chairman of the Conran Group, which has eight Conran Shops around the world and an international interior design and architecture practice. He continues to design furniture for a wide variety of companies, including Benchmark, Content by Conran and Marks & Spencer.

1966 Annual

Annual Design Michael Tucker
Cover Design Alan Aldridge, Lou Klein
Cover Photography Len Fulford

Looking back through rose-tinted spectacles, you could be forgiven for believing that 1966 was one long party, the year the world turned Technicolor. Nancy Sinatra's boots were made for walking, Bob Dylan was upsetting his fans in Manchester by going electric and John Lennon caused a fuss by telling the Evening Standard that the Beatles were now bigger than Jesus. Mary Quant's hemlines couldn't possibly have inched any higher, and she turned up at Buckingham Palace to collect her well-deserved OBE in a micro-mini and black cut-out gloves. She looked magnificent, utterly divine, and we all cheered her when she returned to Chelsea. England took on the world at football and won the World Cup, Harold Wilson swept to power and the space race soared to new heights, with Russian and American probes landing on planets here, there and everywhere. London, the UK and the world were swinging, the seeds planted in the grim post-war years now in full bloom. However, it was set against a backdrop of maniacal political instability across the world: Vietnam, nuclear paranoia and the cold war, the civil rights movement in America. 1966 was a turbulent, colourful and optimistic melting pot.

Against all this, some of us were getting busy – the 60s was an incredible decade for me personally, and 1966 was probably as busy a time as I can remember. We had opened the first Habitat in 1964, and it had been far more successful than we had dared to dream and in a much shorter time. The swinging 60s may have their origins in London but had swept across Britain, and in 1966 we added more stores in Brighton, Glasgow and Manchester, as well as a second in London. Our little Habitat was growing up fast and all the frustration we had felt at the end of the 50s and early 60s – that the establishment wouldn't recognise our ideas, that there was a better style of life for people to live – had a real, tangible focus.

One thing we were constantly told was that what we were doing – our revolution – was only relevant to our small and arty area of London. We didn't believe this, which was why we opened those other branches across the country – and we were right. In many respects, 1966 was a defining year for me personally. We had done the first Habitat catalogue the year before, consisting simply of loose sheets attached in one corner. It was successful, however, and in 1966

Where's The Penguin?

The penguin's not on the man...the man's on the penguin. Spicers Penguin, the superb art paper that prints those birds and beasts as clearly and colourfully as ever they are in the flesh. For high quality full colour, you can't do better than Spicers Penguin white art for letterpress.

Title Where's the Penguin?
Client Spicers
Agency Charles Hobson & Grey

Conran Design Group Art Director Ron Baker produced something much more sophisticated that even caught the attention of the D&AD Annual.

Looking back through the Annual for 1966, it is clear that British design, and specifically graphic design, was growing up and making use of the latest advances in technology. IBM was pioneering computer-aided design automation tools that changed the face of the industry. Design times were sped up, work could be produced more efficiently and the quality of work was on the up and up.

I still believe now, as I did in 1966, that "eye to hand" is the most important part of the design process, as this is where creative ideas are generated, and it is through this creativity that, as designers, we succeed or fail. However, there is no denying that computers have made the work of a designer or architect easier and more efficient – just as long as we do not become their slaves.

In line with the liberated times, graphic design was becoming much sexier and more risqué, pushing boundaries that our parents' generation would have found beyond the realms of good taste. But this was the attitude we railed against to make the 60s so exciting. Helmut Newton's erotically charged black and white photographs for Vogue, working with Terence Whelan, were recognised by D&AD and rightly so.

I don't think any of us at the time were aware of the changes taking place, even if they now seem radical. We were just getting on with trying to make things happen and pay the gas bill, although it has been a pleasure to look back on the exciting time for design it was in 1966.

"One thing we were constantly told was that what we were doing – our revolution – was only relevant to our small and arty area of London. We didn't believe this.

Title ...Has It All Wrapped Up
Client Reed Paper & Board Sales
Agency Charles Hobson & Grey

Title Habitat catalogue
Client Habitat Designs
Agency Conran Design Group

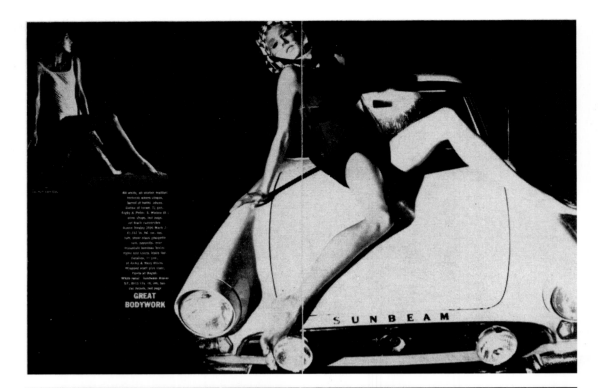

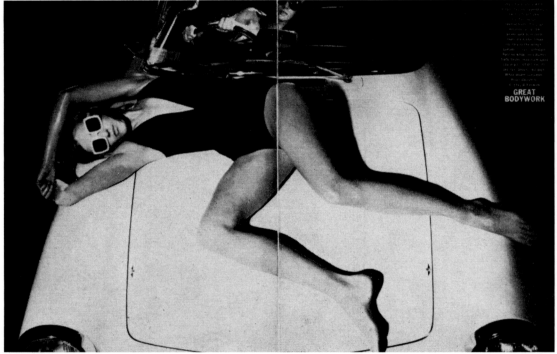

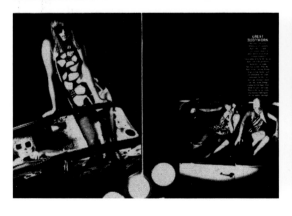
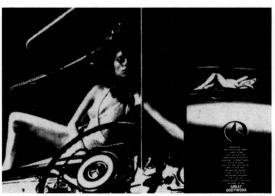

Title **Vogue spreads**
Publication **Vogue**
Publisher **Condé Nast**

Title **William Klein spread**
Publication **Queen**
Publisher **Stevens Press**

"In line with the liberated times, graphic design was becoming much sexier and more risqué, pushing boundaries that our parents' generation would have found beyond the realms of good taste.

1967
David Puttnam

David Puttnam spent 30 years as an independent producer of award-winning films such as 'The Mission', 'The Killing Fields', 'Local Hero', 'Chariots of Fire', 'Midnight Express', 'Bugsy Malone' and 'Memphis Belle'. He was awarded a BAFTA Fellowship in 2006.

He retired from film production in 1998 to focus on his work in public policy as it relates to education, the environment and the "creative and communications" industries.

Puttnam was awarded a CBE in 1982 and a knighthood in 1995, and was appointed to the House of Lords in 1997.

He is the present Chancellor of the Open University, President of the Film Distributors' Association, Chairman of The Sage Gateshead and Deputy Chairman of Profero, and a trustee of the Eden Project.

1967 Annual

Annual Design Briggs & McLaren
Cover Design Mario Lippa, David Newton
Cover Art Peter Blake

I was urged by Colin Millward to become involved. I was appointed to the second ever D&AD jury. I can't think why – I was an account man – but he wanted to spread the load a bit. I was working with a group of very good photographers, and my father had been a photographer, so maybe he thought that I knew a bit about it.

After a few years we were losing money hand over fist with the Annual, and at around year four it looked as though we were going to have to stop publishing it. So probably my greatest single contribution to D&AD was a deal I made with Michael Heseltine – who was running Haymarket Press – whereby we let Haymarket take over the publication of the Annual for a guaranteed royalty each year. The royalty (from memory) was £1,200 a year, plus a percentage on sales over a certain number of copies, plus 50 per cent on any advertising. So we moved to something that was beginning to underwrite the organisation as a whole.

By 1967, the world itself was changing, and Britain seemed to be at the cutting edge of much of that change. The somewhat silly "Swinging London" articles actually began to take on some meaning. I was very much a beneficiary of the swinging 60s, but I was also married and had two children. I didn't have time for anything much beyond work, added to which I've never been much of a party-goer. I don't really like events of any sort, but I do a lot of speeches because I'm passionately interested in the subjects that I speak on (educational reform, media regulation and climate change), and at this point in my life it's the

only way that I can have any impact on anything.

That year, Collett Dickenson Pearce was so dominant that there began to be a bit of a backlash against us. People seemed to think we had somehow got above ourselves. I vividly remember going around the exhibition, and whereas in previous years there had been a lot of congratulations before going off to the pub, the atmosphere had changed. We were doing just a little too well.

As to the most memorable work of what was for me a very memorable year, here are a few things that jump out. I make no apology for including a couple of campaigns I was directly involved with, as 45 years later, aspects of them remain particularly vivid.

The 'Five Girls' campaign for Monsanto was conceived by an American art director named Ed Brigdale, and most of the photographs were done by Helmut Newton. We came back from Majorca with a lot of fantastically good pictures. It wasn't exactly a breakthrough idea – five identical girls in the same swimsuit – but it had a lot of impact.

Then there were the 'Soft' Acrilan knitwear ads, also for Monsanto. As an account man, I had an extraordinarily difficult job getting them into the two dominant women's magazines of that era: Woman and Woman's Own. They were extremely conservative publications, and I had enormous problems over our showing belly buttons! We had these beautiful photographs done by Art Kane in the States, and Jerry Schatzberg, who took the iconic early photographs of Bob

Title Chemstrand ads, featuring
Catherine Deneuve (left)
Client Monsanto
Agency Collett Dickenson Pearce

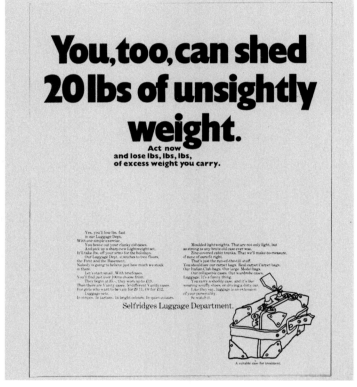

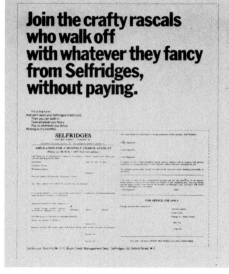

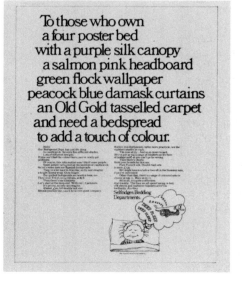

Title Selfridges campaign
Client Selfridges
Agency Collett Dickenson Pearce

> **My favourite is the ad about Selfridges' greatest shoplifting fear: that the beautiful girls might get stolen from their perfume department.**

Dylan, and we used some fantastic models – Charlotte Rampling, Catherine Deneuve and Françoise Hardy. These sweaters, when you photographed them the way we did, with the girls putting them on for the first time, quite naturally showed their stomachs. Believe it or not, we were required to "sensitively airbrush" their belly buttons out.

The other huge negotiation was over the fact that Art Kane only shot on 35mm film, and many of the magazines refused to accept this format because they claimed it was "sub-standard". The real breakthrough was getting them to accept grainy images – the result was ads that were noticeably softer than anything else around at that time.

Similarly, it was only possible to get Robert Freson's very graphic photo essay 'Life Begins Here...' into The Sunday Times Magazine on the grounds that National Geographic seemed to have no problem showing the residents of west Africa suckling their children. Nothing like it had ever been previously published in a British newspaper.

I've chosen the Quaker ad because of the really unusual, and I think quite beautiful, typography. Around that time there was an explosion in the creative use of type, and advertising began to differentiate itself from magazines and newspapers in its use of typefaces. It made the ads really sing.

The Selfridges campaign was very special. It was the first time I had been required to work to that kind of deadline. We started on a Monday, and had to deliver the finished ad by Wednesday night. It had to be a whole page in the Evening Standard – every week. We used to go into Selfridges for inspiration, and there was tremendous jealousy among

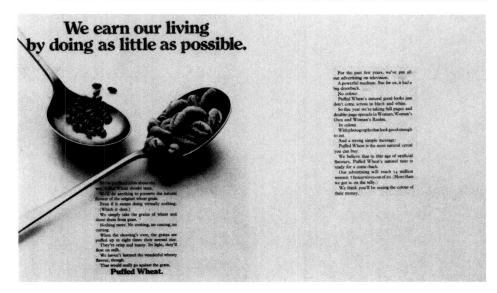

Title Quaker Puffed Wheat
Client Quaker Oats
Agency Doyle Dane Bernbach

the buyers, each of whom was eager to promote their own department. My favourite is the 'Shoplifter' ad, which is about Selfridges' greatest shoplifting fear: that the beautiful girls might get stolen from their perfume department. There was hysteria from some of those at the client end over the word 'shoplifter'. That would not be the problem today – you'd simply get shot for coming up with something so unashamedly sexist, of course.

Lastly, I've chosen Nova magazine, which represented such an extraordinary breakthrough in magazine design. Its Art Director was Harri Peccinotti, and what its arrival did was force us out of our newly acquired comfort zone. Nova and Peccinotti made our ads, which we thought were wonderful, start to look a bit ordinary. He really forced us to raise our game. ●

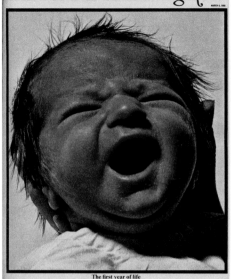

THE SUNDAY TIMES *magazine*

The first year of life

Life begins here…

The baby on the right is five seconds old. The first thing she did when she entered the world was to cry. Next, she moved her hands towards her eyes as if in protest against the light.

These elementary responses are important because they suggest that the baby is physically normal and mean the mother can be reassured. On these pages we publish a unique documentary; we trace the first year of life — from the moment when the umbilical cord has just been cut, to the triumphant moment when a baby can shakily stand on its own feet without assistance.

Paediatricians at the Department of Child Health, Sheffield University, have for years been leading the rest of Britain's medical schools in 'developmental diagnosis'—the method by which a baby's mental and physical capacity can be assessed. To reach a diagnosis, the doctors make a detailed study of the baby's posture, movements, reflexes, special senses and social behaviour and then compare the results with the average for his age. This work is particularly important if there is a suspicion that a child might be mentally handicapped, or when proof of its normality must be obtained for adoption cases. We based this feature on the research carried out at Sheffield, and we produce it with the co-operation of the hospital authorities. Robert Freson set up a photographic studio in Sheffield Children's Hospital where, with the aid of editorial researcher Sylvia Lane, he spent three weeks patiently photographing and 'cataloguing' dozens of babies to record key stages in their development.

We are grateful to the mothers who gave permission for their babies to be photographed — and particularly those who brought children to Freson's hospital studio from outlying districts of Sheffield when we sent taxis out to collect them.

It is vital for parents to remember that no single sign of development can be related to a child's progress. Some are later than others in sitting, talking or walking, and yet are no less clever. These photographs give a general guide to the progress of an average full-term baby.

Photographs by Robert Freson
Commentary by Dr Alfred Byrne, Sunday Times Medical Correspondent
Editorial Research by Sylvia Lane

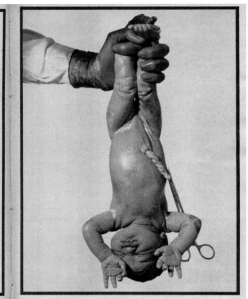

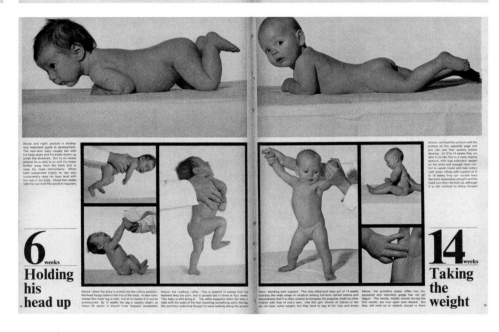

6 weeks
Holding his head up

14 weeks
Taking the weight

Title Life Begins Here…
Publication The Sunday Times Magazine
Publisher Times Newspapers

"
What Nova's arrival did was force us out of our newly acquired comfort zone. Harri Peccinotti made our ads, which we thought were wonderful, start to look a bit ordinary.

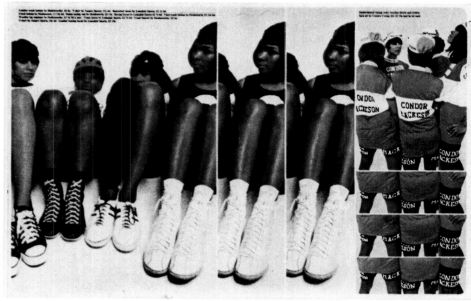

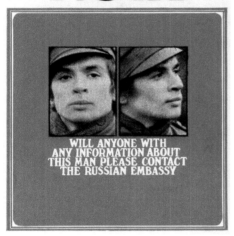

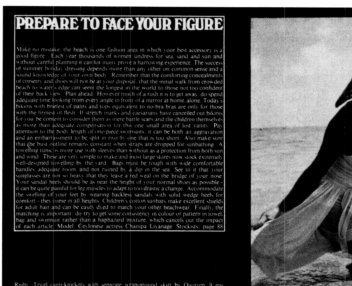

Title **Nova**
Publisher **George Newnes**

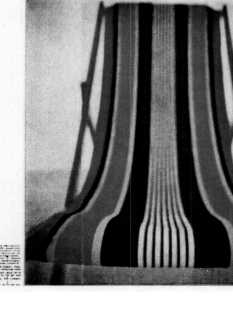

1968
Bob Brooks

Bob Brooks began his advertising career in 1955 at Ogilvy Benson & Mather New York. By 1959 he was Creative Group Head at Benton & Bowles New York. In 1960 Brooks moved to Benton & Bowles London as co-Creative Director with copywriter Bob Gross.

In 1962 he became one of the founders of D&AD.

Brooks opened a photographic studio specialising in advertising photography in 1964. In 1967 he realised, along with future partners Len Fulford and Jim Baker, that the future was with film commercials, and they founded Brooks Baker Fulford, later known as BFCS.

In 1977 Brooks directed the BAFTA-nominated TV film 'The Knowledge' for Thames Television, and in 1981 he directed 'Tattoo' for American film producer Joseph Levine. He then returned to BFCS and continued directing until he retired in the late 90s.

1968 Annual

Annual Design **Bob Gill**
Typography **Malcolm Frost**

Lady Teacher would like to meet foreign students of either sex.

She wants to teach you English.
To speak English quickly and easily and fluently.
At St Giles, we teach in small friendly groups.
We teach with the most up-to-date equipment,
with private tape-recorders and with our
language laboratory.
We take you on weekend excursions.
We teach you English and about England.
It costs about four shillings a lesson.

St Giles School of Languages
Recognised by the Department of Education and Science
192 Oxford St, London W.1. MUS 0618
Write or Phone for Prospectus

Title Lady Teacher
Client St Giles School of Language
Agency John Collings & Partners

In 1962 I was co-Creative Director of Benton & Bowles London along with Bob Gross, but by 1964 I had left the agency world and opened a photographic studio specialising in advertising and editorial photography. So, by 1967 (the year for work appearing in D&AD 68) I wasn't following agency life and output that closely, and found myself working increasingly on the continent.

Going through the 68 Annual, I realised that it was the final phase of print advertising before the onslaught of the television revolution, which exploded on the London scene just a few years later. The print ads and campaigns in this Annual, on the whole, are excellent. Great ideas are written with a light, subtle touch and presented in fresh, exciting layouts. Illustration, photography and typography are outstanding, very different from the work I first saw when I arrived in London in 1960. Though the influence of Doyle Dane Bernbach (DDB) is evident, here was advertising with a new voice and look that was uniquely British. Most of these ads were written and art directed by the soon-to-be stars of British advertising over the next two decades: Abbott, Yeoman, Maxwell, Hegarty, Carruthers, Dale, Cramer, Saatchi, Crosby/Fletcher/Forbes, Godfrey and Webster, to name a few.

It was also the time that the newly conceived colour supplements from The Sunday Times, The Observer and The Telegraph flexed their design muscles and produced some amazing editorial layouts, along with the stunning and influential output of Nova magazine.

Interestingly, I now see this trend towards television commercials in my own work that was included in the 68 show. These photographs marked the end of my stills career, as 1967 saw the birth of Brooks Baker Fulford (eventually BFCS), a film production company formed by Jim Baker, Len Fulford and myself. We felt then, and were proved correct, that the advertising future in the UK would be mainly in television. In 1968, I closed my photographic studio and concentrated full-time on learning the craft of film directing.

As for the work in this Annual, the following are my favourites:

Title The Middle Age of Jackie Kennedy – and You
Publication The Sunday Times Magazine
Publisher Times Newspapers

> It was the time that the newly conceived colour supplements from The Sunday Times, The Observer and The Telegraph flexed their design muscles and produced some amazing editorial layouts.

A campaign from DDB for Uniroyal Rain Tire that deserves its two Yellow Pencils: excellent copy and striking layouts and photographs from Art Director Doug Maxwell and Copywriters David Abbott and Dawson Yeoman.

El Al Israel Airlines, created by John Hegarty and Lindsay Dale at John Collings & Partners: excellent, witty copy and exciting art direction that must have given the jury a difficult decision about the Campaign Award.

The Sunday Times Magazine's 'The Middle Age of Jackie Kennedy – and You'. Artist Michael Leonard was awarded a Yellow Pencil. I remember this issue with great affection for its wit and unusual approach to celebrities. We eventually used the artist for the Brooks Fulford logo.

The Daily Telegraph Magazine's 'The Twelve Days of Christmas': there were many excellent colour supplement articles in this Annual but this was one of the most enjoyable assignments I had as a photographer. I was given the first day of Christmas, and it was the magazine's cover. The overall idea for the article, created by Art Director Geoffrey Axbey and Designer Ian Howes, was charming, and the layout and design was simple yet striking.

Finally, an ad created for St Giles School of Languages by Ross Cramer and Charles Saatchi for John Collings & Partners is a perfect example of the new creative approach to advertising that was evolving in the late 60s. Sly British humour in a strong, direct design. Impossible to miss. ●

Title Uniroyal Rain Tyre campaign
Client Uniroyal
Agency Doyle Dane Bernbach

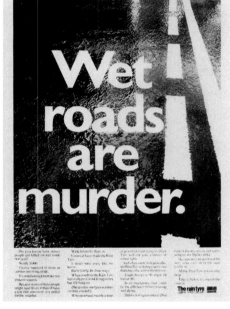

On a Jewish Airline you'd expect cheesecake.

This year, why not spend Hanukah with the folks at home?

Title El Al Israel campaign
Client El Al Israel Airlines
Agency John Collings & Partners

A message from our founder.

You've read a lot about us already.

Just a few of the people who dropped in on us at one time or another.

It took 40 years for our first flight to get here. You can make it in 4½ hours.

The lowest night-spot on earth.

THE TWELVE DAYS OF CHRISTMAS

Christmas each year brings new ideas to the shops, new lights to Regent Street, new extravaganzas to the kitchen. But the ancient traditions hold their own, and if time has lost the secret of their origins, so much the better. *The Twelve Days of Christmas* continues to celebrate the 12 feast days from Christmas to the Epiphany. But what it really means or where it really comes from, nobody knows. It's a carol, a wassail song, a relic of fertility magic, the words of a fireside memory-and-forfeits game, or an "irreligious travesty". There are French versions from the Middle Ages, and the English text was first published in 1780 in a children's book called *Mirth without Mischief*. It has been set to 12 different tunes and sung in pubs and churches alike. To ring a contemporary change on an old song, we asked 12 artists and photographers to illustrate each gift sent by the true love, each present added to the menagerie dreamed up in folklore's strange imagination

"It was the final phase of print advertising before the onslaught of the television revolution, which exploded on the London scene just a few years later.

Title The Twelve Days of Christmas
Publication The Daily Telegraph Magazine
Publisher The Daily Telegraph

1969
Michael Peters

Michael Peters OBE studied graphic design at the London College of Printing, and later won a scholarship to Yale University. He subsequently worked for CBS Television in New York before returning to London to set up the design department for Collett Dickenson Pearce.

In 1970 Peters set up Michael Peters and Partners, which would revolutionise the role of packaging in the marketing of consumer products and count the BBC, British Airways, United Distillers, Unilever, ITV and the Conservative Party among its clients.

In 1992, he founded The Identica Partnership, which specialises in the creation, development, management and design of brands for clients such as Diageo, Nike, Aeroflot, Universal Studios, Pernod Ricard, Russian Standard and Levi Strauss.

Peters left Identica in 2007 and now works as a private consultant.

1969 Annual

Annual Design Trevor Jones, Bob Celiz
Cover Design Lou Klein
Cover Photography Julian Cottrell

Of late a few people have been looking at their regular glass of Bristol Cream in a new light.

They've been taking to a largish glass not normally reserved for our sherry.

Plonking in two or three chunks of ice.

And for good measure, more than a good measure of Bristol Cream.

But make sure it is Bristol Cream.

Bristol Cream is a blend of the very rarest of sherries. So it has the necessary character to withstand the ice treatment.

With a sherry of more tender years the taste tends to melt away with the ice.

Trouble is, Harveys with ice is becoming so popular, we thought it at least should have a name.

Harveys on the rocks seemed a little unimaginative.

Our own humble effort appears below.

So please write in and help us.

Until then we'll just have to call it "The-best-sherry-in-the-world-on-ice".

It's a bit of a mouthful we know.

But what a mouthful.

Iced Cream.

Harveys Bristol Cream. The best sherry in the world. 30/6.
Recommended retail price.

Title Harveys Bristol Cream
Client John Harvey & Sons
Agency Collett Dickenson Pearce

D&AD has changed dramatically. It's really as much design as it is advertising now, but at the time, 1965–69, it was very much about advertising. It's so broad nowadays, with so many different categories – Design, Technology, Spatial Design, the whole design base.

Alan Fletcher was a great man. There were endless people like him that you looked at with enormous respect. And the organisation grew and grew and grew. I won a Pencil very early on in my career, and the feeling was just tremendous. I've won lots of awards, but that one was particularly good.

In 1970 I set up my own design company. I ended up employing 670 people worldwide, in 14 countries. I only started with three or four but it grew tremendously quickly. Our first client was Veet, the hair removal brand.

When I designed the Conservative Party identity in the early 80s, Margaret Thatcher was amazing. She looked at my work, and said, "Which do you like, Mr Peters?" And I said, "I like that one." So she presented it and said, "This is our new logo." And there it was. It was the quickest presentation! We had done it in 50 seconds. No one had said anything, because they were so scared of her – "Do you like it?" "Yes, thank you!"

The 'Ford Squad' advert by CDP is one of the ones I've selected from this year. And it's to do with the incessant nature of the business. It really caused quite a storm. The copy was lovely, talking about all the people who were the backroom boys, really.

The Harveys Bristol Cream one, also by CDP, was just so fresh and so new. It was like, "Wow! We just don't do things that way!", to focus on the product itself like that. It was beautifully written. I remember now that it meant so much to me. That was brilliant work.

The Bowyers sausages one was fantastic. That was an enormous breakthrough at the time, it was so fresh. And there was this great logo – it was fantastic both in the way that it showed the product, and in the design. Wolff Olins deserved a medal for that. At that time – apart from Michael Peters, of course! – I think Wolff Olins was doing the great work.

Title Bowyers campaign
Client Bowyers
Design Group Wolff Olins

The Ford Squad.

The time has come to expose some shady dealings in the motor business. Investigated by the Ford Squad.
What happens is this.
An unsuspecting Ford owner takes his car to a non-Ford dealer to have it serviced.
And the next thing he knows, he's driving around with brake pads, hoses, fan belt, contact points, etc. that aren't Genuine Ford parts.
If they were anywhere as good as our parts, we wouldn't mind so much.
But they aren't. So fitting parts like these usually means you'll have to part with plenty later on.
Admittedly, not every dealer is as sneaky as this. But if you want to be absolutely safe, have your car serviced at a Ford dealer.
Then you can always be sure that some wrong part isn't going to put your car out of action when you're out looking for where the action is.

Ford GENUINE PARTS

Title The Ford Squad
Client Ford Motor Company
Agency Collett Dickenson Pearce

I wasn't well enough to receive my President's Award in 2009 – I was given it for all that I had done over the years – but to win that was the most magnificent tribute that could ever happen. They said, "Michael Peters isn't well, he can't be here – in fact, he nearly died. He's in hospital," and the roar of applause was amazing. It was really big. That was good, even better than that Pencil. I am now recognised as being one of the greats of design in this country.

Every ten years, D&AD changes. In the 1969 Annual, there is work that I produced, and it's 40 years since that way we saw things. Now there are new things coming along, and in 20 years' time we'll look back at our work and it will have changed even more.

D&AD is the utmost of its kind in the world – it's grown everywhere. I remember that they had an exhibition before I was sick, and the publicity it got was unbelievable. I'll leave with one thought. All the greats, be they dead or alive, have grown up through D&AD. And that really is unbelievable. ●

"Wolff Olins deserved a medal for Bowyers sausages... At that time, I think Wolff Olins was doing the great work.

Title **Girl**
Publication **Vogue**
Publisher **Condé Nast Publications**

Title Ogdens' Nut Gone Flake album cover
Client Immediate Records
Design Harry Willock, Derek Burton, Small Faces

"Every ten years, D&AD changes. In the 1969 Annual, there is work that I produced, and it's 40 years since that way we saw things. Now there are new things coming along, and in 20 years' time our work will have changed even more.

1970
Brian Byfield

Brian Byfield studied at the London School of Printing and Graphic Arts before going into advertising. He was Art Director at McCann-Erickson, Grey and Doyle Dane Bernbach (DDB), where he was Head of Art. In the early 70s he formed his own agency. In 1978 he started Brian Byfield Films, where he directed many award-winning commercials.

Over the years, his work as art director, writer, designer and director has appeared in numerous D&AD Annuals.

In 2005 he thought he had retired, but found himself writing a series of books on chess and other games.

1970 Annual

Annual Design **Skyner/Wallis**
Cover Design **Shirt Sleeve Studio**
Cover Photography **Alain Le Garsmeur**

1963   1964   1965   1966   1967   1968   1969   **1970**   1971   1972   1973   1974   1975   1976   1977   1978   1979   1980   1981   1982   1983   1984   1985   1986   1987

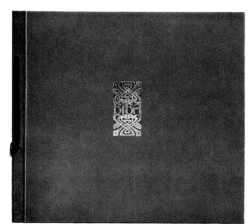

Title Biba
Client Biba
Design Group John McConnell

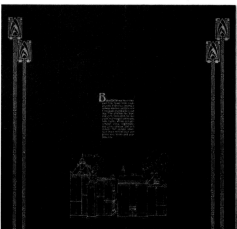

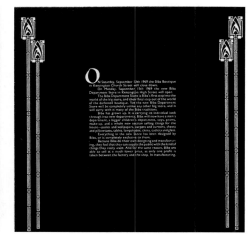

The 60s was the decade that changed English advertising and design. The 1970 D&AD Annual showcased the work that brought ten exciting years to a close.

New advertising agencies and design groups were rattling the cages of the old guard. DDB, Collett Dickenson Pearce, Boase Massimi Pollitt, Papert Koenig Lois and CramerSaatchi in advertising. Crosby/Fletcher/Forbes, John Gorham, John McConnell, Klein Peters and Shirt Sleeve Studio in design.

The Chairman of the jury sessions that year wrote of his worry that the work lacked flair. Apparently the entries were disappointing. Maybe the fact that his own agency managed to get only one piece of work accepted fuelled his comments. Looking back, it is clear to see that the work was of a very high standard, and many of the names who had their early work accepted have gone on to prove that they were no one-night wonders.

David Abbott, Tim Delaney, John Hegarty, Peter Mayle, Alan Parker, Charles Saatchi, Ridley Scott, John Webster and Robin Wight – all of them went on to change

the course of English advertising.

Every young art director, writer and designer was working hard on his "book". Teams were pairing up to forge partnerships that would propel them into the best agencies.

American magazines were bought to check out the latest ads from the city of the 'Mad Men'. DDB was doing groundbreaking work for Volkswagen, Polaroid and Avis. Herb Lubalin was changing New York graphics.

Meanwhile, London agencies and design groups were finding their own. CDP in particular was creating a very English style of its own.

If you have a copy of the 1970 Annual, it's worth reading an ad for account men by DDB. It was written by David Abbott, and will give you an insight into what a creative agency was all about.

I was lucky enough to get into DDB in 1967. I took a pay cut just to be there. It was very competitive, but with a great team spirit. We worked long hours and never complained. It was a chance to work with some of the best art directors,

"They say if you remember the 60s, you weren't there. But for some of us, being there was something we'll never forget. A decade of such creativity it would have been impossible for some of it not to rub off.

Title Posters
Client Health Education Council
Agency CramerSaatchi

Would you be more careful if it was you that got pregnant?

Anyone married or single can get advice on contraception from the Family Planning Association
Margaret Pyke House, 27-35 Mortimer Street, London W1 N 8BQ. Tel. 01-636 9135.

The Health Education Council

This is what happens when a fly lands on your food.
Flies can't eat solid food, so to soften it up they vomit on it. Then they stamp the vomit in until it's a liquid, usually stamping in a few germs for good measure. Then when it's good and runny they suck it all back again, probably dropping some excrement at the same time. And then, when they've finished eating, it's your turn.

Cover food. Cover eating and drinking utensils. Cover dustbins.

The Health Education Council

work and with an uncanny ability to sell it to clients. No wonder Abbott Mead Vickers went on to become the biggest agency in the UK.

They say if you remember the 60s, you weren't there. But for some of us, being there was something we'll never forget. A decade of such creativity it would have been impossible for some of it not to rub off.

Bob Dylan, the Beatles and the Rolling Stones. Long-haired photographers with miniskirted supermodels as girlfriends. Angry young playwrights. Young men from Oxbridge being rude to politicians. A golden-haired young painter from the Royal College of Art exhibiting pictures of naked boyfriends. It certainly changed the way young people saw life. All of this was reflected in the work that was being produced in advertising and design.

I believe 1970 was a great year. But in the real world it had its ups and downs. The jumbo jet landed for the first time in Heathrow, Jimi Hendrix and Janis Joplin died, Paul McCartney left the Beatles, Glastonbury held its first festival and Germaine Greer wrote 'The Female Eunuch'. Four students were killed by National Guardsmen at Kent State University, Ohio, while demonstrating

against the US invasion of Cambodia. 'Midnight Cowboy' won Best Picture Oscar and an earthquake in Peru killed 50,000 people. For the D&AD Annual, however, it was a very good year. Here are some of my personal favourites.

The Health Education Council campaign by CramerSaatchi led the way with a Yellow Pencil for the most outstanding poster. It was certainly one of the best things of the year. A pregnant young man stares woefully at the viewer. The headline reads, "Would you be more careful if it was you that got pregnant?"

The Yellow Pencil for Best Poster Copy was written by Charles Saatchi for the Health Education Council. It's a brilliant piece of writing which is enough to put you off your food.

There were only 19 commercials credited. Commercial TV production was only just getting into its stride. Alan Parker won the Yellow Pencil for his TV campaign for the Post Office. Besides being Copywriter, he was credited as Consultant Director. Early days indeed. Not being a member of the Association of Cinematograph Television and Allied Technicians, he was not allowed to take the Director credit. That would thankfully come later with movies such as 'Bugsy Malone', 'Midnight

Express', 'Angel Heart', 'Mississippi Burning' and 'The Commitments'.

With Alan Parker and Ridley Scott leading the way, TV commercial production would reach new heights. For the first time since television advertising was introduced, viewers were happy to sit down and watch a commercial break. The kettle would only be put on once the programme restarted.

The Sunday Times dominated the Design section, with Michael Rand and David King producing outstanding spreads. Their work in the magazine was required viewing for all aspiring art directors and designers on an easy Sunday morning.

One piece of Print and Direct Mail I particularly like was for Biba. The Designer was John McConnell, with the wonderful photography of Sarah Moon. The Copywriter was Leslie Lake.

I enjoyed looking through the 1970 Annual again. Sadly, the quality of printing and the lack of colour do not help to present the work in its best light. I hadn't seen it since my copy had been stolen from my office in 1994. It was nice to get my hands on one again. If you ever find a copy, give me a call. I'll gladly pay through the nose for it. ●

Title Please, Get a TV Licence
Client General Post Office
Agency Collett Dickenson Pearce

Title Chairman of China
Publication The Sunday Times Magazine
Publisher Times Newspapers

Title Everest
Publication The Sunday Times Magazine
Publisher Times Newspapers

Title 1000
Publication The Sunday Times Magazine
Publisher Times Newspapers

"The Sunday Times dominated the Design section... Required viewing for all aspiring art directors on an easy Sunday morning.

1971
Michael Wolff

Photo **Charles Best**

Michael Wolff is a founder of Wolff Olins, still among the world's most iconic design companies. Now, as Michael Wolff and Company, he works with clients around the world both as a designer and creative advisor. He's a visiting Professor at Central Saint Martins in London and Cape Peninsula University of Technology in Cape Town, South Africa, a Senior Fellow at the Royal College of Art, a member of the Royal Designers for Industry and the UK Government's Inclusive Design Champion.

1971 Annual

Annual Design **Ron Costley**
Cover Design **Gray Jolliffe**

Title Anti-smoking campaign
Client Health Education Council
Agency Saatchi & Saatchi

By 1971, it was mostly all over.
By which I mean the spirit of the 60s.
The 60s, particularly in London, was the decade during which talent, originality, audacity and sheer brilliance were free from domineering account-handling, restraint and, worst of all, "reasons why not". Among many brilliant things that George Bernard Shaw said was: "Nothing is ever accomplished by a reasonable man." The 70s marked the beginning of reasonableness entering into the world of creativity.

Of course, every year since then there's been some great work, much of it rewarded by D&AD's Pencils. Sadly, however, the torrent of meaningless, unoriginal and superficial work drowns it. While creativity in films, drama, food and literature flourishes, generally speaking, the way business uses creative advice to assist with its self-expression has become dispiriting – a bundle of stale and well worn clichés.

So much of what I see from our industry now is visualised reiterations of cautious briefs. In my experience, briefs are usually a client's best shot at expressing what they want. But I don't think just getting what you want gets you very far. Achieving what you couldn't have imagined is the only point of working with creative people. Finding yourself in a different place in your mind from where you started is what should happen when you invite creativity to work for you. Creativity is always about surprise – always about the unexpected.

I remember the juries as simply a question of "in or out". Edward Booth-Clibborn, D&AD's first Chairman, would tear his hair out as he saw our thumbs go down again and again and again. The juries were made up of a handful of discerning people, and sometimes work of a high enough standard was so scant that we feared there would not be enough to hold an exhibition or print an Annual. Now that there is far more work from around the world, more diverse categories and multiple juries with international judges, it's harder to maintain the standards that D&AD was created to uphold and celebrate. That's a big challenge for our future.

Milestones in 1971 were in advertising and specifically in brilliant copywriting. The work that Charles Saatchi, Ross Cramer, Bill Atherton and John Hegarty did for the Health Education Council, inspired by the transformational work of Doyle Dane Bernbach in New York, was to my mind the key creative work of 1971. I thought Fletcher/Forbes/Gill and then Crosby/Fletcher/Forbes produced some milestones in design, and so did Michael Peters.

In 1971, we had a milestone of our own at Wolff Olins. I asked Charles Campbell, the brilliant maître-d' of Terence Conran's Neal Street Restaurant, which had opened in London to great acclaim the year before, to design our food. His brief was to plan a year's menus based on seasonal and extraordinary ingredients.

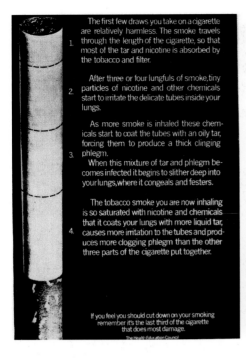

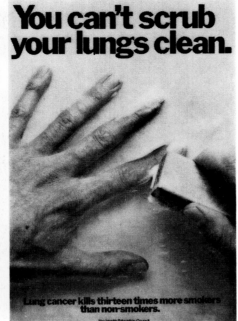

Title Anti-smoking campaign
Client Health Education Council
Agency Saatchi & Saatchi

"

Achieving what you couldn't have imagined is the only point of working with creative people.

The idea was simple food that tasted sublime. We didn't want to be like a restaurant, but like a kitchen where you tasted delicious things as they were being prepared. It was a metaphor for choice and taste, and for our clients to be able to celebrate themselves and not to succumb to "we know better" graphic design.

As far as I was concerned, "no brilliant food, no brilliant ideas". The results of Campbell's influence still delight Wolff Olins's people and their clients and friends today. Our food was a catalyst for our ideas, and for the wit and craft with which we carried them out. We were unabashed and joyous populists in the early days, when many designers were cool and tidy elitists.

One day in 1971, sitting at the huge table designed by David Bristow in our offices, we were having lunch with Graham Searle. Searle had founded Friends of the Earth in San Francisco in 1968, and we were discussing how it would become an international organisation. 1971 was the year Greenpeace started – it was a landmark year, and I, together with much of the advertising and design world, didn't even know there was an environmental movement. From that perspective, 1971 was a milestone year for me, for Wolff Olins, for our industry and for the world. The environmental movement was waking us up.

The enduring landmarks that I associate with 1971 came from the copywriters, photographers and art directors who recognised and didn't interfere with simple and strong ideas. That's why great ads, like those created and written by people such as David Abbott, Tony Brignull and others, are so enduring. The sheer wit and simplicity of being absolutely direct hadn't yet been replaced by the often verbose, self-indulgent and grossly extravagant ads of today.

At that time, Nova magazine was wonderful – Art Director David Hillman was a giant, and both Tony Evans and Harri Peccinotti brought Editorial Photography into the milestone category; and they did it as graphic designers and as painstaking photographers without the glib moves of Photoshop.

Designs that had already endured for decades were the real milestones for me. In 1971, Pan Am's brand identity was a powerful example of what design could do. Despite all the efforts of design companies since then, not one airline brand designer has exceeded Pan Am's elegance, simplicity and respect for the aircraft themselves. That's why Stanley Kubrick chose the Pan Am brand for the spaceship in his '2001: A Space Odyssey'.

The excitement, exuberance and promise of the 60s still burned in 1971, but business, bean-counting and cautious processes were blunting the blades of creativity. 1971 was the beginning of many of us slithering down the gentle slopes into reasonable and client-pleasing work. Don't be disheartened. I think we're at the beginning of a new epoch in which human creativity is needed more than ever. Creative design is happening all over the world. No country is supreme. The opportunities today are greater than they've ever been. Let's see what you'll make of them. ⬡

Why your first cigarette made you feel giddy.

Cigarettes contain tiny quantities of nicotine, a nerve poison.

The symptoms of mild nicotine poisoning are dizziness, rapid pulse, cold clammy skin, nausea and vomiting.

Smokers experience some of these symptoms with their first few cigarettes.

But once smoking becomes a regular habit, these side effects soon disappear.

Unfortunately, there are other side effects that don't disappear.

The tiny particles of nicotine, and other chemicals that are inhaled, cling to the tubes inside your lungs or enter the blood.

These chemicals gradually form a coating of oily, liquid tar that irritates the tubes, forcing them to produce a thick clogging phlegm.

Heavy smoking increases the irritation in the tubes. When they become infected they start to swell with pus, and sometimes this mixture of infected tar, pus and phlegm rises up in the throat and is swallowed.

But the rest of it slithers deep into the lungs where it congeals and festers.

And that's why smokers cough, and are short of wind, have bad breath, and are more susceptible to crippling incurable diseases.

The Health Education Council

Title Anti-smoking campaign
Client Health Education Council
Agency Saatchi & Saatchi

Title Anti-smoking campaign
Client Health Education Council
Agency Saatchi & Saatchi

What makes a cigarette so enjoyable?

Hydrogen Cyanide. The potentially harmful gases in cigarette smoke include Hydrogen Cyanide in a concentration 160 times the amount considered safe in industry. Hydrogen Cyanide is a powerful poison.

Ammonia is commonly used as a household cleansing agent, and in the manufacture of explosives.

Carbon Monoxide, the same deadly gas that is emitted from car exhausts, combines with haemoglobin in red blood cells, thereby reducing the oxygen-carrying capacity of the blood. Since Carbon Monoxide has a much greater affinity for haemoglobin than does oxygen, it literally drives oxygen from the blood.

Nicotine is a colourless oily compound, which in concentrated form is one of the most powerful poisons known. It is marketed as a lethal insecticide (Black leaf 40) and injection of one drop, 70 milligrams, will cause the death of a man of average weight within a few minutes.
Nicotine is probably the addictive agent in cigarette tobacco. When you smoke, it temporarily stimulates the nervous system, and causes the craving for tobacco.

Butane, the gas used in camping stoves and cigarette lighters. Apart from cigarette smoke, it's also found in natural gas and crude petroleum.

Tar. Tobacco tar contains more than 200 compounds, many of them toxic. Among these are at least 10 hydrocarbons that have produced cancer when administered to animals.
As you inhale a cigarette the smoke coats your lungs with this liquid tobacco tar. The further down you smoke your cigarette, the more tar and nicotine it produces. In fact, the last third of the cigarette produces more tar and nicotine than the other two thirds put together.

Phenol has not been proved to cause cancer on its own. However, it does destroy the protective action of the cilia, the small hairlike projections that line the respiratory tract. It is a corrosive poison, and a severe irritant. Used to make glue, paint, plastic and explosives.

Fortunately the poisons in tobacco smoke are counteracted and discharged by the natural defences of the body.
However, the accumulative effects of many years smoking often breaks these defences down.
If you feel you should cut down on your smoking remember it's the last third of the cigarette that does most damage.

The Health Education Council

The tar and discharge that collects in the lungs of an average smoker.

Every time you inhale a cigarette tiny particles of nicotine and other chemicals are left inside your lungs.

These particles gradually build up into an oily tar, that irritates your lungs till they become infected and clogged with pus and phlegm.

Then, as more of this septic discharge forms, the mixture of tar pus and phlegm sometimes rises up into the throat and is swallowed.

But the rest of it slithers deep into the lungs, where it congeals and festers.

It's not surprising that smokers cough, are short of wind, have bad breath, and are more susceptible to crippling incurable diseases.

The Health Education Council

Title Anti-smoking campaign
Client Health Education Council
Agency Saatchi & Saatchi

" The excitement, exuberance and promise of the 60s still burned in 1971, but business, bean-counting and cautious processes were blunting the blades of creativity.

1972
David Hillman

Photo **Kevin Davies**

Educated at the London School of Printing and Graphic Arts, David Hillman began his career as a Designer on The Sunday Times Magazine. In 1968 he became Art Director of Nova magazine, and in 1975, through his own practice, he designed a new French daily, Le Matin de Paris. In 2006, after 29 years as a Pentagram partner, he set up the eponymous Studio David Hillman. In addition to his work in signage, identity, editorial, promotional and communication design, he has designed 30 Royal Mail stamps celebrating the London 2012 Olympics. Hillman is a past International President of Alliance Graphic International, a Royal Designer for Industry and a Senior Fellow of the Royal College of Art.

1972 Annual

Annual Design **Ron Costley**
Cover Art **Allen Jones**

Title Menu card
Client Mr Freedom
Design Group Nicholas Thirkell Associates

Perhaps it's the fact that it is printed entirely in black and white, but there is a sombre tone to the 1972 D&AD Annual. There aren't really any jolly bits, with the exception of one or two pieces, both of them personal favourites: George Hardie's illustration for Mr Freedom (Yellow Pencil for Outstanding Design of a Menu Card) and Tony Meeuwissen's letterhead for Kinney Records. It was probably a cost thing, black and white being considerably cheaper than printing over 300 pages in four-colour, but given the events of that year – the miners' strikes, power cuts, the three-day week, the expulsion of the Ugandan Asians by Idi Amin, the killing of Israeli athletes by terrorists at the Munich Olympics, Bloody Sunday in Ireland – it seems fitting.

The Black Pencil for Photography that year was won by Don McCullin, whose powerful images of poverty and starvation in West Bengal and unrest in Northern Ireland for The Sunday Times Magazine helped to set the tone, and while the Black Pencil was shared with photographer Sarah Moon for atmospheric fashion shots for Nova magazine, these were styled against a backdrop of urban decay. That said, I was art directing Nova at the time and remember it as rather a colourful period.

Perhaps it's because the D&AD Awards were still in their infancy, but I recall a great generosity between the various disciplines at the time. No rivalry between design and advertising was in evidence, although on looking at the Annual, design did seem to dominate in terms of page numbers. I also don't recall any of the interdisciplinary and interagency rivalry that crops up from time to time. Perhaps we were less competitive or there were fewer of us to compete then, but as judges we didn't care who had done the work, only that the work was good.

Looking at the book as a whole, there is a notable balance between illustration and photography, making it perhaps one of the rare periods when the two were on a par. There are wonderful examples of collaboration and certain curiosities, such as illustrations by Wurlitzer for photographer Roger Stowell's letterhead, a purely graphic and typeface-based letterhead for photography firm Robert Montgomery & Partners and Geoffrey Hockey's letterhead for photographer Andrew Cockrill.

Title Kinney Records letterhead
Design Group Kinney Records

Of course, in the days before Photoshop the crossover was sometimes pragmatic, while montage was a matter of a deft hand with a scalpel, and special effects – reflections, "sweat" on bottles and the like – were the domain of model-makers and painstaking studio set-ups, with little or no retouching. There's a spread in the Annual in Editorial Art and Photography: Consumer Magazines that exemplifies a state of the art moment in each of these two disciplines. On the left is a wonderful image by Tony Evans for Nova of pickled onions in a glass onion with a reflection of a window in the glass. We'd persuaded Caroline Conran to write a cookery piece prompted by our idea for the image and she made the actual onions. The glass is real and the reflection was set up in the studio using a complicated lighting rig. On the facing page is an article from Nova about underwear, with girls standing at highly reflective glass bar tables. It uses illustrations by Celestino Valenti, not only because it was less expensive than a complicated studio photoshoot, but because, had we used live models, there was a danger it would have been labelled pornography.

Interestingly, Packaging Design at the time was quite a low-key affair, not the dynamic category it is today. The selection is small: a mere eight pages buried in the Annual under the heading of Advertising Design. Again, illustration proliferates, with only three of the 12 featuring photography, and while most of the products have long since vanished, the original Alpen packaging by ad agency Masius Wynne-Williams looks very familiar.

Another phenomenon that seems to have changed dramatically is the sheer quantity of copy in the advertising. Did we read more in those days? Are we more visual now? Or demanding of more instant gratification? It's not just evident in the large Copy: Consumer Advertisements, Posters section at the end of the Annual, but throughout. It reminds me of how difficult it was at the time to integrate images and copy in editorial design. A couple that stand out are the Times Educational Supplement, under the art direction of Jeanette Collins, and one of my personal favourites, the magazine for Coventry Football Club, art directed and edited by John Elvin. Both make great use of cut-out photographs. Not only did this require painstaking scalpel work, but it

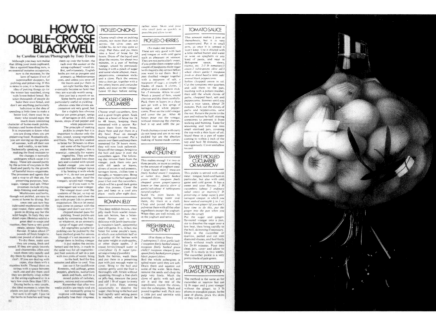

HOW TO DOUBLE-CROSSE BLACKWELL

by Caroline Conran/Photograph by Tony Evans

YOUR BODY IS SOFT AND ROUND AND COMES WITHOUT SEAMS

> Perhaps we were less competitive or there were fewer of us to compete back then, but as judges we didn't care who had done the work, only that the work was good.

Title Nova
Publisher IPC Magazines

Title Pirelli calendar
Client Pirelli
Agency The Derek Forsyth Partnership

Title A Land Beyond Comfort
Publication The Sunday Times Magazine
Publisher Times Newspapers

> "The list of winners in the D&AD Annual 1972 is quite the roll call of today's industry heavyweights and icons.

also called for the cooperation of a block maker who had to rout out the hot metal plates by hand. In some cases, it even meant negotiating with the block maker's union over the extra hours.

It reminded me that as art directors on magazines and newspapers, our input was not just about visual considerations but of economic matters too. At Nova I was allowed three images per page, maximum, and they all had to be in pro. As a "cheat" we often chopped up images and put them together before turning them into "film". It's why I enjoyed collaborating with the brilliant photographer Harri Peccinotti, who wasn't precious about his photographs being hacked about a bit and took a proactive part in the process of manual Photoshopping!

Our battles to make these publications more visually exciting weren't always appreciated by the management, and not just because we kept pushing the budgets on a daily basis. I remember the day after Nova won a Black Pencil and a Yellow Pencil, I was called into the

publisher's office. Thinking it was to be praised, I was taken aback when they gave me a serious dressing down, telling me that the magazine didn't exist for design glory but to make money.

The list of winners in the D&AD Annual 1972 is quite the roll call of today's industry heavyweights and icons: young talent like John Hegarty, Terence Conran, Terence Donovan, Alan Fletcher, Michael Rand and Michael Peters, to mention a few. On the jury were names like Herb Lubalin, Herbert Spencer and Peter Mayle (of 'A Year in Provence' fame). Scattered throughout are those who ultimately made their name in different, albeit related, industries: Alan Parker and Ridley Scott, who both went into feature filmmaking, illustrator Roger Law, who went on to make the satirical TV series 'Spitting Image' with partner Peter Fluck, illustrator Jan Piekowski and graphic designer David Pelham, who both independently went on to design wonderfully imaginative pop-up books, and Terry Gilliam of 'Monty Python' fame, who judged Art and Photography and was described simply as "Artist".

1973
Chris Wilkins

While still at Cambridge, Chris Wilkins was lucky enough to fail the McCann-Erickson copy test, which is how he found himself at J Walter Thompson, where his work for Guinness carried off the D&AD TV campaign of the year and won more Lions at Cannes than you could shake a chair at. (His children immediately cut up the certificates to make a cardboard zoo.)

His 'Smash Martians' commercial, written at Boase Massimi Pollitt (BMP) for Cadbury's Smash, was named Ad of the Century in Campaign's millennium issue. Which makes him, he supposes, copywriter of the century. The last century.

1973 Annual

Annual Design **Ron Costley**
Cover Art **Tony Meeuwissen**
Art Direction **John McConnell**

How to beat the Army Officer Selection Board.

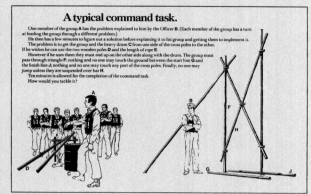

It's a fact that only about 20% of the candidates applying to the Army Officer Selection Board pass. In spite of what some disgruntled applicants may tell you however, the Board isn't bent on keeping people out.

Quite the opposite. While setting a necessarily high standard, the Board goes out of its way to help applicants show their stuff.

So we're only going an inch or two further by giving you a few tips that could improve your chances.

Are you a fit person?

First off, don't be in a hurry to present yourself to the Board if you can't run up stairs without blowing like a geyser. Get fit first.

While none of the tests used by the Board demand Olympic standards, they all call for considerable mental effort. And you can't think at your best if you're exhausted by the previous obstacle.

Take the task illustrated for instance. Study it now while you're calm and collected and doubtless a number of possible solutions will occur to you. You can probably imagine yourself giving crisp, explicit orders to your team and them moving across the obstacle with their equipment in a smooth flow of action.

It won't be like that if you're jack-knifed on the grass wheezing for breath. The Board will not have the chance to see how good you really are.

Another thing that will help you over the obstacles is an understanding of levers, pendulums and inclined planes. So if you're rusty brush up.

You don't need a plum in your mouth.

We'd hate anybody who has been to a public school to get the idea that the Board is prejudiced against them.

So if you went to Eton don't waste time hanging around the East End trying to pick up the accent. It will do you no good. And the converse is equally true if you happen to come from the East End.

The Board isn't interested in your style of speech. But it will be keenly interested in what you have to say.

During the time that you spend with the Selection Board you will be interviewed by a Major, a Lieutenant-Colonel, and a Brigadier: possibly by a Major-General and certainly by an Education Officer.

You had better have plenty of material. Like most people, they enjoy chatting to somebody who has had a bit of experience.

Somebody who has been around and who has met different sorts of people.

They don't want to hear a rundown of the week's television programmes. And if this is the limit of your experience hold off your application until you've branched out a bit.

Buy a rucksack and start working your way around the country. Talk to the crew on your father's yacht. Anything to broaden your contacts.

Understandably, officers like talking to candidates about the Army. So it's worth considering joining the Cadet Force or the University Officer Training Corps. These outfits can give you access to the regiment or corps that interests you. All grist to the mill. You might even consider reading a few books on military subjects.

All the interviewers will be looking for evidence of a keen interest in the Army. And they are not easy to fool. If you aren't interested, really interested, please don't bother them.

One of their favourite questions is 'What will you do if you get turned down by the Board?' Think about it. What are you going to say?

If you can impress your fellow candidates you'll impress the Board.

Besides talking to members of the Board, you'll be talking to your fellow candidates. There will be a group discussion on current affairs which will be led by the group leader and watched by other members of the Board.

So start reading the papers a bit more avidly than you do at the moment.

Later you'll be given a choice of subjects and a quarter of an hour to prepare a lecturette.

You'll also have to present persuasive arguments in favour of your solution to a variety of problems.

So, if you have trouble talking to groups of people, take steps right away. Join a debating society or a drama club. Take a soap box to Speaker's Corner. It won't take you long to overcome the communication problem.

And if you haven't had any experience of organizing groups of people at school you should try your hand with a youth group.

Don't think from all this that the Board expects you to appear before them ready and prepared to take command of a regiment. It's just that we felt that you'll make a better showing if you have some idea of what you're in for.

Remember, the Board want to pass you. But to be worth training at Sandhurst you have to display the qualities (however latent) required of an Army Officer.

If you think you're ready to face the Army Officer Selection Board, and you're under 29, write to: Major K. S. Robson, Army Officer Entry, Dept. F1, Lansdowne House, Berkeley Square, London, W1X 6AA. Tell him about your educational qualifications and your life in general so far.

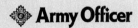 **Army Officer**

Title How to Beat the Army Selection Board
Client Ministry of Defence
Agency Collett Dickenson Pearce

Maybe it really was a golden age. In his preface to the 1973 Annual, Peter Mayle laments the absence of fresh names among the credits, and asks, "Where are all the new young art directors and designers and writers?" Looking back with the benefit of almost 40 years' hindsight, aren't we still waiting for them to show up? The names in the index of filmmakers with lots of numbers after them – that's the first thing you checked when the new Annual came out – are Ridley Scott, Alan Parker and Hugh Hudson. Whatever became of them? Or Peter Mayle, for that matter? We were really good back then.

Look at John Salmon's masterly press advertisement for army recruitment. When Collett Dickenson Pearce won the army account, it was widely rumoured that the creatives mutinied and refused to work for what they described as a bunch of warmongering fascists. (Remember that this was the year the Vietnam war finally ended, and all right-thinking creatives were Woodstocked into a kind of stoned pacifism.) Up until this time, army recruitment ads promised rewards like foreign travel and free skiing lessons, but this one ad turned everything around. It was fiercely intelligent, immaculately argued and crafted and, on the morning it ran, was the most interesting page in the newspaper. It changed the way young men saw a career in the army, and it changed the attitude of the advertising industry to military recruitment. In my time as Creative Director at Young & Rubicam, we worked our butts off to win the Royal Navy and Royal Marines recruitment account, and I have rarely worked with a more intelligent, decisive or sympathetic client. This ad made it all possible.

Now consider Michael Peters' design award for his work on Winsor & Newton. The brief to redesign the packaging for the firm's range of coloured inks must have looked like a gift. Here's a target market of sophisticated, design-conscious artists. What an opportunity! Hang on, though. Here's a target market of picky, opinionated, frustrated artists. Nightmare! The solution was almost unthinkably bold – a completely different pack design for every colour in the range. The orange ink had a portrait of Nell Gwynne, the black had a cartoon spider drawing his web, and the 20 or more designs ran right round the cubes of the boxes in 3D. Today, almost 40 years on,

Cosmopolitan

Couple chatting at cocktail party.

MAN (amazed): I don't believe it!
Where did you hear that about
Richard Burton?
VO: Cosmopolitan, page 82.

Couple having intimate dinner.

MAN (starry-eyed): That was
great! Where did you learn to cook
like that?
VO: Cosmopolitan, page 113.

Man stepping into girl's new Ferrari.

MAN (impressed): How did
you raise the money to buy a
car like this?
VO: Cosmopolitan, page 60.

Couple sunning themselves on
French beach.

FRENCH MAN (seductively):
Tell me, where you get zee idea of
coming 'ere for your 'oliday?
VO: Cosmopolitan, page 23.

Cosmopolitan magazine.

VO: Cosmopolitan. A sensational
new magazine for women who're
interested in men, love, fashion,
food, men, travel, films, beauty,
and themselves. And men.

Young married couple in bed.

He looks at her astonished.
WOMAN: Cosmopolitan, page 114.

SUPER/VO: Cosmopolitan.
First issue out today.

Title Cosmopolitan
Client National Magazines
Agency Saatchi & Saatchi

Title Wait Till She Finds Out It's Only a Volkswagen
Client Volkswagen
Agency Doyle Dane Bernbach

> It ran with just a mute shot of the man's questioning face and cut to the woman saying… 'Cosmopolitan, page 114'. A rare example in the history of advertising where the censors made things not only better, but sexier.

those designs are still selling the client's product. There was a scurrilous rumour back then that Michael Peters' training scheme for his reps was to teach them to say to a client, without laughing, "That will be £30,000." Worth every penny.

The Volkswagen ad is my favourite example from the Annual of the use of wit in advertising – yes, there used to be wit in advertising. Here's the Karmann Ghia, a Volkswagen which looks like a sports car. Look at that word "only" in the headline. The glorious girl who is all over the driver will dump him, we are led to believe, when "she finds out the car is only a Volkswagen". What a client! What confidence! It's a kind of verbal aikido, using the strength of our prejudices against us. Any advertiser with the nerve to take themselves this lightly will forever win our affections. To get this ad, you have to conspire with the advertiser to agree that this has to be one remarkable motor vehicle – and look at the collectors' market for that car today.

There was a hell of a lot of sex around in 1973. Allen Jones's Yellow Pencil-awarded Pirelli calendar brought glossy fetishism to the garage walls of thousands who could not even spell "fetishism". It was the year too when Cosmopolitan magazine launched itself into the British market. One of Saatchi & Saatchi's earliest clients, its launch commercial won Jeremy Sinclair a page in the Copy section of the book for his script. A series of vignettes (or, as an old client of mine used to call them, "vinaigrettes") of snippets of conversation like "Where did you hear that about Richard Burton?" – to which a male voiceover would confide, "Cosmopolitan, page 82". The original

Title **Pirelli calendar**
Client **Pirelli**
Design Group **The Derek Forsyth Partnership**

VERMILION
ZINNOBER

ORANGE
ORANGE

BLUE
AZUL

SUNSHINE YELLOW
BRILLANTGELB

NUT BROWN
AVELLANA

CARMINE
CARMIN

BURNT SIENNA
GEBRANNTE SIENA

CANARY YELLOW
KANARIENGELB

ULTRAMARINE
ULTRAMER

VIOLET
VIOLETA

COBALT
COBALTO

CRIMSON
CARMESI

BRICK RED
LADRILLO ROJO

VIRIDIAN
VIRIDIAN

PEAT BROWN
BRUN TOURBE

EMERALD
VERDE VERONES

SCARLET
ESCARLATA

WHITE
BLANCO

APPLE GREEN
VERDE MANZANA

965 · ORANGE

BLACK INDIAN INK
NOIR (ENCRE DE CHINE)
BLACK INDIAN INK
SCHWARZ
BLACK INDIAN INK
NEGRO
BLACK INDIAN INK
NERO

Title Winsor & Newton Inks
Client Winsor & Newton
Design Group Michael Peters & Partners

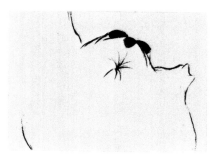 

> "
> We had made the product
> famous overnight. That's what
> admen used to do in those days.

script ended with a couple in bed,
where the astonished man asks his
female partner, "Where did you learn to
do that?" (or words to that effect – it's
all a long time ago, you understand).
The Independent Television Companies'
Association was having none of it and
demanded the line be cut. So it ran with
just a mute shot of the man's questioning
face, then cut to the woman saying, with
the most smugly innocent of expressions,
"Cosmopolitan, page 114". A rare
example in the history of advertising
where the censors made things not
only better, but sexier.

Cresta was a weird one, and I include it
among my favourites largely in memory
of the great and sadly late John Webster.
BMP was in its infancy as an agency and
John had just hired me as his writer.
I arrived early one morning at the agency
and John showed me a crude line
drawing he had done of a polar bear in
sunglasses and explained this vague idea
he'd had about a rebellious teenage bear
who has left home in search of Cresta.
Could I, he asked, write some words for
the character? After an hour or so, I told
him I was having difficulty connecting the
character to the product in a way that
didn't seem contrived, and John said,
"Why don't we open with him saying,
'Hi, I'm a polar bear and this is an
amazing new soft drink called Cresta'?
That'll work." I had five scripts by the end
of the morning. The night after the ads
broke, Dave Trott was in an East End pub
where a burly stevedore was served a pint
with a huge head on top. "What's that?"
he demanded of the timorous barman.
A man standing next to him, said,
"It's frothy, man." We had made the
product famous overnight. That's what
admen used to do in those days. ⬡

Cresta – 'Jumpin' Off Icebergs'

1½ seconds silence.

SFX: Rock music.

BEAR: Y'know what I dig, about
the south, man? There's so much
to do – the groovy sounds and
frothy Cresta…

WOW! Ooh, that orange flavour…

EEEH!

Y'know my old man's idea of
entertainment?

Jumpin' off icebergs into the sea.

Cluck-cluck-cluck…

I mean, it's so undignified.

(Whistles.)

MVO: Cresta – in four fruity flavours.

BEAR: It's frothy, man.

Title Cresta – Jumpin' Off Icebergs
Client Schweppes
Agency Boase Massimi Pollitt

1974
Alfredo Marcantonio

English-born but of Italian parentage, Alfredo Marcantonio began his advertising career as a client, at Volkswagen. He left to become a copywriter, joining French Gold Abbott (FGA) and, later, Collett Dickenson Pearce.

In 1981 he helped CDP bosses Frank Lowe and Geoff Howard-Spink to found Lowe Howard-Spink, and became Creative Director. In 1987 he joined WCRS but left to run BBDO until its merger with Abbott Mead Vickers reunited him with David Abbott.

By 1998 he was Vice-Chairman of AMV BBDO in London and Creative Vice-President of BBDO Milan. More recently, following a stint in Rome as Creative Director of Leagas Delaney Italy, he has been running Marcantonio Plus Hobbs with creative services guru Steve Hobbs.

As a writer and creative director, Marcantonio has been involved in some of Britain's most iconic campaigns for clients like Hamlet, Heineken, Stella Artois, BMW, British Telecom and Carling Black Label. He is the author of 'Well-written and Red: The Story of The Economist Poster Campaign', and co-author with David Abbott of 'Remember Those Great Volkswagen Ads?'

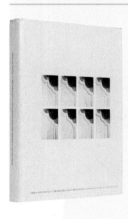

1974 Annual

Annual Design **John McConnell, David Hillman**
Assistant Designer **David Pearce**

Following my two or three stints on the Executive Committee, some wag described me as "the best President D&AD never had", which I took to be a compliment. The sad passing of the 1974 incumbent, the mightily talented and mighty nice Alan Fletcher, has afforded me the honour of assuming office for a page or two.

Whenever I do my 'Remember Those Great Volkswagen Ads?' spiel, I put the work into "tail-finned Cadillac" context. I decided to do the same here.

Believe it or not, much of 1973's prized work was probably created by candlelight. New Year's Day had seen the UK's entry into the Common Market, with Prime Minister Edward Heath rejoicing at the prosperity it would bring. Eleven months later he was nursing the nation through an energy crisis and "a harder Christmas than we have known since the war." (Sounds familiar, doesn't it?)

Following the Yom Kippur war, OPEC had cut our oil supply. Petrol rationing loomed, with tokens being issued – a measure that J Walter Thompson celebrated with a 'Guinness Rationing' spoof that made it into the Annual.

The electrical and miners' unions, yet to be broken by Thatcherism, seized the opportunity to ban overtime and organise strikes. Energy became so scarce that companies were only allowed power three days a week. For retailers, it was indeed a hard Christmas. Between 17 and 30 December, they could only light up for a total of five days.

Fear not, there was brightness aplenty in the Book. Alan Fletcher not only enjoyed the 1974 Presidency, he also earned one of the year's three Black Pencils with a charming exploitation of his "pointillist" Reuters logo. A game idea if ever there was one.

The Design jury also gave a Yellow Pencil to Gert Dumbar's work for Dutch railway Nederlandse Spoorwegen, though for me Marcello Minale's Milton Keynes entry was more deserving. Arthur Robins and Peter Mayle were also left Pencil-less. Their book 'Where Did I Come From?' was not only beautifully illustrated, designed and written, but delightfully controversial too.

The title sequence for Leonard Bernstein's opera 'Trouble in Tahiti' also received a well-deserved Yellow Pencil for Pat 'South Bank Show' Gavin.

Title **Reuters logo**
Client **Reuters**
Designer **Alan Fletcher**

Our thanks to Ben Godfrey age seven for the use of his favourite dishes.

Fish Finger train with carrots, mashed potato, Peas and Sweet Corn.

Beefburger hippo in a swamp of French Beans.

Brunchie tank with Sweet Corn.

Chicken Rissole sun with Crinkle Cut Chips.

Sausage and mash hedgehog.

Fish Cake fish in a sea of Broccoli.

BIRDS EYE

Title Our Thanks to Ben Godfrey
Client Birds Eye Foods
Agency Collett Dickenson Pearce

Nova earned its rightful place in Consumer Magazines for the umpteenth year running, no one suspecting that this universally admired nine-year-old would not reach its teens.

Print advertising saw a raft of such repeat appearances from the likes of Dunn & Co, Benson & Hedges Special Filter, Army Officer Recruitment and my two ex-employers, Colt Ventilation and Volkswagen. (I was now a rookie writer at Burson-Marsteller.)

The big winner was Tony Brignull and Neil Godfrey's Birds Eye campaign, with two Yellow Pencils and a Black Pencil. It was outstanding work in a tough category and forged a trail that Tony's writing rival David Abbott was to follow elegantly and eloquently for Sainsbury's, a decade or so later.

The Film jury passed over two of the most iconic British commercials ever made for the Black Pencil, giving it to a somewhat obscure US anti-drug spot. The two – 'Smash Martians' from Boase Massimi Pollitt (BMP) and CDP's 'Lifeboat' spot for Cockburn's – were Yellow Pencil-winners and each of them represented the very pinnacle of their agencies' differing approaches to the creation of memorable advertising.

From the late John Webster and director Bob Brooks, 'Smash Martians' gave us an early form of the "created character", while in the late Geoffrey Seymour and Sir Alan Parker's 'Lifeboat', we have a double dose of "30-second theatre".

Unigate's Humphreys, Cresta's bear, Sugar Puffs' Honey Monster – all these and more were to follow in the metal men's footsteps, while B&H's 'Istanbul' film, the Olympus 'Wedding Photographer' and Parker's 'Finishing School' were strongly influenced by the Cockburn's commercial.

Was the US Black Pencil-winner an early example of the Brit-against-Brit rivalry that sees judges more comfortable rewarding work from around the world rather than around the corner? Competition has ever been fierce, but it also used to be fair.

Mind you, there were far fewer creative adversaries. BMP, CDP, BBDO, FGA, Saatchi & Saatchi and Doyle Dane Bernbach represented a magic roundabout of hot shops that saw the Awards divvied up between them.

A warm "well done, you bastards" was the standard greeting as a rival brushed past your table en route to the podium, as your own agency was likely to enjoy a "shake and take" before the night was out.

By this time, the man wants to get as close to the woman as he can, because he's feeling very loving to her. And to get really close the best thing he can do is lie on top of her and put his penis inside her, into her vagina.

This is the closest two people can get.

Title Spread from the book 'Where Did I Come From?'
Publisher Lyle Stuart

It was not the Awards night but the Annual's index that decided D&AD's Victor Ludorum; who had the most page numbers after their name?

Top honours for 1973 went to CDP with 47 entries, BBDO with 29 and BMP with 14. The figures reflect BMP's concentration on TV and BBDO's position as CDP's bête noir et blanc when it came to newspaper ads.

I can only show five pieces of work and have selected ads you need to see to appreciate fully. I can however salute a few of the Annual's brilliant headlines from ads not shown here.

First, a favourite from Birds Eye: "We are the first to admit nothing tastes as good as the pie you bake yourself." Now, two of Terry Bunton's great Sony lines: "Does your turntable hum along with the music?" and "Remember when you first heard your voice on tape and said, 'That doesn't sound like me?' Well, it didn't." Next, young Jeremy Bullmore's still prescient Guinness poster: "I've never tried it, because I don't like it." And lastly, a small-space hotel ad by Tim Mellors: "Honestly now, when was the last time you had a great night out in Slough?"

Marvellous work from a miserable year.

"Believe it or not, much of 1973's acclaimed work would have been created by candlelight.

Title Cockburn's – Lifeboat
Client John Harvey & Son
Agency Collett Dickenson Pearce

Cockburn's – 'Lifeboat'

SFX: Sea and mouth organ.

CAPTAIN: Dashed shame really, she was a fine old ship.

SPRATT: They didn't mention the old bit when I booked my passage.

FIRST OFFICER: Oh come off it, Spratt old chap. Still, pity she went down before we finished dinner. Missed the liqueurs, what!

SPRATT'S LADY: Could've done with a drop myself.

LADY: Hear! Hear!

DAVIS: (whispers to captain)

CAPTAIN: I'm afraid I might have some rather bad news for some of you. Davis only had time to bring the port. It's my after-dinner tipple, but what about the rest of you?

FIRST OFFICER: I should say so, sir.

SPRATT: Cockburn's, is it?

CAPTAIN: Cockburn's?

FIRST OFFICER: Cockburn's – very good.

CAPTAIN: Oh, you mean Cockburn's. Yes – Special Reserve.

FIRST OFFICER: Cockburn's.

VO: After dinner, a bottle of port is really all you need. Cockburn's Special Reserve, a very fine bottle of port.

> " A warm 'well done, you bastards' was the standard greeting as a rival brushed past your table en route to the podium.

Title **Smash – Smash Martians**
Client **Cadbury Typhoo Foods**
Agency **Boase Massimi Pollitt**

Smash – 'Smash Martians'

1½ seconds silence.

QUESTIONER: On your last trip, did you discover what Earth people eat?

SPEAKER: They eat a great many of these…

SFX: Muttering.

SPEAKER: They peel them with their metal… knives…

SFX: Murmuring, laughter.

SPEAKER: …boil them for 20 of their minutes…

SFX: Louder laughter.

SPEAKER: …then they smash them all to bits.

CHAIRMAN: They are clearly a most primitive people.

SFX: Helpless laughter.

VO: For mash, get Smash.

1975
David Abbott

On his first and last days in advertising, David Abbott wrote a piece of copy. In the intervening 40 years, he worked in two excellent agencies (Mather & Crowther and Doyle Dane Bernbach (DDB)) and helped start two more (French Gold Abbott and Abbott Mead Vickers). It is rumoured that he had a fine old time.

1975 Annual

Annual Design **Neil Godfrey**
Cover Photography **Tony May**

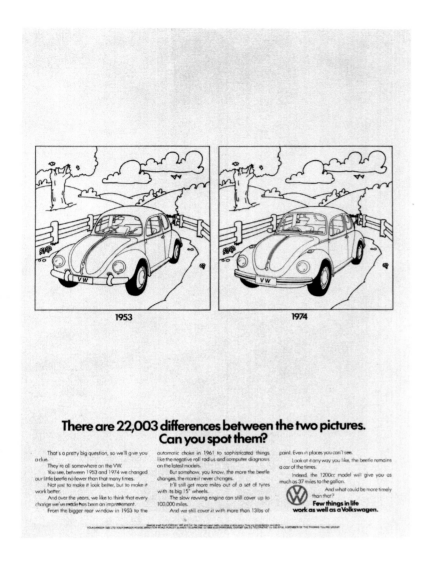

There are 22,003 differences between the two pictures. Can you spot them?

1953 / 1974

Title Spot the Difference
Client Volkswagen
Agency The Drawing Room

I am sitting down to write this and realise I don't remember one thing about 1975. Of course, I could get on Google and check it out, but for some reason I am reluctant – what's worth remembering is remembered, and by that test it seems that 1975 doesn't make the grade.

I have another reason, too, for not delving too aggressively into the past – I am not that interested. For 40 years, advertising was not only my job, but also my passion. I loved everything about it – the people, the fun, the meetings, the shoots, the long nights in the studio, the pitches, the togetherness and, above all, the craft – the "happiness of getting it down right" as the writer Frank O'Connor used to say.

And now?

Fourteen years into my retirement, I rarely give it a thought. When I do think of it, it's with great fondness. I live a comfortable life because of advertising, but for me, the thrill was doing it, not talking about it.

Were there any advertising milestones in 1975? How would I know? My nose was too close to the layout pad to notice. And anyhow, I believe the great sweep of history is made up of the small brushstrokes of the everyday. By concentrating on the task in hand, we move things on. When DDB created the Volkswagen campaign in America, it was to sell cars and get the account, not to change the face of advertising – though it surely did. What you do is the only testament that counts.

I will never write a book on advertising because there's nothing to say that hasn't been said before. If you want to learn how to do great ads, my advice is to study the great ads. Everything that John Webster wanted to say about advertising is in his work.

Now there's an idea. I turn to my bookshelves to see if John had any work in the 1975 D&AD Annual and I remember that I no longer have any Annuals. A while ago, I gave all of them away to the AMV library.

I email D&AD and they promise to send me their only copy. I can keep it for 24 hours.

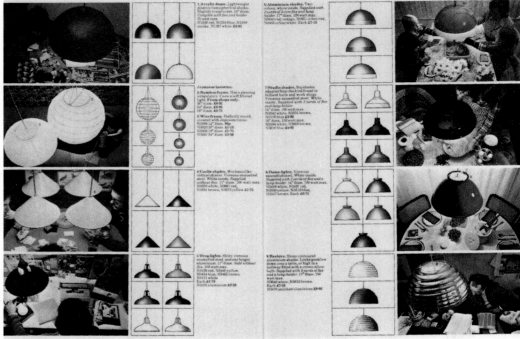

Title Habitat catalogue
Client Habitat Designs
Design Group Conran Associates

"

I start to reconsider the 70s.
It never had the tag of a
revolutionary decade – none
of the glamour of the 60s –
but for all that, it was a time
of start-ups and adventure.

I have it in front of me now. I flick
through the pages. It seems very wordy
(never a problem for me) – all those
classic long-copy ads for the Army and
the Metropolitan Police. John Salmon,
Tony Brignull, Arthur Parsons and Neil
Godfrey in all their pomp. How good the
campaigns are – intelligent, involving
and persuasive.

Another surprise. On page 32, I see that
the judges honoured the iconic Hovis
television campaign. Three commercials
are illustrated – the one with the boy
wheeling his bike up the cobbled hill
the most familiar, and the most loved.
The surprise is that the jury gave it
a Yellow Pencil for Outstanding Film
Photography and not a Black Pencil
for outstanding everything.

I begin to feel good about my year
as President.

There's a VW Beetle ad I admire and a
campaign for the Jamaica Tourist Board
where glorious art direction, writing,
photography and branding combine
to get you on the plane.

And on page 128, the Habitat catalogue gets a mention. Like the products and the stores themselves, the catalogue is useful and beautiful. (In 1975, I had been married for 13 years and lived in a Span house with a wife, four children and lots of Terence Conran furniture. So yes, I am biased.)

The next day, D&AD send a courier to retrieve the Annual. I hand it over, but not before I have jotted down a list of names of some of the judges who were on the D&AD juries in 1975:

David Driver
Michael Rand
David Hillman
Neil Godfrey
Alan Parker
John Webster
Colin Millward
Ronnie Kirkwood
Arnold Schwartzman
Martin Boase
John Salmon
Dawson Yeoman
Michael Wolff
John Larkin
Alan Fletcher
Nancy Fouts
David Pelham
Rod Springett
George Hardie

I am humbled. How could I have forgotten such a galactic gathering?

I start to reconsider the 70s. It never had the tag of a revolutionary decade – none of the glamour of the 60s – but for all that, it was a time of start-ups and adventure. The talented youngsters of the 60s were now running things and making their mark in all the creative industries. It was like a Lyndon Johnson after a JFK.

Most of the judges in 1975 were running or helping to run their own companies, so why did they give so much time to D&AD?

I suspect, like me, they thought it was good for business. They turned out to honour the brave and good work, and by honouring it, they helped to increase it.

I still think that's the point of D&AD, but as I said at the beginning, I'm out of it now and never look back.

And in case you're wondering, John Webster did get something in the Book. ⬤

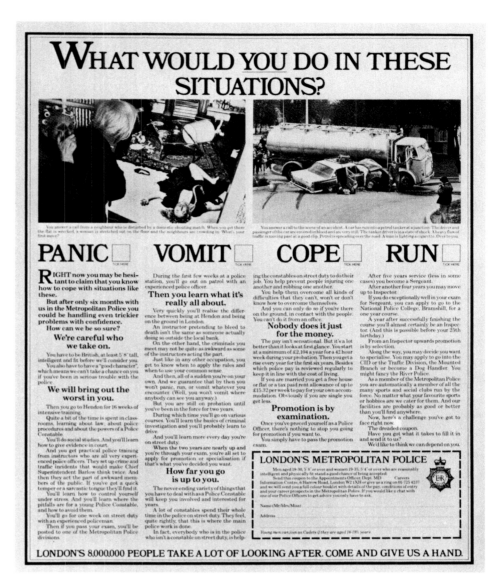

Title What Would You Do in These Situations?
Client Metropolitan Police
Agency Collett Dickenson Pearce

There will be an area of high pressure centred over Cornwall, Middlesex and Surrey. Temperatures will be in their 100's with occasional tropical showers in hilly districts.

Jamaica is no place like home.

Our Kingston is upon Caribbean. Not upon Thames.

And there's no mistaking our Falmouth, either.

The sea there is 80°F. All year round.

Whilst in Cornwall, go fishing. For Marlin. Off Montego Bay.

Or, if you're up at dawn watch the fishermen land their catch.

It could be your supper.

To further your education of Jamaica go up to Cambridge.

It's 1,000 feet up, in rain forests as green as jade.

Here you can catch the 'Governor's Coach', our once a day train. To Middlesex.

Find more English names like Ian Fleming and Noel Coward, who lived here.

And some names not so English like 'boonoonoonoos'.

It simply means a happening that's a good time.

Pronounce it right, and you could find yourself climbing up Dunn's River Falls.

Or paddling up a torchlit White River.

To a feast in a jungle clearing.

Come back to civilisation and you'll find Hampton Court.

In case you didn't know, it's in Surrey.

As is our Sherwood Forest.

Only a horn's call away from where Errol Flynn made his home. And his name in the 'Adventures of Robin Hood'.

If you like the sound of our Jamaican names, go to Middlesex, and catch a 'plane out of Heathrow.

You can spend two weeks in Jamaica for as little as £250.* (Includes hotel, breakfast, dinner and airfare.)

For more information see a travel agent or write to us, the Jamaica Tourist Board, 6-10 Bruton Street, London, W.1. (01-493 3647.)

Fishing in C...

Eating out in N...

If you come and stay at one of our hotels, you'll probably find it's better to eat out every night.

We'll seat you in a restaurant with a ceiling as high as the stars.

And with walls that sway in the gentlest breeze. (Palm-trees.)

Try some coconut chips as you ponder over the menu.

Maybe for starters, pick the fruits of our island: Guava, Watermelon, Papaya, Pineapple, Orange and Grapefruit.

Then follow them with the fruits of our sea: Red-snapper, Grouper, Lobster. Or Flounder, stuffed with crab.

As an accompaniment we'll add the food of love.

Music.

Be lulled by our Calypso bands. Let the sound of Jamaica fill your ears.

For afters there's another feast.

This time for your eyes.

Witness the Limbo. The Bamboo dance. Reggae dancers. Bellydancers. And men playing with fire.

When the floor show comes to an end, sit back and listen to the sea playing on the beach. (It's a non-stop show.)

Feeling romantic?

Then take to the floor yourselves. Get into the rhythm of Jamaica.

After you have, you'll need something refreshing.

Ever tried our sea?

It's still luke-warm at midnight.

Whatever night, you'll find there's something about eating out in our country you won't find anywhere else in the world.

If you fancy eating out in Jamaica we can fly you out for two weeks for as little as £250.*

(Includes hotel, breakfast, dinner and airfare.)

For more information see a travel agent or write to us, the Jamaica Tourist Board, 6-10 Bruton Street, London, W.1. (01-493 3647.)

Mantalent Inn.

Richmond Hill.

Title Jamaica
Client Jamaica Tourist Board
Agency Doyle Dane Bernbach

Title Hovis TV ads
Client Hovis
Agency Collett Dickenson Pearce

Hovis – 'Bike Ride'

SFX: Music.

MAN'S VOICE: Last stop on round was old Ma Pegerty's place.

'Twas like taking bread to the top of the world.

'Twas a grand ride back though.

I knew baker'd have kettle on. And doorsteps of hot Hovis ready.

Get this inside you boy, he'd say, and we'll have you going up that hill as fast as you come down.

MVO: Hovis still has many times more wheatgerm than ordinary bread. It's as good for you today as it's always been.

Hovis – 'Alarm Clock'

SFX: Music.

MAN'S VOICE: Before it were light I'd hear our dad getting up to get oven going.

He were a right good baker were our dad… and right proud of his Hovis.

Son, he'd say, there's more wheatgerm in that there loaf than in half a dozen others put together.

I knew nowt about that. But I knew I liked it – hot from the oven.

And when smell crept upstairs I knew it were ready and time I were up.

It were better than any alarm clock.

MVO: Hovis still has many times more wheatgerm than ordinary bread. It's as good for you today as it's always been.

Hovis – 'Coronation'

SFX: Music.

MAN'S VOICE: I were just a nipper when old King came to throne.

Everyone in street had day off, 'cept me mam and dad.

Ee… they put in some hours that day…

… baking Hovis and getting sandwiches ready for party. Come tea time they looked fair jiggered.

I told me dad what he was allus telling me 'bout Hovis and wheatgerm and how it does you good and that.

Cheeky monkey! He said. But all t'same he didn't half gun into them sandwiches.

MVO: Hovis still has many times more wheatgerm than ordinary bread. It's as good for you today as it's always been.

> **"**
> I believe the great sweep of history is made up of the small brushstrokes of the everyday. By concentrating on the task in hand, we move things on.

1976
Alan Parker

Sir Alan Parker CBE is a director, writer and producer. He began his career as a copywriter and went on to direct many prize-winning commercials, as well as feature films such as 'Midnight Express', 'Mississippi Burning', 'The Commitments', 'Evita', 'Fame', 'Birdy', 'Angel Heart', 'Pink Floyd – The Wall' and 'Angela's Ashes'. His films have won 19 BAFTA awards, ten Golden Globes and ten Oscars. Parker was the founding Chairman of the UK Film Council and is a past Chairman of the British Film Institute. He received the CBE in 1995 and a knighthood in 2002. He is also an Officier Des Arts et Lettres (France).

1976 Annual

Annual Design **Colin Craig**
Cover Sculpture **Liam Neary**
Cover Photography **David Thorpe**

Title Bestseller
Client Penguin Books

The 1976 Annual was not the best. This was probably because 1975, when the work was done, was a pretty gloomy year. Harold Wilson was Prime Minister and the economy was in tatters, as we borrowed from the IMF "to avoid wholesale domestic liquidation of the economy". This went unheeded in the advertising creative community, where "domestic liquidity" meant a couple of bottles of very good red at dinner.

D&AD must have been hard-up too, as the 1976 Annual is very cheaply printed compared to its predecessors. Flicking through these mildewed pages, what struck me, sadly, was how many of my friends and contemporaries are no longer with us: Geoff Seymour, John Gorham, John Webster, Ron Collins, Arthur Parsons, Vernon Howe, Phil Mason. Also a man who was responsible for much of the good work of the period, but rarely credited: Colin Millward. A quiet, diffident Yorkshireman, Millward was the undisputed Creative Director of Collett Dickenson Pearce and our mentor and frequent tormentor. He ruled with a benign but singular authority, keeping giant egos in their place, from Lowe to Puttnam and Saatchi to, well, Parker. John Pearce, the eccentric CDP boss, deferred to him on all matters creative and promptly fired the clients who were rash enough to reject the work. Millward is included in the pages of the 1976 Annual because he, so rightly, received the President's Award.

First up, there are two cracking Hovis commercials directed by Ridley Scott: variations on the iconic, original film of two years before, of the Hovis delivery boy pushing his bike up the cobbled Yorkshire hill (actually shot in Dorset). I was amused to see that it won for Best Use of Music. The famous brass-band piece, from Dvorak's New World Symphony, had originally been used on a CDP pilot commercial for Birds Eye pies. Alan Marshall had pinched the music from a documentary on the Charlton brothers, directed by Frank Cvitanovich. Good ideas were often regurgitated at CDP – or maybe each creative group was nicking from the other!

The Black Pencil for Commercials was given to the new Heineken campaign. My own vicarious connection with the campaign was that I was originally meant to direct it. My producer, Alan Marshall, and I prepared the commercials, but I didn't get along with the copywriter, Terry Lovelock, during the quarrelsome run-up to the shoot and so I was fired. Just as well, because Lovelock's Art Director, Vernon Howe, had directorial ambitions of his own, and went on to direct them so well that they won the year's top award. Their masterstroke, apart from getting rid of me, was to choose Danish-American comedian Victor Borge to do the voiceovers.

In the Design section, my eye went immediately to the work of a friend, the late John Gorham. He was one of the great pioneering heroes of British graphic design, the like of which can only be counted on one hand – an idealist and purist. He was also a great illustrator and, in a pre-computer age, everything he did, from type to illustration, was drawn by hand. As computers gradually took over, he did a self-promotional poster that had a picture of a pencil and, underneath, the words "My Mouse". He was a unique talent and a self-effacing genius in a vainglorious business.

> "Harold Wilson was Prime Minister and we borrowed from the IMF 'to avoid wholesale domestic liquidation of the economy'. This went unheeded in the advertising creative community, where 'domestic liquidity' meant a couple of bottles of very good red at dinner.

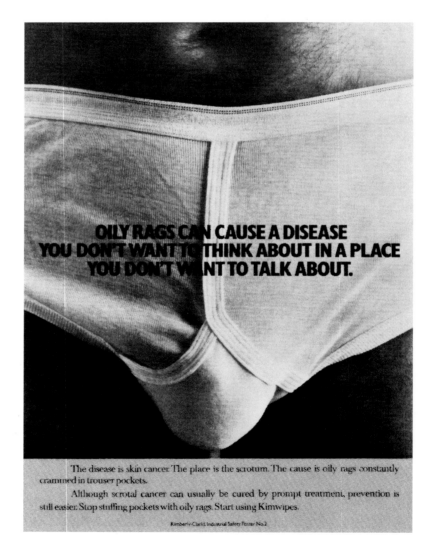

OILY RAGS CAN CAUSE A DISEASE YOU DON'T WANT TO THINK ABOUT IN A PLACE YOU DON'T WANT TO TALK ABOUT.

The disease is skin cancer. The place is the scrotum. The cause is oily rags constantly crammed in trouser pockets.

Although scrotal cancer can usually be cured by prompt treatment, prevention is still easier. Stop stuffing pockets with oily rags. Start using Kimwipes.

Kimberly-Clark Industrial Safety Poster No.2

Title Oily Rags Can Cause a Disease You Don't Want to Think About in a Place You Don't Want to Talk About
Client Kimberly-Clark
Agency Fletcher Shelton Reynolds & Dorrell

Title Heineken – Illogical
Client Whitbread
Agency Collett Dickenson Pearce

The Art and Photography sections are always my personal favourites in D&AD Annuals and there is some good work in this one. In Venice, there's a terrific shot for Benson & Hedges – an account that saw the oddball Alan Waldie grow into a great art director. Storm Thorgerson's unique Hipgnosis work for Pink Floyd was always way ahead of its time, and in an era of iTunes the kind of graphics for music that the Annual will not be seeing again. There's the powerful Elliott Erwitt 'Mother and Child' photograph for The Sunday Times Magazine, a publication that opened all our eyes to photographic reportage. My particular favourites are by the illustrator Arthur Robbins for Nova and Peter Mayle's books. In an era when everyone was slavishly copying Magritte and Matisse, Robbins drew his inspiration from The Beano and The Dandy.

In the year that I made my first feature film, 'Bugsy Malone', I was surprised so many of my commercials were included in the Annual. Mind you, I also notice that my producer, Alan Marshall, was on the jury that year, which might explain it. Of my own work, I immodestly mention the Parker pens commercial with Penelope Keith, for which I appear to have won Best Director. It was shot very quickly in the Pinewood Studios restaurant. I can't remember why two creative teams are credited: Paul Weiland / David Horry and David Brown / Ronnie Turner. Thereafter, Weiland pestered me to take him on as a director, which we eventually did and he went on to forge a great career and company of his own.

When it comes to Copywriting, there are some lovely examples that set the tone for the times. John Salmon and Tony Brignull's work is well worth a re-read – entertaining but never flashy, always literate and right on the money. And there's a lot of work from the greatest exponent of smart, succinct copy, David Abbott. Because Abbott went on to found and sell his own agencies a few times, it's easy to think of him as a figurehead and frontman. The work here, when copywriting was still his day job, reminds us that he was the George Best of British advertising writers. •

Parker – 'Finishing School'

TUTOR: Well girls, your last day at the Zermatt School for Young Ladies. And your final and most important lesson…

How to spend daddy's lovely money.

Chequebooks open, girls. Pens at the ready…

No, no, no, Felicity… One couldn't possibly stop in Knightsbridge with one of these.

(The tutor drops the cheap ballpoint pen into the bin and takes out her own pen – a Parker Lady.)

A pen with style… A pen with elan… A Parker Lady, in white rolled gold.

Noughts just seem to rrrroll from its tip.

Signatures flow with a flourish.

Now then, all together girls…

Yes, Celia?

CELIA: Does one spell 'pence' with an 'S' or a 'C', Madame?

TUTOR: I don't think you need worry about that, my dear.

MVO: The Parker Lady in white rolled gold. £9.95.

Title Finishing School
Client Parker Pen Company
Agency Collett Dickenson Pearce

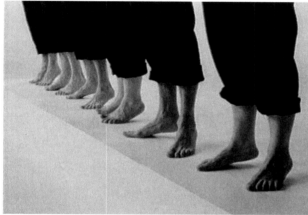

Heineken – 'Policemen'

MVO (Victor Borge): In this simple experiment, we examine the effect of beer on the feet.

Now, these feet have been walking all day and are very tired…

We see that there is no movement in them…

…which is due to lack of refreshment.

So we administer the cold Heineken…

…wait a few seconds…

…and we observe that the Heineken is already refreshing the feet…

…causing lively movement of the toes and activating the arches.

Heineken is the only beer able to do this…

…because it refreshes the parts other beers cannot reach.

> "D&AD must have been very hard-up too, as the 1976 Annual is very cheaply printed compared to its predecessors.

Title Heineken – Policemen
Client Whitbread
Agency Collett Dickenson Pearce

1977
John Salmon

John Salmon's first job in advertising was as a typographer at Erwin Wasey, London. When commercial TV began in Britain, he morphed into a writer/producer. In 1957, having failed to get a job in New York, he moved to Canada and became a copywriter at Ronalds-Reynolds. He moved to Young & Rubicam Toronto to gain experience, and was later transferred to the firm's New York office. In 1961, he was hired by Doyle Dane Bernbach to write copy in the agency's first overseas office, in London. In 1967, he moved to Collett Dickenson Pearce as Creative Group Supervisor under Colin Millward. Two years later, he was made Creative Director. He retired in 1999.

1977 Annual

Annual Design David Driver,
Robert Priest, Derek Ungless,
Claudine Meissner, Peter Laws
Cover Photography Tony Evans

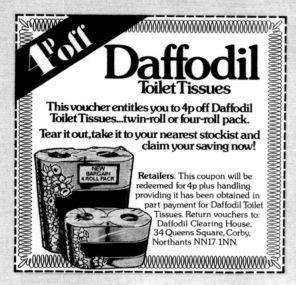

Save money on toilet tissue.

Use this piece of paper.

Title Daffodil Toilet Tissues
Client Modo Consumer Products
Agency Saatchi & Saatchi Garland-Compton

Compared to current Annuals, 1977's is a slim volume, almost entirely in black and white. The relative size of the Annuals isn't the only indication of how much D&AD has grown. The membership list in the old volume occupies a bit less than a page. Currently, it occupies four and a half pages, and includes members from all over the world. Clearly, D&AD is expanding in all directions, but the aim remains the same: to improve the standard of design and advertising by education and example.

When I was a copywriter, I was primarily interested in developing ideas that would sell. In order to do that, advertising has to meet the usual criteria – it has to get the attention of the target audience, communicate a powerful selling idea, and stick in the mind. I rarely succeeded in producing such work but, when I did, it quite often got into the show. I encouraged the people in my department to produce selling ads, but some creative people follow a different path – they want awards more than anything else. They don't care too much about effectiveness. After all, effectiveness is often hard to measure, and some clients aren't too confident when judging advertising. They tend to see awards as a confirmation that they were right to approve winning work. (And they enjoy the Awards Dinner.) Promotion, riches and fame sometimes result from adopting an all-out pursuit of awards, but it isn't what D&AD set out to foster.

The largest category of work in the 1977 Annual was Print Advertising, and I was happy to be reminded that it included more work from CDP than any other agency. However, not all the judges felt that year's entries showed improvement. Some were disappointed by the lack of progress, and said so in the Annual.

Art Director Mike Dempsey's reaction was typical of several judges. He said: "Not a vintage year, nothing really outstanding, general lack of originality... No one daring to break new ground... No more impressive than those of the 76, 75 and 74 shows." Designer Rod Springett said: "The work submitted was disappointing... It's time we all stopped juggling with well-tried techniques and extended our activities as inventors."

Creative Director Len Weinreich asked plaintively: "But is it not saddening that one agency scoops the pool? If D&AD's objective is to raise the standard of British creative work, then it cannot have succeeded." He goes on to say, rather

Title Is It Fair to Force Your Baby to Smoke Cigarettes?
Client Health Education Council
Agency Saatchi & Saatchi Garland-Compton

Title Makes Bagpipes Sound Like Music
Client Seagrams Distillers
Agency Collett Dickenson Pearce

enigmatically: "Maybe one day Edward (Booth-Clibborn) will publish the rejects and garner a little sympathy for the jury." I'm not altogether sure whether he is suggesting that seeing the appalling rejected work would elicit sympathy for those who were called upon to judge it, or if he is hinting darkly at some hidden influence that allowed so much CDP work to get in. For those of a suspicious turn of mind, I must emphasise that the only part played by the President was to chair the Committee that selected jurors. Furthermore, only one juror out of the ten worked for CDP, and those who did were forbidden to vote for the agency's work.

The judging criteria have been a bit problematic from time to time. Entries are not judged on their effectiveness in the marketplace. The decision of whether to accept or reject a given piece is highly subjective. I have been a juror a number of times, and a question often raised by jurors is, "Does it work?", which could mean any of a number of things from "Is it aesthetically pleasing?" to "Is it something not seen before, something truly original?"

One year, I was on a jury judging magazine advertisements, alongside Charles Saatchi. As usual, Edward Booth-Clibborn held up the entries for consideration one by one, and called on the jury to vote. Every entry was voted out, and the session ground to a halt. Apparently, none of the work

Title Cold Kills the Old
Client Health Education Council
Agency Saatchi & Saatchi Garland-Compton

was deemed worthy of a place in the show, let alone an Award. Booth-Clibborn confessed that the jury's failure to find anything worthy of an Award would affront the sponsor of that Award, who was contributing money that D&AD always needed desperately. He begged the jury to review the work to see if there was not something that could pass muster.

The discarded work was in a heap under a bench. After a brief discussion, we agreed to re-judge items that anybody present felt deserved a second chance. Saatchi pulled out a campaign for Dunn's, a chain of old-fashioned men's outfitters, which I had produced with Arthur Parsons. He asked me why it had been discarded. I couldn't remember why. He then said: "I'm going to put it in for re-judging. Will you vote for it?" I said that I couldn't, because I had written it. In the event, it was voted in.

I mention this to illustrate the kind of thing that can influence a jury other than the quality of the work. Fashionability, for instance. The client was a tired old chain of shops that sold well-made but unfashionable men's clothing and hats. When we acquired the account, I remember touting it around the creative department to see if any of the trendy young art directors or writers would rise to the challenge. I can still recall the looks of horror they gave me as they recoiled from the very idea of associating themselves with something so severely uncool. ⬡

Title Everybody Laughed When John Introduced Me as His Wife's Little Sister
Client Ryvita Company
Agency Doyle Dane Bernbach

"Some clients aren't too confident when judging advertising. They tend to see awards as a confirmation that they were right to approve winning work.

Ovaltine – 'Goodnight Ovaltineys'

Open on a mid-30s recording studio. Uncle Henry and the Ovaltineys are standing round microphones.

UNCLE HENRY: Goodnight Ovaltineys.

OVALTINEYS: (singing) And now the happy Ovaltineys bid you all adieu... And don't forget your Ovaltine. It's very good for you.

Mix through to 30s-type radio in sitting room, family sitting round drinking Ovaltine.

OVALTINEYS: And we'll be here again next Sunday with songs and stories too...

MVO: (Over singing) Ovaltine. Has there ever been a better way of ending the day?

OVALTINEYS: ...The Ovaltineys bid you all adieu.

SUPER/VO: Has there ever been a better way of ending the day?

Title Ovaltine – Goodnight Ovaltineys
Client Wander Foods
Agency TBWA

"Promotion, riches and fame sometimes result from adopting an all-out pursuit of awards, but it isn't what D&AD set out to foster.

Daily Express: 'Howard Hughes Tissue Trail'

(A door opens into a hotel room and one of Howard Hughes's aides enters.)

AIDE 1: Mr Hughes wants to go to the bathroom.

(Aide 2 enters darkened bedroom. The windows have been blackened out and a film is being projected.)

AIDE 2: I'm right here, Mr Hughes.

(He picks up a box of tissues from the bedside table and lays a trail of tissues on the floor to the bathroom.)

VO: If there was anything that Howard Hughes trusted less than people it was floors. He thought they were all contaminated. His last 15 years as a total recluse were full of strange quirks like this.

This Sunday in the Sunday Express and all next week in the Daily Express you can read 'Howard Hughes – The Hidden Years'. The true story of those 15 years, revealed by two of his closest aides. You won't believe it until you read it. Even then you still won't believe it.

Title Daily Express – Howard Hughes Tissue Trail
Client Beaverbrook Newspapers
Agency Collett Dickenson Pearce

1978
Gerry Moira

Gerry Moira got his first proper copywriting job at Ogilvy & Mather. He won some prizes including a Lion and a Pencil so they made him a Creative Director, and that was the beginning of the end.

He became Executive Creative Director of the agency that became Publicis and won quite a few Arrows, but most of his time was spent in meetings and pitches. Then he started his own agency, which was really hard. He went back to his old job at Publicis, which was probably a mistake. Then, he took a year out of advertising only to be sucked back in by Euro RSCG. Now, he's Creative Chairman, doing more of what he does best, which is writing.

1978 Annual

Annual Design **Brian Webb, Colin Sands**
Cover Photography **Tony Evans**

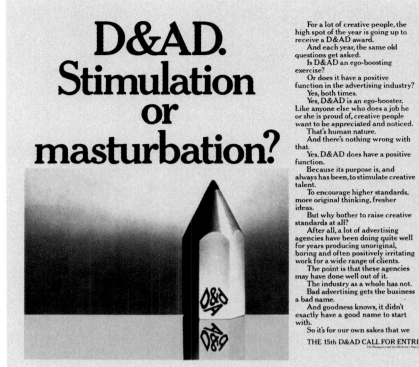

Title Call for Entries
Client Design & Art Direction
Association of London
Agency Collett Dickenson Pearce

"It was the best of times, it was the worst of times..." Although the 1978 D&AD Annual was published less than half a century ago, it does not seem wholly inappropriate to quote the opening of Charles Dickens' 'A Tale of Two Cities'. Both books mark the beginning of the end of one dynasty and the birth of another. 1978 was the year the Conservative Party appointed Saatchi & Saatchi. The firm's subsequent 'Labour Isn't Working' poster came too late for the D&AD Annual of that year, but it signalled the arrival of Thatcherism as the dominant political and social force in Britain. For good or ill, this country would never be the same again. 1978 also marked the acme of Collett Dickenson Pearce's dominance of the UK's creative advertising scene. The agency that created the way this country came to market was never to enjoy quite the same monopoly of Awards shows thereafter.

Before we examine the Annual that boasted a huge cock on the outside of the book, and one or two between the covers, it is important to set some context, a benchmark of achievement in other commercial creative fields. Remember, in those days D&AD was almost an entirely British affair.

'The Deer Hunter' won Best Picture at the Oscars but 'Grease' smashed box office records. Kate Bush scored her first and only No. 1, but Boney M and 'Grease' (again) dominated the charts. 'The Sweeney' were still chasing villains across our television screens, interrupted by commercial messages from the PG Tips chimps and the sultry sultans of Fry's Turkish Delight. James Callaghan clung to power in a government at war with the unions and the IRA. By general consensus, and as evidenced by the Award jury photos in this book, Britain was enduring its worst fashion crisis since the Middle Ages.

What of the work itself? Those of you who have served on a D&AD jury will know the time-honoured ritual of head-shaking that concludes every judging session. "This is not a vintage year," we mutter, reassuring ourselves of our own impeccable standards while subtly questioning the talent of our peers. True, the 1978 juries could not find it in themselves to award more than a couple of Black Pencils. True also that many of that year's winning campaigns – Hovis, the Smash Martians, Parker pens, Olympus cameras, Heineken – were not exactly in their first flush of youth. All these were following formulae laid down by earlier, much-lauded executions. I am not saying maintaining high standards is easy, but it helps if everyone is in on the joke before you have to tell it.

History will record that 1978 was a vintage year for Côte-Rôtie but not, it would appear, British advertising. Michael Rand was President. The celebrated Art Director of The Sunday Times Magazine had a good year.

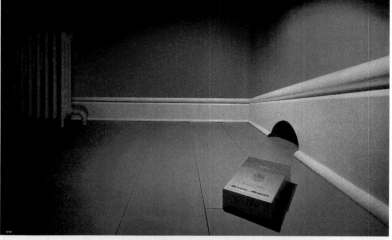

MIDDLE TAR As defined by H. M. Government
EVERY PACKET CARRIES A GOVERNMENT HEALTH WARNING

MIDDLE TAR As defined by H. M. Government EVERY PACKET CARRIES A GOVERNMENT HEALTH WARNING

MIDDLE TAR As defined by H. M. Government EVERY PACKET CARRIES A GOVERNMENT HEALTH WARNING

Title Benson & Hedges
Client Gallaher
Agency Collett Dickenson Pearce

He won a Yellow Pencil. His President's Award went to Jeremy Bullmore, one of the very few working survivors from the alumni of 78. The list of creative personnel no longer on active duty in the business reads like a roll call from the Battle of the Somme. The list of defunct agencies is equally poignant. Whatever happened to Cherry Hedger Seymour, Zetland, Davidson Pearce, Fletcher Shelton, French Cruttenden Osborn, French Gold Abbott (FGA) and Colman & Partners? Not to mention CDP and Boase Massimi Pollitt (BMP)? In 1978, these agencies were winning prizes, oblivious to the mergers and acquisitions that would erase their names from future Annuals.

By far the most important initials were C, D and P. This exceptional agency racked up a staggering 74 entries in 1978. Nearest competitors BMP and FGA each languished in the mid-teens. That was the measure of CDP's dominance. Perhaps the best evidence of this supremacy is the agency's Yellow Pencil-winning Benson & Hedges poster campaign.

Shocking perhaps to our modern sensibility to see such talent lavished upon proven carcinogens, but as Silk Cut was to prove in the 80s, creativity is not always good for your health.

Other standout work for me includes the Central Office of Information Ordnance Survey ads and the Scottish Health Education Unit work. Like the majority of press campaigns in the book, these are long copy. Their creators had the confidence in their material and their ability to engage you in a long conversation. All that information would be parked online today. But this is not just information, this is persuasion. I think David Bailey and David Litchfield's Ritz Newspaper stands the test of time, no small achievement. I love John Kelley and John O'Driscoll's ad for D&AD itself – provocative headline and an argument as compelling today as in 1978.

One of the two rather underwhelming Black Pencils went to a radio script.

"

By far the most important initials were C, D and P. Shocking perhaps to our modern sensibility to see such talent lavished upon proven carcinogens in the agency's Benson & Hedges poster campaign, but as Silk Cut was to prove in the 80s, creativity is not always good for your health.

Radio Scripts were augmented by the inclusion of a floppy 45rpm record. It is ironic that this attempt at innovation would be the very technology that locks this Annual in the 70s. The other Black Pencil was for Illustration. Frankly, it could just as well have been a photograph, but it did herald the only entry from a young Art Director called John Hegarty, who was to do rather well in the next decade.

Perhaps Tony Evans's crowing cock on the front cover was not just a knob gag after all. Perhaps it reflects a cockiness and swagger about much of the best work in this book. Many campaigns take sideswipes at the competition, like Barbara Nokes and Peter Harold's punchy Volkswagen work, but I think the Black Pencil for chutzpah goes to David Abbott. We are used to designers commissioning their own onanistic house campaigns for D&AD, but Abbott gets two in this book: one swearing his allegiance to FGA, and one announcing the birth of the agency he formed on leaving FGA. Both are impeccably written, of course. ●

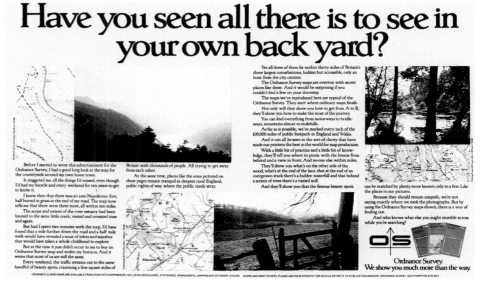

Title Ordnance Survey
Client Central Office of Information
Agency French Cruttenden Osborn

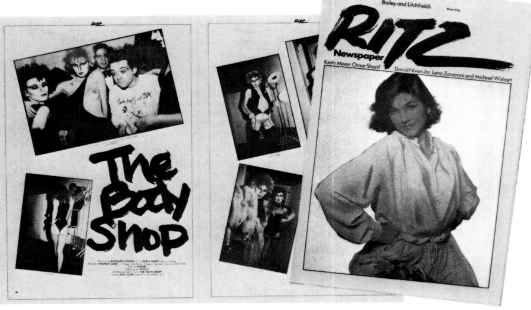

Title/Publication Ritz Newspaper

> By general consensus, and as evidenced by the Award jury photos in this book, Britain was enduring its worst fashion crisis since the Middle Ages.

Ford Fiesta.

Underneath, it's still a Ford.

Volkswagen Polo.

Underneath, it's still a Volkswagen.

Polo.

Shown here: Polo N £1999, Fiesta L £2079. Prices include car tax and VAT. Delivery and number plates extra. Seat belts extra on Polo.
For a facts analysis on the Polo, Fiesta and other competitors, write to Volkswagen (GB) Ltd, Pembroke House, Campsbourne Road, London N8 7PT.

Title VW Polo
Client Volkswagen
Agency Doyle Dane Bernbach

1979
Andrew Cracknell

Started at the top, at Collett Dickenson Pearce as a baby Copywriter in 1968. Creative Director of Kingsley Manton & Palmer (KMP) in 1973 via Pritchard Wood and boutique Aalders Marchant Weinreich. Then French Cruttenden Osborn (FCO), a jewel of an agency, until the then grandeur of Foote Cone & Belding called. WCRS presented an insane but accepted challenge, as did Dorland – which led to Bates New York and an inevitable parting. Chairmanship of Ammirati Puris Lintas was followed by a stint back at Bates before it was subsumed into WPP. Of the 14 agencies Cracknell has worked at, only one still exists – and the only thing they all have in common is that he worked there.

1979 Annual

Annual Design **Christopher Impey; Stodden Hughes**
Cover Design **Eric Pratt**
Cover Photography **Steve Garforth**

There are a few good reasons to be ambivalent about awards. There's the hype, the self-importance, the reverential postures and attitudes they engender. The vanity of people lauded and applauded out of all proportion as a result, for example, of writing once a year the sort of line a Sun sub-editor would write at least twice a week…

But the wonderful legacy of 50 years of D&AD Annuals is a record of the rise and fall in quality of the very best work of any and every year. There is no going back and changing it now – we have all moved on. And now we all look back and see where we were, and more importantly, who we were. What the 1979 Annual tells us is that we were a year of careful people doing careful work, very carefully.

Copy – lots of it, *my* how we read a lot in those days – is beautifully crafted, honeyed sentence after honed phrase. Art directors clearly worked long into the night with forensic delicacy on sculpting type of precisely the correct weight and size around exactly the right photograph or illustration by the best possible choice of illustrator or photographer.

TV commercials had scripts as sharp as any of the cream of TV sitcoms of the era – something we miss today. Radio was witty and the design of both ads and packaging was sumptuous and sophisticated.

There was absolutely nothing wrong with just about all of it, and if we were around then, we would all like to have done most of it ourselves.

Can you sense the faint praise, though? It is only when you come across the thrilling and confusing and mouth-droppingly gorgeous Hugh Hudson 'Swimming Pool' Benson & Hedges commercial that you realise the ordinariness of everything else you're examining.

How often has a piece of work stopped you dead, transfixing every sense and pinning you to your seat and making you think maybe it was time you chose a different career? For me, 'Gercha', 'Points of View', 'Surfer' perhaps – and 'Swimming Pool'.

There's a relentless mystery about it. It is ominous and frightening – maybe it's the unbending, insistent music – and it is bewildering. But also beautiful. In a cinema, it was just unthinkable to move while it

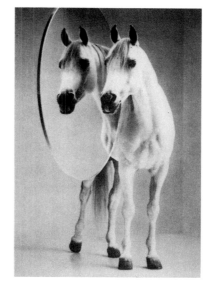 

SCOTCH ON THE ROCKS.

SCOTCH AND GINGER.

NEAT SCOTCH.

Title White Horse
Client White Horse Distillers
Agency French Cruttenden Osborn

Title Labour Isn't Working
Client Conservative Central Office
Agency Saatchi & Saatchi Garland-Compton

"What the 1979 Annual tells us is that we were a year of careful people doing careful work, very carefully.

was on. It is impossible to forget and it is so outstandingly far ahead of everything else in that year that it actually seems unfair. The jury were equally besotted – it won one Black and three Yellow Pencils.

It was a good year for posters: 'Labour Isn't Working', often erroneously attributed to Charles Saatchi, Jeremy Sinclair or even, preposterously, Maurice Saatchi, but actually written by Andrew Rutherford, marked the beginning of a mutually profitable relationship between Saatchi & Saatchi and the Conservative Party. 1979 was the year Margaret

Thatcher ascended to the throne – incidentally, at more or less the same time as Saddam Hussein in Iraq.

Again from Saatchi, Benson & Hedges won a Poster Yellow Pencil with shots by Jimmy Wormser and Adrian Flowers for the Gold Box campaign. And another Yellow Pencil went to a lovely and utterly original White Horse whisky campaign. With no pack shot and just the line 'Scotch and American', one image showed an immaculate white horse next to a black basketball player in an all-American outfit; 'Scotch and Ginger' had

the horse next to a punkish but smart young woman with bright ginger hair; 'Scotch on the Rocks' was the horse appearing to be sculpted from the pile of rocks around its feet – and so on. It also won gongs in print, and as Creative Director of the agency, FCO, I can take some pride in this startlingly simple but complete idea by Graeme Norways and Nick Hazzard. I cannot take any credit, though – to my eternal shame, it took Richard French, the F of FCO, to find the roughs in a pile of also-rans and promote it as the campaign to run. Exquisitely shot by Lester Bookbinder, it ran for only a

Title Benson & Hedges – Gold Box
Client Gallaher
Agency Collett Dickenson Pearce

B&H – 'Swimming Pool'

SFX: Low, pulsating music builds up tension throughout.

The commercial opens with a shot of iguanas, lying beside a empty swimming pool in the dazzling sunlight. The scene cuts to a view of a desert from a helicopter. The helicopter carrying a box attracts the attention of an iguana. The swimming pool starts to fill up and one of the iguanas moves slowly towards the point of intrigue. A snake notices the helicopter and lifts its head. Then a camera turns towards the helicopter and zooms in. The iguana enters the pool and, as it swims, grows bigger, transforming into a diver. The helicopter drops the box in the pool and the diver approaches. The camera continues to follow the action. The diver peels back the surface of the box to reveal an image of Benson & Hedges cigarettes. The camera snaps, zooms out and reveals an enormous billboard poster for B&H.

Title Benson & Hedges – Swimming Pool
Client Gallaher
Agency Collett Dickenson Pearce

> "It is only when you come across the thrilling and confusing and mouth-droppingly gorgeous Hugh Hudson 'Swimming Pool' Benson & Hedges commercial that you realise the ordinariness of everything else you're examining.

year, pulled by a sales force who couldn't understand why the woman wasn't older and wearing an evening gown, made racist remarks about the basketball player and described the 'Scotch on the Rocks' shot as "messy". They wanted, and got, large bottle-and-glass shots. For the brand, the rest is history. Ignominious, anonymous history.

On TV there was a commercial through the Central Office of Information – how sadly will it be missed – for the Youth Opportunities Programme that could and should, if we had a youth opportunities scheme, run today. Potential employers stand dispassionately bemoaning the state, doing nothing about the young adults drowning in the pool at their feet, while a voiceover tells them that without openings for jobs from employers such as them, too many young people are going to go under.

The stellar stuff is difficult to find, though, and it's difficult to say why. UK creative work certainly took off in the early 70s, fuelled by brave new agencies like French Gold Abbott and Boase Massimi Pollitt and the continuing brilliance of CDP. Maybe by the end of the decade, we were just tired.

Since researching and writing 'The Real Mad Men', about the creative revolution in 60s New York, I've become interested in the effect that social events and demographic changes within agencies can have on advertising. 1978, when the work in this Annual was done, was certainly a time of upheaval and uncertainty. As we entered the Winter of Discontent, a period of acute and angry industrial unrest, we were the Sick Man of Europe. Northern Ireland was particularly bloody, while the Yorkshire Ripper stalked our streets and imaginations.

Within the creative departments, the rout of the "old school tie" was complete and the lower-middle and working class takeover, started with such energy and vibrancy by the "cockney" photographers in the 60s, was complete.

You would never know it from the work of 79, though – polite, erudite and considered, but with little exuberance.

As I said, careful. ⬢

There's one thing worse than being unemployed at sixteen.

That's still being unemployed at seventeen.

And eighteen.
And nineteen.
All over Britain there are thousands of young people unable to find jobs, as many as one in three in some areas.

It's not that they are work-shy. In many cases they have tried for dozens of jobs - only to find that, without experience or a skill, they haven't a hope.

How can we stop these young people ending up on the scrap heap before they've even had a chance?

We think we've found a way.

Youth Opportunities Programme.
The Youth Opportunities Programme is a new plan to help employers help young people, even if they can't offer any permanent jobs.

It's based on the best elements of existing schemes that have succeeded in helping as many as 8 out of 10 participants into jobs.

The idea is extremely simple: If you can take in young people for up to six months, introducing them to the benefits and disciplines of work, we will pay them £19.50 a week.

And there are no National Insurance contributions or tax returns to worry about.

The alternative.
The only alternative is a growing number of young people who feel discarded by 'the system' and a smaller pool of trained and enthusiastic people for industry to draw upon. And, if nothing's done, the inescapable truth is that by the end of this year the situation will be even worse.

Which is why the Programme is backed by the government, the CBI and the STUC.

How it works.
We have offices all over the country and our staff are eager to give employers every detail of the scheme. At the same time, these offices keep in close touch with all the bodies concerned with unemployed young people in your area.

Which makes them uniquely qualified to help you help young people.

If you're interested in participating in the Programme, our staff will help you plan an introduction to work for young people that will benefit them without disturbing the normal running of your business.

You are then free to choose the young men and women you feel have the most to offer - and whose future will be brighter as a result of training and experience under your guidance.

Then it's up to the Youth Opportunities Programme to make sure that your involvement is as trouble-free and rewarding as possible. Give a young person a chance, and we will do the rest.

What to do.
Get the full story from Roger Panton, Manpower Services Commission, Department SCI, Selkirk House, 166 High Holborn, London WC1V 6PF Tel. 01-836 1213.
Our future workforce depends on it.

YOUTH OPPORTUNITIES PROGRAMME MSC

Is this the best future we can offer our school leavers?

There are now more young people out of work than at any time since the war.

In some areas that's 1 in 3. And they're not work-shy hooligans, they're victims of the economic facts of life.

They've applied for jobs - in some cases they've applied for dozens - and they've been told that without a skill or work experience they haven't a chance.

Which makes them teenage rejects. Turned down without trial.

Youth Opportunities Programme.
The Youth Opportunities Programme is a new plan to help employers help young people, even if they can't offer any permanent jobs.

It's based on the best elements of existing schemes that have succeeded in helping as many as 8 out of 10 participants into jobs.

The idea is extremely simple: If you can take in young people for up to six months, introducing them to the benefits and disciplines of work, we will pay them £19.50 a week. And there are no National Insurance contributions or tax returns to worry about.

They get invaluable experience, training and the chance to earn a reference that proves their worth. You get a chance to give them a future without having to take anyone on permanently unless you want to.

The alternative.
The only alternative is a growing number of young people who feel discarded by 'the system' and a smaller pool of trained and enthusiastic people for industry to draw upon.

And, if nothing's done, the inescapable truth is that by the end of this year the situation will be even worse.

Which is why the Programme is backed by the government, the CBI and the TUC.

How it works.
We have offices all over the country and our staff are eager to give employers every detail of the scheme. At the same time, these offices keep in close touch with all the bodies concerned with unemployed young people in your area.

Which makes them uniquely qualified to help you help young people.

If you're interested in participating in the Programme, our staff will help you plan an introduction to work for young people that will benefit them without disturbing the normal running of your business.

You are then free to choose the young men and women you feel have the most to offer - and whose future will be brighter as a result of training and experience under your guidance.

Then it's up to the Youth Opportunities Programme to make sure that your involvement is as trouble-free and rewarding as possible. Give a young person a chance, and we will do the rest.

What to do.
Get the full story from Roger Panton, Manpower Services Commission, Department Selkirk House, 166 High Holborn, London WC1V 6PF Tel. 01-836 1213.
Our future workforce depends on it.

YOUTH OPPORTUNITIES PROGRAMME MSC

Youth Opportunities Programme – 'Swimming Pool'

1½ seconds silence

Open on group of adults watching young people drowning.

MVO: This is a Manpower Services Commission announcement.

1ST EMPLOYER: They shouldn't allow it.

2ND EMPLOYER: Why don't they do something about it?

3RD EMPLOYER: It's a disgrace.

MVO: This is how it feels to be young, willing and out of work.

How it feels when through no fault of your own you can't get a job.

Without help, thousands of teenagers are going to go under.

It's your help they're crying out for.

Because if you're an employer you can give them up to six months' work experience and we'll pay them.

So if you can't give them a permanent job, you can still give them a chance.

Telephone the Youth Opportunities Programme on Glasgow 331-2751 and help them to help themselves.

YOUTH OPPORTUNITIES PROGRAMME
MSC · Manpower Services Commission Special Programmes

COI/MSC YOUTH OPPORTUNITIES PROGRAMME 'Talkover'

All spoken rhythmically to music with sung chorus.

When I left the school I scouted round for jobs but there was nothing doing anywhere unless you got experience. And when I met my friends all they ever said was...

CHORUS (Sung): Aint you gotta job yet? Aint you gotta job?

So I trotted round the offices and factories but all they said was 'sorry'. So I went home for a cuppa tea, but when I walked in there's me mother at the sink saying...

CHORUS (Sung): Aint you gotta job yet? Aint you gotta job?

So I'm reading in the paper about this Youth Opportunities Programme whatsit, says you spend maybe six months trying out different work and learn a bit and pick up some experience as well as over twenty quid a week which is better than a poke in the face. Then me dad starts... go on, dad...

CHORUS (Sung): Aint you gotta job yet? Aint you gotta job?

So I'm in this Careers Office and I'm saying to the bloke in the suit 'What about your Youth Opportunities Programme?' and he says 'Can you start Monday?' and I felt really chuffed.

So if people keep saying to you...

CHORUS (Sung): Aint you gotta job yet? Aint you gotta job?

Get on your actual Youth Opportunities Programme, brothers and sisters. Wander down the old Job Centre or Careers Office. Have a word with the bloke in the suit. (end music). Then everyone'll shut up.

...I can't get a job without experience ...but I can't get experience without a job...

Vicious, isn't it?

All over Britain there are thousands of unemployed young people trapped in this vicious circle.

In some areas it's as many as one in three. They are not work-shy: in many cases they have tried for dozens of jobs, only to find that, without experience or skills, they haven't a hope.

Yet we know for certain that if they could get some experience of working for a living or acquire a skill, their prospects would be much brighter.

Which is precisely why we have created the Youth Opportunities Programme.

Youth Opportunities Programme.

The Youth Opportunities Programme is a new plan to help employers help young people even if they can't offer any permanent jobs.

It's based on the best elements of existing schemes that have succeeded in helping as many as 6 out of 10 participants into jobs. The idea is extremely simple: if you can take in young people for up to six months, introducing them to the benefits and disciplines of work, we will pay them £19.50 a week.

And there are no National Insurance contributions or tax returns to worry about.

They get invaluable experience, training and the chance to earn a reference that proves it's worth. You get a chance to give them a better start without having to take anyone on permanently - unless you want to.

The alternative.

The only alternative is a growing number of young people who feel discarded by 'the system' and a smaller pool of trained and enthusiastic people for industry to draw upon. And, if nothing's done the inescapable truth is that by the end of this year the situation will be even worse.

Which is why the Programme is backed by the government, the CBI and the TUC.

How it works.

We have offices all over the country and our staff are eager to give employers every detail of the scheme.

At the same time, these offices keep in close touch with all the bodies concerned with unemployed young people in your area.

Which makes them uniquely qualified to help you help young people.

If you're interested in participating in the Programme, our staff will help you plan an introduction to work for young people that will benefit them without disturbing the normal running of your business.

You are then free to choose the young men and women you feel have the most to offer - and whose future will be brighter as a result of training and experience under your guidance.

Then it's up to the Youth Opportunities Programme to make sure that your involvement is as trouble-free and rewarding as possible. Give a young person a chance, and we will do the rest.

What to do.

Get the full story from Roger Punton, Manpower Services Commission, Department FT2, Selkirk House, 166 High Holborn, London WC1V 6PF. Tel 01-836 1213.

Our future workforce depends on it.

YOUTH OPPORTUNITIES PROGRAMME
MSC

Youth Opportunities Programme – 'Pinball'

Youth is shot across an enormous pinball table.

MVO: It's not much of a game...

SFX: Boing!

...being young and unemployed.

1ST EMPLOYER: Sorry, no vacancies.

SFX: Boing!

MVO: ... Being shunted from pillar to post.

2ND EMPLOYER: No experience.

3RD EMPLOYER: No qualifications.

2ND EMPLOYER: No experience.

3RD EMPLOYER: No qualifications.

MVO: ... Knowing you're one of the thousands who can't find work. There is a way out.

SFX: Flipper.

A way to get...
...the work experience, training and references...
...that could help you...
...to a permanent...

The Youth Opportunites Programme...
...is a new, no-nonsense scheme...
...to help you help yourself.
And we'll pay you £19.50 a week.

If you're beginning to think you'll never get a job, ask at your Careers Office of Jobcentre about the new Youth Opportunities Programme.

KID'S VO: It's a whole new ball game, innit?

Title Youth Opportunities Programme
Client Central Office of Information
Agency Saatchi & Saatchi Garland-Compton

1980
Snowdon

Photo **Roger Keller**

London-born Antony Armstrong-Jones, better known as Lord Snowdon, started taking photographs as a professional in 1951.

In 1960 he married Princess Margaret, and during the 1960s he had his studio on the roof of The Sunday Times Magazine.

In 1961 he, Frank Newby and Cedric Price designed the Aviary at London Zoo, which is now a listed building. In 1965, 'Private View', the seminal book on the 1960s London art world, was published with photographs by Snowdon and writing by Bryan Robertson and John Russell. Over the course of the 60s and 70s he made several film documentaries, and 'Don't Count the Candles' (1968), a film about old age made for CBS, won seven awards, including two Emmys.

In the 1970s he moved from Kensington Palace and built a small studio and darkroom at the bottom of his house in Kensington. Over the last 40 years he has photographed many people there, including Margaret Thatcher, Tony Blair, David Cameron, David Bowie, Freddie Mercury and The Queen, to mention a few. He still lives and works there today.

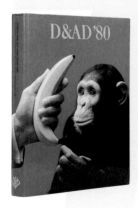

1980 Annual

Annual Design **Pete Green; Rod Springett Associates**
Cover Photography **John Clarke**

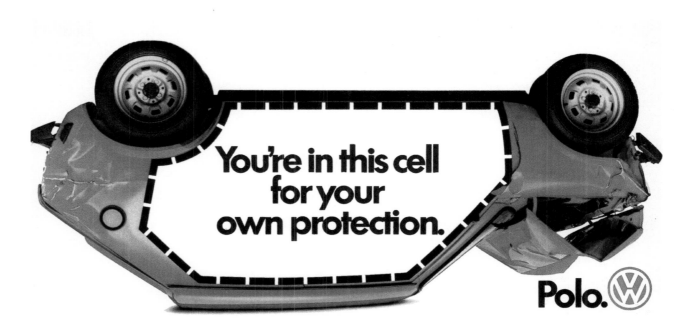

You're in this cell
for your
own protection.

Polo. VW

Title Polo – 'Protection'
Client Volkswagen
Agency Doyle Dane Bernbach

God knows what I would have been looking for when we were judging the work in 1980. What would have caught my eye? Probably the girl sitting next to me. But I think it's good to have an Annual that collects the best of the year's work together. And it's a very good idea for there to be awards for excellence in one's field – it's always nice to be recognised, isn't it?

At the time, I was very close to Mark Boxer, the editor of The Sunday Times Magazine. He died far too young – he was wonderful. I remember once when he rang his wife, Anna Ford, and I heard him on the phone – they had been married quite a long time – "Hello? Oh, it's Mark here… Boxer." It was Mark who was the leader of the whole thing; he was frightfully good and he did very good cartoons. And he was wonderful looking. As far as I am concerned, it always goes back to Mark Boxer. And the magazine was revolutionary at that time.

People sometimes frame photographs. I'm against all that. It's pretentious. The best photographers were people like Henri Cartier-Bresson. He used to go round in a little suit, you would never notice him. A lot of photographers are too self-important – it's a fairly menial profession really, only just above window cleaners. Photography should stay a trade.

I don't get up as early in the morning as I used to… that's why I'm not as good a photographer as I was. Photographers should get up earlier. When I was doing a piece with Marjorie Wallace on mental health, we used to go to the institutions at six o'clock in the morning. We would then just get the night staff, so we got interviews with them, which was far more interesting than if we'd gone there at 11 o'clock in the morning. That's a good tip for young photographers… and old ones. ⬡

When Mrs Marion Gibson first planned the evening's meal, nothing could have been further from her mind than hot-plate flambé.

In fact, the family dinner that night had started life as steak and chips.

But, by 6.20, there had been a dramatic change in the menu.

Moments earlier, the oil in the chip pan had been bubbling away quite merrily: so it was with every confidence that Mrs Gibson turned her back to lay the table.

It was then that the oil reached boiling point and instantly caught light.

Within seconds the entire cooker was ablaze.

Thankfully though, the fire brigade arrived in time to drown the kitchen, before the flames had a chance to take hold in the rest of the house.

The following morning, with the gloomy prospect of weeks of Chinese takeaways ahead of them, the Gibsons took little comfort from the fact they were insured.

After all, as everyone knows, it takes more than a completed claims form to restore life

The following day, we gave Mrs Gibson another chance to burn the dinner.

to some sort of normality after a serious fire.

It takes people who are prepared to put themselves out.

At Commercial Union, we pride ourselves in the knowledge that we have these sort of people working in our midst. As the Gibsons were soon to discover for themselves.

Barely an hour after reporting the fire to our local branch office, Mr Gibson found himself opening his front door to one of our claims inspectors.

No sooner had he assessed the damage, than he agreed to a settlement. On the spot.

That afternoon a second surprise appeared on the Gibsons' doorstep.

Quite simply, a brand new cooker. Identical in every way to their original.

Courtesy of Commercial Union.

In the normal course of events, we would replace a cooker with a cheque. Not a cooker.

But then, there are always exceptions to the rule.

Being down to earth insurance folk, we would never claim to work miracles.

Though Mrs Gibson would doubtless disagree with us.

We won't make a drama out of a crisis.

To stem the flood from the attic, all our man had to do was turn off a tap.

On December 31st last year, when most of the country was in the grip of a severe blizzard, one of our policy holders, Mrs Dean, had a problem of another kind.

She was in the grip of a severe flood.

Caused, not by the elements. But by a pipe that had sprung a leak in a section leading from the cold storage tank.

The ceiling in one of the upstairs rooms of her sixteenth century cottage had collapsed, and cold water was pouring through onto the bed.

To add to her problems, Mr Dean was 5500 miles away at the time. On a business trip to Riyadh.

With great presence of mind, Mrs Dean decided there wasn't much point in phoning her husband.

Instead, she phoned her local Commercial Union District Sales Manager who lived but three miles away.

Having worked for Commercial Union for a good number of years, our man can tell a crisis a mile away (or, in this case, a little further).

More than that, though, he's a dab hand at knowing what to do in such nerve-wracking circumstances.

So, instead of getting into his car and setting off to the New Year's Eve party to which he had been invited, our quick thinking District Sales Manager got into his car and set off through the blizzard to Mrs Dean's house.

To cut a long story short, when he arrived, he first organised buckets to catch the water coming through the ceiling.

Then, he tracked down the main stopcock to a point in the front garden that was by now under several inches of snow.

Having turned that off, he turned his mind to getting hold of a qualified plumber.

Needless to say, by the time all this had been taken care of, he was more than a trifle late for his New Year's Eve celebrations.

But our story doesn't stop here.

The next day, our knight in shining gumboots was back.

This time, to disperse an air-lock that the plumber had inadvertently overlooked.

To be perfectly honest, it's not every day of the week that we can quote you such examples of devotion to duty.

And indeed, neither would we want to.

Since we'd much rather you looked upon us as a highly efficient insurance company.

And not a highly efficient plumbing service.

We won't make a drama out of a crisis.

Financial Times

Seven days later, we bought a brand new red Volkswagen for the man who'd just bought a brand new red Volkswagen.

On 2nd April 1975, the morning weather forecast happened to mention there would be gusty showers around the South East.

For once, the clairvoyants at the Met Office were right.

But while other people were simply getting blown about, one man was getting more than he bargained for from the elements.

Though modesty prevents him from lending his name to our story, we can reveal that he was a school teacher in Guildford at the time. And the proud owner of a new

Volkswagen Beetle.

No sooner had he parked it, locked it and turned his back on it than a ton and a half of tree trunk crashed down onto the bonnet.

With the result that his new red Volkswagen was effectively a new red write-off.

The teacher called his local branch of Commercial Union.

As his insurance company, we of course needed to see the damage for ourselves.

By late morning we had the claim form signed, sealed and on

its way to head office for final approval.

This we received within two days, on 4th April.

Then came the tricky part.

We told the teacher that we'd be happy to replace his Volkswagen immediately with a new one, whereupon he told us he had this thing about red.

Then red it is, we said. But it may take a little time.

As it turned out, very little time indeed. On 9th April, just 7 days (not to mention scores of phone calls)

later, our learned friend took delivery of a brand new Volkswagen.

And, we're happy to say, the colour was such you'd be hard put to spot a ripe tomato on the bonnet.

Of course, we can't always promise to deal with every claim with such speed and so little fuss. But we'll do our level best.

Whether you suddenly find yourself without a car or a colour television, your home or your health: armed with the right policy, you'll find us more than willing to help.

And if that means a cheque within days, rather than weeks, we'll be the first with a first class stamp.

We won't make a drama out of a crisis.

Title Commercial Union Assurance campaign
Client Commercial Union Assurance
Agency Doyle Dane Bernbach

'Monty Python's Life of Brian' – 'Mrs Cleese'

MRS CLEESE: I?... Into this?...

SFX: Noise of microphone.

MRS CLEESE: Hello. My name is Muriel Cleese and I live in a very nice elderly people's home in Weston-super-Mare.

My son John is in the new Monty Python film 'Life of Brian'.

I do hope you'll go and see it, because he's on a percentage and he says if it doesn't do well he won't be able to keep me on in the home any longer.

So see 'The Life of Brian' now because I'm 102 years old and if I have to leave here it'll kill me. (laughs)

MVO: If you want to help Mrs Cleese please go and see 'Monty Python's Life of Brian'.

(Mrs Cleese laughs.)

Title Monty Python's Life of Brian – Mrs Cleese
Client Cinema International Corporation
Agency Lonsdale Advertising

"People sometimes frame photographs. I'm against all that. It's pretentious.

"It's good to have an Annual that collects the best of the year's work together... It's always nice to be recognised, isn't it?

Title Crabtree & Evelyn range of packaging
Client Crabtree & Evelyn
Design Group Peter Windett & Associates

Fiat Strada – 'Handbuilt by Robots'

SFX: Rossini's 'Figaro' from 'The Barber of Seville' throughout.

The commercial traces the manufacture of a Fiat Strada from start to finish. The process is systematic, efficient and precise – and it is performed entirely by robots. The ad promotes meticulous craft on an industrial scale.

Title Handbuilt by Robots
Client Fiat Motor Company UK
Agency Collett Dickenson Pearce

1981
Martin Boase

Martin Boase was born in 1932 and educated at Bedales and New College, Oxford. He came into advertising in 1958, joining first The London Press Exchange, then Robert Sharp & Partners and Pritchard Wood.

In 1968 he formed Boase Massimi Pollitt (BMP), which grew to be number two in the UK and went public in 1983. The agency joined Omnicom Group in 1989, and Boase chaired the Advertising Association for six years in the early 90s.

Since retiring from advertising in the mid-90s, he has served on the boards of Emap and Taunton Cider and chaired Maiden Outdoor, Heal's and Herald Investment Trust.

1981 Annual

Annual Design Alex Maranzano,
Dimitri Karavias; Minale Tattersfield
Cover Photography Ian Stokes
Art Direction Marcello Minale,
Brian Tattersfield, Alex Maranzano

My memories of that time are less about D&AD but of all the other things happening in my own life, like the company I was working in and what we were doing. It was a much-lauded agency at the time, called Boase Massimi Pollitt, and Stanley Pollitt had died in 1979 aged 49. We had sold half of our company to Univas, which was part of the huge French company Havas, and we were in the midst of extracting ourselves from it. We managed to buy back the half that we'd sold for the same amount that we'd sold it for, and as a result of that we spread the shares much further down the line to lots of other people in the company. It was democratic stuff. People didn't get bonuses, they got shares in the public company – the tea lady and everybody. They were known as Boasie bonds. Eventually we went public in 1983, two years later.

The D&AD Awards night was at Grosvenor House, and I turned up in my dinner jacket, as usual, to hand out the prizes. When I arrived there, they said, "No no no! No black tie!" So, I scuttled all the way back to St John's Wood and put on something less posh.

I was flattered to preside over D&AD as the first non-creative to take the chair, and expressed that in my words at the beginning of the book. I suppose, looking at the book from the perspective of the digital age, with all the multi-faceted transparency that it brings, 1981's work looks a bit stilted and doesn't have the elbow room that we now enjoy.

Specifically, four things strike me about the work from that year.

First, how modern and undated it still looks, considering the passing of the years, both in terms of the quality of the ideas and their execution.

Second, in the Advertising field, how certain agencies dominate so comprehensively – Collett Dickenson Pearce across the media gamut, BMP in TV and Abbott Mead Vickers in print.

Third, that really persuasive, beautifully written long copy featured a lot and has now largely disappeared, perhaps as a result of the rough and ready nature of communication in the electronic age.

Fourth, the Book looks so much less comprehensive in terms of the

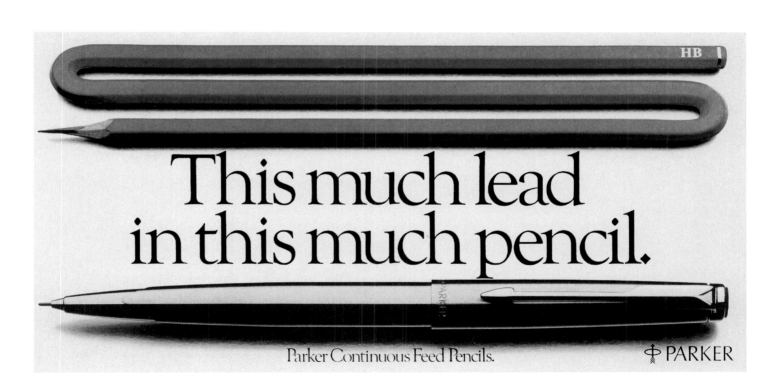

This much lead in this much pencil.

Parker Continuous Feed Pencils.

☦ PARKER

Title Parker Continuous Feed Pencils
Client Parker Pen Company
Agency Collett Dickenson Pearce

manifestation of good design it features.
In those days, there were only 14
sections in the Annual; now, there are
many more as D&AD has broadened
its remit.

The medal work I particularly admire is
the first Lego ads from TBWA, a campaign
that is still more or less running now
all these years later, supervised by the
same agency principals, now called Bartle
Bogle Hegarty.

Then, Benson & Hedges from CDP, the
beginning of the campaign that was to
become fully surreal at Saatchi & Saatchi,
before the eventual banning of tobacco
advertising. The 'Rabbit' commercial from
the wonderfully original black and white
Courage Best campaign, from BMP's
John Webster. And another finely crafted
campaign with long copy for Albany Life –
effectively a piece of CDP work.

I was keen that D&AD should go on
admiring good work. Looking forwards
after that time, I'm not so comfortable
as many people are with the extension
of the remit – opening it up to all sorts
of design. It isn't particularly admirable,
but one does focus on one's own craft.
Broaden it out into other crafts and
suddenly it becomes less interesting,
it waters the thing down. ●

> "It isn't particularly admirable,
> but one does focus on one's
> own craft. Broaden it out into
> other crafts and suddenly it
> becomes less interesting,
> it waters the thing down.

Courage Best Bitter – 'Rabbit'

The commercial uses an adaptation
of Chas & Dave's 'Rabbit' to suggest
that a trip to the pub for a pint of
Courage Best is a perfect escape
from a rabbiting wife.

SUNG: Rabbit x 20

When your old girl starts talkin',
And she won't give it a rest,
If you want my advice mate,
I'd have a pint of Courage Best.
It's so gold and clear and beautiful
that I can hardly wait,
Without a doubt it's one o'the things
That makes this country great.
They ought to have a pint
On exhibition in the Tate –
You can't get nothing like it –
A lovely pint of Courage Best.

Rabbit x 20

MVO: Remember a pint of Best.
Courage do.

Title Courage Best Bitter – Rabbit
Client Courage Brewing
Agency Boase Massimi Pollitt Univas

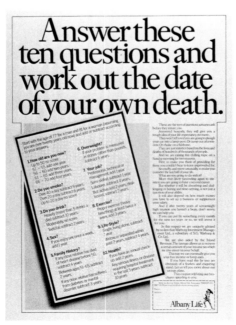

"

Really persuasive, beautifully written long copy featured a lot and has now largely disappeared, perhaps as a result of the rough and ready nature of communication in the electronic age.

Title Albany Life
Client Albany Life Assurance
Agency Advertising and Marketing Services

Lego – 'Kipper'

MVO: You see, I was standing outside my mouse hole the other day and all of a sudden along comes this cat. So quick as a flash, I turn into a dog. (barks) But the cat turned into a dragon, (breathes fire) so I turned into a fire engine. (laughs) And then, and then he turned into a submarine, so I became a submarine-eating kipper. I said a kipper, not a slipper – never mind. (chuckles) But he turned into an anti-kipper ballistic missile! So I turned into a missile cruncher… crunch, crunch, crunch crunch, crunch. Just in time to see him change into a very, very big elephant… so do you know what I did then? I turned back into a mouse and gave him the fright of his life – just like that. (evil laugh)

Title **Kipper**
Client **Lego UK**
Agency **TBWA**

1982
Steve Henry

Steve Henry was Founder/Creative Director of Howell Henry Chaldecott Lury, which was voted Campaign's Agency of the Year three times and then Agency of the Decade in 2000.

In 2009, he joined Albion as non-executive Creative Director. In both 2010 and 2011, Albion was shortlisted for Campaign's Digital Agency of the Year. In his career, Henry has won most of the major creative awards, including the D&AD Black Pencil and the Grand Prix at Cannes.

He has spoken at over 50 major advertising conferences around the world. In 2008, he was included in Campaign's inaugural Hall of Fame, a collection of the 40 most influential people in British advertising. He blogs on the Campaign website.

In 2011, Henry launched Decoded, a company that teaches anyone to "code in a day".

1982 Annual

Annual Design **Larkin May**
Cover Design **Chris Lower**
Cover Photography **Peter Hall**
Typography **Sue Carter**
Art Direction **John Larkin, Gordon Smith**

1982. Blimey. Rowntree's Fruit Pastilles. Aztec chocolate bars. Bell-bottom trousers. Harold Macmillan was Prime Minister. George Formby was top of the charts with his ukulele.

Actually I may have got some of my chronology a bit off, but if the past is another country, then 1982 looks like the western Solomon Islands.

Was I even alive back then? Sadly, yes. The proof is on page seven of the 1982 Annual.

Looking back at this Annual had me so overcome with nostalgia, I wanted to get monumentally pissed at lunchtime. That's what people used to do back then.

Advertising back then was all about flair, arrogance, larking about. If you look at the photo of the TV jury for 1982, Frank Lowe is having a huge laugh with Alan Parker while leaning his head on Mike Cozens – they all look like they've fully enjoyed whatever fine wine was provided for lunch that day.

It's the photos of the juries that are most fun and most revealing. Ridiculous haircuts, cockiness, odd clothes, laddishness – advertising really was one of the last bastions of rock'n'roll. There was even a client called Frank Cokayne – in fact, he was the client behind the brilliant John Smith's TV campaign.

Even though a lot of the Press work looks like it belongs in your dad's shed, the important point is this – back then, the work was much more loved. Which is kind of ironic, if you think about it. Right now, advertising is trying to invade culture in every way it can. Back then, it was happy to sit in a little box called advertising – but it feels like it was much more a part of culture than it is nowadays.

Perhaps that is because there was much more focus on the industry as a creative one then, rather than just as an adjunct to accountancy.

The Design Black Pencil was amazing (Gert Dumbar's witty work for a hospital in The Hague), and John Smith's TV work was outstanding.

Actually, very little TV got in that year – maybe because the jury was having too much of a laugh to press their buzzers. But the Press jury went mad and put in loads.

Title Good Food Costs Less at Sainsbury's
Client J Sainsbury
Agency Abbott Mead Vickers SMS

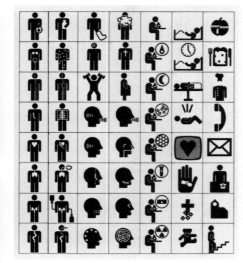

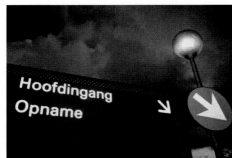

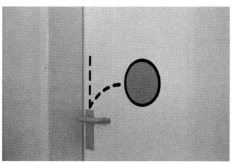

Title Westeinde Hospital
Client Westeinde Hospital, The Hague
Design Group Studio Dumbar

"The Design Black Pencil was amazing – Gert Dumbar's witty work for a hospital in The Hague.

**John Smith's Yorkshire Bitter –
'Arkwright'**

(Dog's head is just visible above the
bar. It does not move.)

MAN: Like your new dog Arkwright.
Here boy, hup, hup. Down. Sit. Heel.
(whistles) Dun't do much, does he?

ARKWRIGHT: Fancy a drop o' John
Smiths?

(Dog somersaults, does a
handstand, juggles, lifts bar stool.)

ARKWRIGHT: He just needs the right
motivation.

Title John Smith's – Arkwright
Client Courage Brewing
Agency Boase Massimi Pollitt Univas

The best of this came, of course, from David Abbott, who was writing elegantly irresistible headlines as effortlessly and silkily as... well, I can't actually think of anything silkier than David Abbott's copywriting skills.

His arch-rival for the title of most respected creative in London, John Webster, apparently used to throw Campaign into the bin if David Abbott was on the front page – such was the rivalry between the two gods of the industry.

Webbo won the big plaudits that year with his beautifully simple ad for John Smith's that had the hero's dog doing tricks while hidden below the pub bar. Sheer genius, and it would blow the lid off YouTube if it was made today. Unbetterable.

Mr Abbott, meanwhile, was writing lines for Sainsbury's that would help to change Britain's shopping habits more or less overnight.

London Weekend Television (LWT) was doing the most interesting posters (I got my share of a Yellow Pencil for that one, I thought I'd mention that), but the real breakthrough was the media thinking. Mike Gold asked the media contractors if they could change the poster sites every week, rather than the usual monthly cycle.

They said no, so he hired two blokes with a van to do it. As a result, the ads felt fresher than anything else happening in the London ad scene that year.

Gold Greenlees Trott, where I was working at the time, felt like the sexiest place to be – Collett Dickenson Pearce was losing its dominance, mainly because Frank Lowe had left, but Boase Massimi Pollitt, Abbott Mead Vickers and Saatchi & Saatchi were all great, and a slew of amazing new agencies like Bartle Bogle Hegarty, Lowe Howard-Spink and WCRS were hoving into view. But GGT was the bad boy on the block.

Working for Dave Trott was tough, but he taught me loads. He was implacable in his dedication to a creative vision. So of course (in their different ways) were people like John Hegarty, David Abbott, Robin Wight, Tim Delaney, Paul Arden, Jeff Stark and so on. Back then, creative directors were creative directors, and they didn't need a poncey "executive" in their titles, either.

So... what looks dated about the work? The puns. All those puns.

"Even at 20 degrees below, Chris Bonington has no problems with exposure."

(Olympus.)

"For perfect home baking... watch for 105 minutes without stirring."

(BBC Video.)

"When you're on holiday, be prepared to be stung by the locals."

(Anthisan.)

"Is there a snag in your tights?"

(Pretty Polly.)

"Eat the same pasta they eat on the Via Veneto. (Via Sainsbury's.)"

(Tesco. No, I'm joking...)

Trotty hated puns but I quite liked them and even wrote one myself for an LWT poster – "Retiring to the seaside. Is it the last resort?" I topped it off with a visual pun showing an old person's foot kicking a sandcastle bucket. You see, if you didn't have a verbal pun, you had to have a visual one. That kind of WAS advertising back then.

One powerful campaign that wasn't too punny was the one for Albany Life Assurance, which included an execution that asked: "Can you afford to live to a ripe old age?" It forecast the prices of various goods in 2001 allowing for inflation running "at only 10%" (!) – so an average family car would cost £30,000, a loaf of bread three quid and so on.

Pretty wrong for 2001 – pretty wrong even now, thank God, or else nobody would ever be able to retire.

Maybe the puns were just a sign of the fun most people were having. It certainly seemed like a terrific way to waste your life back then, and that's what appealed to me. If I dip my Proustian madeleine (two slices of peanut butter on brown toast) into my Proustian cup of tea (a cappuccino from Patisserie Valerie), I can still remember the glamour, the fun, the improbability, the sheer larkiness of the whole thing. Where the hell has all that gone? ⬡

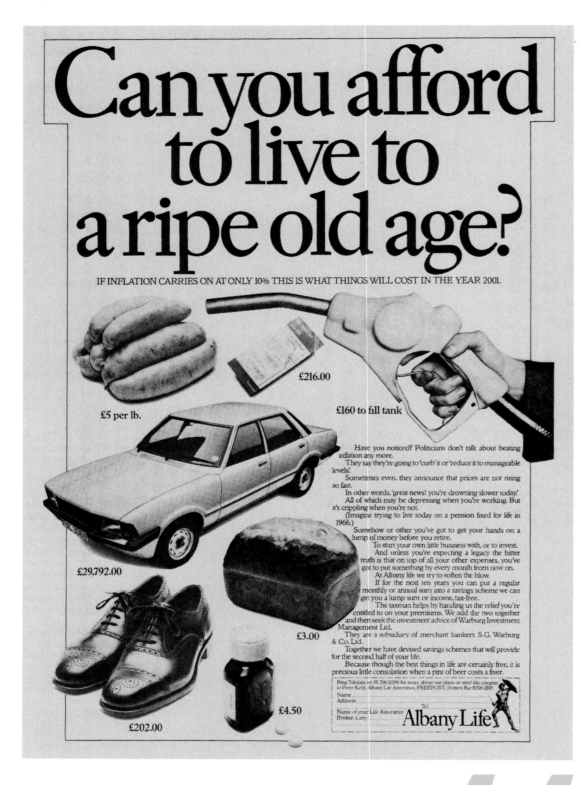

Title Albany Life
Client Albany Life Assurance
Agency Advertising & Marketing Services

"
Mike Gold asked the media contractors if they could change the LWT poster sites every week, rather than the usual monthly cycle. They said no, so he hired two blokes with a van to do it.

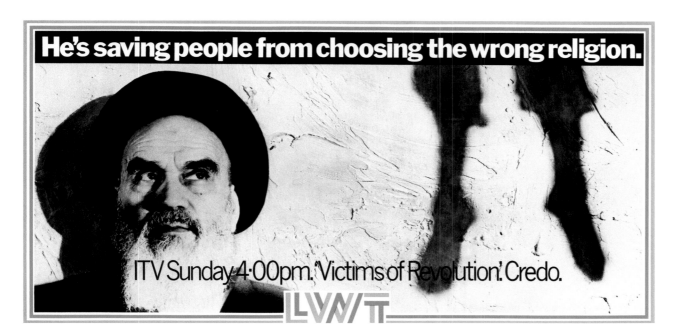

Title LWT
Client London Weekend Television
Agency Gold Greenlees Trott

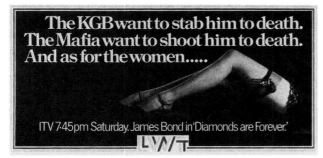

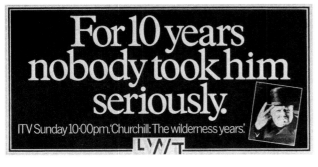

1983
Tony Brignull

Tony Brignull spent most of his career at Collett Dickenson Pearce. With his partner, Neil Godfrey, he won three Black Pencils and 17 Yellow Pencils for work on such accounts as Parker pens, Army Officer Recruitment, Birds Eye, Fiat, Clarks and the Great Ormond Street Wishing Well Appeal. He also worked for Doyle Dane Bernbach (DDB), Abbott Mead Vickers and, for an exhilarating couple of years, ran his own agency, Brignull Le Bas.

On leaving advertising after 35 years, he read English at Oxford, then went to King's College London to study Life Writing.

1983 Annual

Annual Design **Malcolm Gaskin; TBWA**
Typography **Nigel Dawson**

It also sticks handles to teapots.

Title Araldite
Client Ciba Geigy
Agency FCO Univas

On reflection, the committee's decision to hold the Awards Dinner at the Royal Albert Hall was not the greatest of ideas. We had to sit on tip-up seats and eat airline meals on our laps. The dry cleaning bills must have been enormous, but we pulled it off, just. And many found the event louche and wild in a "studenty" sort of way, and said we were crazy mavericks, which we liked. The truth was we had little choice. The Grosvenor House was booked and all the other capacious watering holes were full.

I was determined that we would have the Annual to give out on the night and, thanks to Malcolm Gaskin who designed it, a porter brought a trolley-load of them on to the stage. Perhaps the only time the book has been out that early.

To the work. The juries gave two Black Pencils. They define, I think, what that Award should be. Not merely the best of the Yellow Pencils, but work that is so groundbreaking it changes our perception of its genre for the better and forever.

One was for Araldite adhesive. The agency, FCO Univas, decided to blow the big part of a tiny budget on one huge poster in the Cromwell Road. To it they stuck a Ford Cortina. The headline said: "It also sticks handles to teapots." Some days they paid a model to sit beneath it reading a newspaper. It became an event and went viral before the word was ever applied to works made famous on the web, which of course did not exist commercially yet. Featured in newspapers and on TV, it repaid its costs many times over.

Its triumph lay not merely in a remarkable coup de foudre but because it took demonstration, until then the exclusive property of television, and moved it outdoors.

The other 1983 Black Pencil illustrates what great design can do for a company, even to one as anonymous at the time as Channel 4 (dodgy programmes, few viewers, fewer advertisers). Martin Lambie-Nairn's signature graphics, which showed the number "4" forming itself out of primary-coloured children's blocks, made it fresh and new and modern. It could be argued that the company we know today grew into it.

The budget for the Book that year was limited, and so was the number of coloured pages. As a result, many campaigns were not shown at their best. One that suffered was for Sainsbury's. This campaign was, I believe, the best collection of advertisements ever to run in magazines. The ads, all of them good, just kept on coming, month after month, year on year. This meant that the

> One Black Pencil was for Araldite adhesive. The agency, FCO Univas, decided to blow the big part of a tiny budget on one huge poster in the Cromwell Road. To it they stuck a Ford Cortina.

Title SAS Airlines campaign
Client Scandinavian Airline System
Agency Brignull Le Bas

> On reflection, the committee's decision to hold the Awards Dinner at the Royal Albert Hall was not the greatest of ideas. We had to sit on tip-up seats and eat airline meals on our laps.

campaign gained an onward transitive momentum – each new ad benefiting from the last and contributing to the next – and thus it became part of the magazines it appeared in. The pictures were always mouthwatering, the copy factual and informative, the art direction immaculate.

The client must take some credit, for he initially allowed David Abbott to choose the products he knew would make good advertisements for Sainsbury's, not necessarily the ones which needed promoting. Sadly, by the time I got to AMV, the brand managers had balked at this loss of power – now they called the shots. The product they wanted featured was a silk shampoo with no silk in it. So great campaigns die.

And then there was a national press full page for Albany Life. If you've ever had to write an ad for a life assurance

company you will know how hard it is, for essentially you are reminding people of the fragility of their lives. I had written the original campaign, and it was with mixed feelings that I saw some new ads coming along I wish I'd done. This one featuring Ronald Reagan made me most green.

1983 was a particularly significant year for me personally. In the summer before I had started Brignull Le Bas with the late Caroline Le Bas and Philip Gould (yes, the Lord Gould to be) and the very much alive and wonderful Rob Morris. I am proud of the work we did. That year we got even more in the Book than the agency I loved but left, CDP.

Perhaps the pick of our work was a campaign for Scandinavian airline SAS, which was offering business class travel for the same price as other airlines' economy tickets. The ads we did illustrate the things I value most: concepts that

Will you be as fortunate finding a second career?

Heaven knows, you are going to need a second career more than this gentleman.

Compulsory retirement at 55 is on its way.

No matter how long your service, no matter how high your position, you could be out of a job, come your 55th birthday.

The company car will disappear.

The expense account will disappear.

The private health insurance will disappear.

Sadly, your mortgage won't. You may well find yourself repaying that until you are 60 or 65.

Civil servants should be alright. They have indexed-linked pensions, courtesy of the poor old taxpayer.

Members of trade unions should make out too. They often have an army of negotiators to battle on their behalf.

No, it's the private sector businessman who will be in trouble.

His retirement age is going down, but his life expectancy is on the up and up. Today's 40 year olds can expect to reach 80. You could easily be faced with 25 years in retirement.

How will you manage?

That fixed company pension that looked oh-so-generous ten years ago, won't be worth much in another ten year's time, never mind twenty or thirty.

State pensions aren't famous for keeping up with inflation either.

Of course, with the two added together, you may just have enough to survive.

But is that all you want to do? Survive?

Wouldn't you prefer to do something positive with the second half of your adult life?

Albany Life and the Inland Revenue can help you.

Start salting away a regular sum each month. £15, £50, whatever you can spare.

We will bump up your contributions by claiming back from the taxman every last penny of tax relief we can.

We will then invest the total amount on your behalf.

We receive what is arguably the best investment advice there is. We retain Warburg Investment Management Ltd., a subsidiary of S. G. Warburg & Co Ltd., the merchant bank.

Start saving in your thirties or forties and you will amass a considerable sum, well before your 55th birthday.

When you are pensioned off, you will have a wad of tax-free money to cushion the blow.

Enough to set up shop in some sleepy Devon village.

Enough to pursue some half-forgotten craft, like working with cane or stained glass.

Enough to buy you a stake in some successful small business near your home.

Whatever you decide to do, you'll be better off mentally as well as financially. People vegetate if they have nothing but the garden to occupy their minds.

There is no reason why you shouldn't be active and working at 73, like Mr. Reagan here.

Though hopefully you won't have to carry the worries of the world on your shoulders.

To learn more about our plans send this coupon to Peter Kelly, Albany Life Assurance, FREEPOST, Potters Bar EN6 1BR.

Name

Address

Tel:

Name of your Life Assurance Broker, if any

Albany Life

Title Albany Life
Client Albany Life Assurance
Agency Lowe Howard-Spink

1988   1989   1990   1991   1992   1993   1994   1995   1996   1997   1998   1999   2000   2001   2002   2003   2004   2005   2006   2007   2008   2009   2010   2011   2012

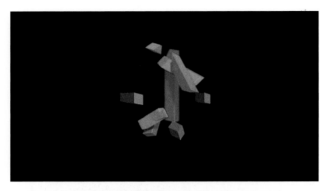

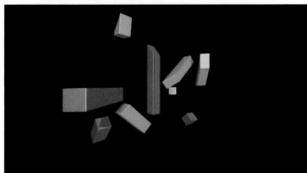

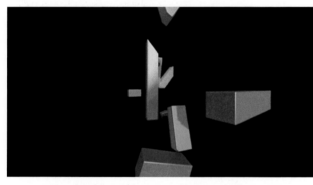

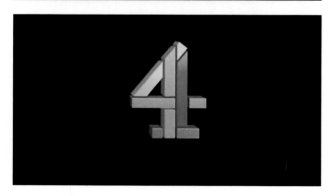

touch a nerve (here the resentment of businessmen at being ripped off), visuals that are unmissable, ads with a razor blade in the headline.

I hoped that with work like this and other examples of ours in the same Annual, we'd go on to be, if not a big agency, then a very good small one. Alas, that year we didn't win a single piece of new business and we had to sell to DDB. 1983, then, was both the high and low point of my career.

To write this review for D&AD's 50th anniversary, I had to open the Annual for the first time in years. It's still painful to read. But I see photographs of all my brilliant, talented (and so young) contemporaries and I think yes, I was part of you and it was an honour to be your President.

That's how it goes sometimes. You do your very best. You work very hard. You encourage each other. The rest is out of your hands. ⬡

" You do your very best. You work very hard. You encourage each other. The rest is out of your hands.

Title **Channel 4 graphics**
Client **Channel 4**
Design Group **Robinson Lambie-Nairn**

Sainsbury's have a peach of an idea for Parma ham. But it isn't peach.

Announcing Sainsbury's own burgers. With 0% beef.

The Côtes du Rhône boasts several Goliaths amongst its red wines. (Can Sainsbury's claim at least one David?)

The safest thing to serve at any dinner party is a good roast from Sainsbury's.

For sale, Sainsbury's fresh English pork. No previous owners.

A good Stilton from Sainsbury's will make your mouth water. (Not your eyes.)

Just when you thought you understood Brie, Sainsbury's create delicious confusion.

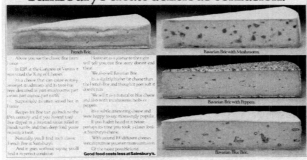

Who knows better than Sainsbury's how dryness can age the skin?

Title Sainsbury's campaign
Client J Sainsbury
Agency Abbott Mead Vickers SMS

Pelham and Jeremy Cox won a Yellow Pencil for Complete Book with their pop-up book 'The Human Body'. Nowadays, this kind of "pop-up, pull-out, cut-away" publishing is common, but in 1984 this treatment for biology was stunning. Boase Massimi Pollitt was nominated for its Sony TV campaign, which ushered in the genre of "good mechanicals" – something we see today perfected by Honda et al. Raymond Briggs's illustration for the Financial Times involved a witty use of the ubiquitous snowman that brought seasonality and a little smile to the FT's serious brand personality. Nichola Bruce and Mike Coulson were nominated for Illustration for 'The Draughtsman's Contract', which I've singled out for the darkness of the story and my love of Michael Nyman's music for the film.

I can't say I enjoyed my Presidency all that much – being a figurehead just didn't suit me. The highlights were two dinners. Back then, the past President held a small, private dinner for the incoming man. Tony Brignull hosted for me. We were a small group of talented, like-minded people telling stories, offering advice, sharing experiences and talking about what mattered. They say history is a different country, and past-President dinners certainly are. Today the Presidents' Dinner is a big, noisy affair, more corporate than creative, where it's doubtful that past Presidents even get to meet the new President. Perhaps a metaphor for contemporary D&AD? That said, after 50 years, where would we be without it? ⬢

Title The Draughtsman's Contract poster
Client British Film Institute
Agency Kruddart/Muscle Films

Sainsbury's have a peach of an idea for Parma ham. But it isn't peach.

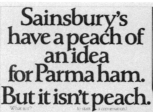

Announcing Sainsbury's own burgers. With 0% beef.

The Côtes du Rhône boasts several Goliaths amongst its red wines. (Can Sainsbury's claim at least one David?)

The safest thing to serve at any dinner party is a good roast from Sainsbury's.

For sale, Sainsbury's fresh English pork. No previous owners.

A good Stilton from Sainsbury's will make your mouth water. (Not your eyes.)

Just when you thought you understood Brie, Sainsbury's create delicious confusion.

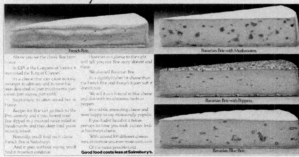

Who knows better than Sainsbury's how dryness can age the skin?

Title Sainsbury's campaign
Client J Sainsbury
Agency Abbott Mead Vickers SMS

1984
Rodney Fitch

Rodney Fitch founded his design consultancy, Fitch, now owned by WPP, in 1972. He left the consultancy at the end of 2009 and now works in higher education and as an independent adviser, consultant and non-executive to a broad portfolio of clients. Fitch is a Senior Governor of the University of the Arts London, and has served on the Design Council, the Council of the Royal College of Art (RCA) and the Chartered Society of Designers (CSD). He is Chairman of V&A Enterprises, and was awarded a CBE in 1990 for his influence on the British design industry.

1984 Annual

Annual Design Dawn Clarkson,
Shawen Haymen, Martyn Hey,
John Lloyd, Linda Loe, Jim Northover;
Lloyd Northover Lim

NOËL

...NO COMMENT.

Copyright Snowmen Enterprises.

Best wishes to all newsagents and wholesalers for Christmas and the New Year from the FT circulation staff.

Title Raymond Briggs illustration
Client Financial Times
Agency Ogilvy & Mather

What on earth can I remember of 1983? I was doing pretty well. The blessed Margaret Thatcher was cracking on. The nation, hitherto choked politically and socially by Luddite lefties, was coming to its senses. My agency was top of its game. Our work was winning everywhere, with new clients, new projects and awards... except of course from D&AD, but that's a different story. Fabulous, clever, talented people were at every desk, delivering mould-breaking work, and the fourth estate told us we were "reshaping Britain's high streets". I had taken the business public the year before and here we were, design darlings of the London Stock Exchange. In retrospect, the former mattered and the latter didn't.

I flattered myself as being at the heart of British design – the CSD, the Design Council, Saint Martins, the RCA, even a private chat with the Prime Minister that went, "Rodney, how can we help?" And yet of D&AD itself I knew little. Yes, I had sat on a jury and designed a lovely exhibition for D&AD in New York called 'It's Great! Britain' (I wonder where the 2012 people got their idea from), but it was something of a surprise to get a call from Edward Booth-Clibborn telling me I was to be the next President.

I don't remember any election or ballot, inaugural speech or welcome dinner, just a notice at the AGM in a grotty walk-up office in Carlton House Terrace, and bingo, I was the President. I guess this is how it happens for some entire nations.

As President, I recall having two agenda items. First, to review the judging system – it seemed flawed to me, with vested interests keeping some of the best work out. Second, to overhaul D&AD's finances. Well, little progress happened on my watch, not least because there was no appetite for it. It was a braver President than me who did sort it out a couple of years later.

As to the book... seeing the Lloyd Northover-designed 1984 Annual for the first time in many years, it seems so ordinary. Thank goodness for that. At bottom, it's a piece of print in which the content matters – a far cry from later Annuals where, for some egotists, the book design became more important than what was in it.

Among a lot of lovely work, my favourite pieces, starting with 'The Post Office' by Minale Tattersfield, which won a Yellow Pencil for Graphics. It is simplicity personified, a lovely idea. If only the Post Office had as much wit today. David

Pelham and Jeremy Cox won a Yellow Pencil for Complete Book with their pop-up book 'The Human Body'. Nowadays, this kind of "pop-up, pull-out, cut-away" publishing is common, but in 1984 this treatment for biology was stunning. Boase Massimi Pollitt was nominated for its Sony TV campaign, which ushered in the genre of "good mechanicals" – something we see today perfected by Honda et al. Raymond Briggs's illustration for the Financial Times involved a witty use of the ubiquitous snowman that brought seasonality and a little smile to the FT's serious brand personality. Nichola Bruce and Mike Coulson were nominated for Illustration for 'The Draughtsman's Contract', which I've singled out for the darkness of the story and my love of Michael Nyman's music for the film.

I can't say I enjoyed my Presidency all that much – being a figurehead just didn't suit me. The highlights were two dinners. Back then, the past President held a small, private dinner for the incoming man. Tony Brignull hosted for me. We were a small group of talented, like-minded people telling stories, offering advice, sharing experiences and talking about what mattered. They say history is a different country, and past-President dinners certainly are. Today the Presidents' Dinner is a big, noisy affair, more corporate than creative, where it's doubtful that past Presidents even get to meet the new President. Perhaps a metaphor for contemporary D&AD? That said, after 50 years, where would we be without it? ⬡

Title The Draughtsman's Contract poster
Client British Film Institute
Agency Kruddart/Muscle Films

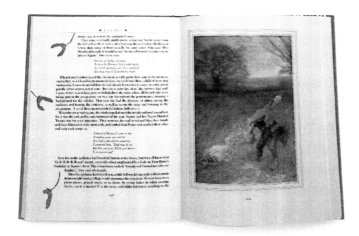

> They say that history is a different country, and past-President dinners certainly are. Today the Presidents' Dinner is a big, noisy affair, more corporate than creative, where it's doubtful that past Presidents even get to meet the new President.

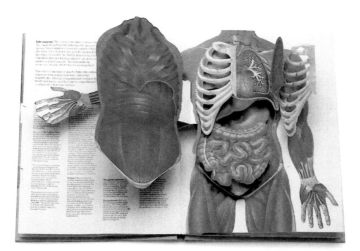

Title **The Human Body**
Publisher **Jonathan Cape**
Design Group **Pentagram Design**

Title The Post Office
Client Post Office
Design Group Minale Tattersfield

"

What on earth can I remember
of 1983? The nation, hitherto
choked politically and socially
by Luddite lefties, was coming
to its senses.

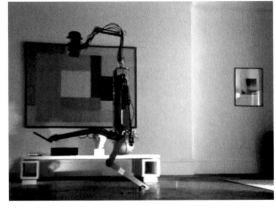

Sony – 'Robot'

SFX: Engine noise.

A metal box enters the room and starts beeping. A robot emerges limb by limb from the box.

ROBOT/JOHN CLEESE: Hello! Remember me? Yes, you do… you know… ring any bells?

(Robot does the Monty Python silly walk across the room.)

ROBOT/JOHN CLEESE: Well, you know those Sony people computerise anything. Take the new compact disc – one hour of Mozart out of a beer mat. Pure sound played by laser. (plays Mozart) Just listen to that – no hisses and crackles of course, but if you do want that, munch a biscuit, sip a cup of cocoa and it'll sound just like your old record player.

SFX: Slurping and crunching noises.

ROBOT/JOHN CLEESE: Know what I mean? (to lamp) Fancy a dance?

MVO: Sony. Whatever will they think of next?

Title Sony CD Player – Robot
Client Sony UK
Agency Boase Massimi Pollitt

1985
Jeremy Myerson

Jeremy Myerson has been a writer, academic and activist in design and communication for more than 30 years. Today, he is Director and Chair of the Helen Hamlyn Centre for Design at the Royal College of Art, which explores design for social change. In 1985 he was Editor of Creative Review and working on plans for Design Week, which he launched as Founder-Editor the following year. In 2002, he co-authored and co-curated the 'Rewind' book and exhibition at the V&A, which featured material from 40 years of the D&AD Awards. His many publications include books about Alan Fletcher, IDEO, Martin Lambie-Nairn, John Makepeace and Gordon Russell.

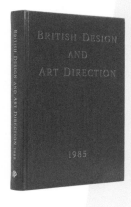

1985 Annual

Annual Design **Roger Pearce**
Assistant Designer **Stephen Kettell**

Title Spitting Image puppets
Programme Company Central Independent Television
Production Company Spitting Image Productions

At the midway point in a decade notorious for dead-eyed conspicuous consumption fuelled by a boom in design and advertising, the 1985 D&AD Awards demonstrated that the creative community could also bite back at consumerist excess, political divisiveness and social inequality.

True, there were plenty of Awards for smartly packaged goods, designer shops and music videos with luxuriant production values that reflected the prevailing individualist ethos of the time. The sharpest knives in the drawer, however, left an overriding impression of 1985 giving a countercultural two fingers to the relentless promotion of a winner-takes-all approach.

I watched the whole story of 1985 take shape from a perfect vantage position, as Editor of Creative Review. That year, the magazine marked its fifth birthday by asking the good and the great of design and advertising to take the temperature of their industry. Adland great John Webster used his column inches in Creative Review to bemoan a decline in TV advertising, describing 1985 as "the time of the great piss-take". He added, despairingly: "Perhaps it's inevitable that things become cynical in a once-great country now in decline with massive unemployment, widening class differences, and sitting on a sediment of broken promises."

'Spitting Image', which won two Yellow Pencils in 1985, for Television Graphics and Best Design of a Comedy Programme, tapped into widespread public cynicism about the ruling political classes. Based on an original idea by Martin Lambie-Nairn, this weekly Central TV programme became renowned for the savagery of its humour – its venomous puppets targeted everyone from pompous rock stars and manic politicians like Margaret Thatcher and Ronald Reagan to the Royal Family.

The show featured the puppet-making skills of Peter Fluck and Roger Law, who had risen to prominence in the 60s and 70s as illustrators and cartoonists. Some of their victims, such as Liberal leader David Steel, depicted as a particularly tiny and ineffectual puppet, saw their poll ratings fall; others asked Fluck and Law if they could buy their puppet after particular episodes were screened, including Michael Heseltine, then Defence Secretary. Law apparently told a Ministry of Defence flunky: "Tell him if he sends Cruise back he can have his puppet for nothing."

To Martin Lambie-Nairn, the originator of this feast of roughhouse creative mayhem, the 1985 D&AD Awards offered another tribute. Lambie-Nairn's famous computer-animated onscreen identity for Channel 4, launched in 1982 and a Black Pencil-winner the following year,

> "Some of Spitting Image's victims, such as Liberal leader David Steel, depicted as a particularly tiny and ineffectual puppet, saw their poll ratings fall.

Title Imagine What London Will Be Like Run by Whitehall
Client Greater London Council
Agency Boase Massimi Pollitt Univas

was affectionately parodied in a Hamlet cigar TV spot made by Collett Dickenson Pearce. In the commercial, which won a Yellow Pencil for Animation, the coloured blocks come together but mistakenly form a 5 instead of a 4; then they try again but make nothing in particular; finally they make a face, which gives up and lights a cigar. Lambie-Nairn himself directed the ad with Anna Hart, having sought permission for the spoof from Channel 4 boss Jeremy Isaacs first. The great piss-take, indeed.

Elsewhere in the communication jungle, photographer David Bailey announced his anti-fur campaign for Greenpeace to admiring D&AD juries with a poster art-directed by Yellowhammer's Jeremy Pemberton. ("It takes up to 40 dumb animals to make a fur coat. But only one to wear it.") Both idea and execution were perfect in their mix of glamour and viciousness. The following year, Bailey would turn it into a Black Pencil-winning cinema commercial.

There was, of course, an inescapable paradox in the creative industry advancing image-making techniques to deal in ever more alluring dreams, while simultaneously telling it how it really was. Astute advertisers selling conventional consumer goods were quick to catch on to the more strident and direct mood engendered by the growing taste for

sharp social satire. Gold Greenlees Trott's 'Hello Tosh, Gotta Toshiba?' campaign, which was directed by Richard Sloggett and won a D&AD Yellow Pencil in 1985, epitomised this cut-through approach in TV advertising.

The ad's powerful penetration was not just down to the appearance of comedian Alexei Sayle, who starred in 80s TV comedy series 'The Young Ones' – it owed its elevated status in public consciousness to GGT's Dave Trott, who had studied Madison Avenue closely and brought a tough-minded, proletariat approach to the business of creating ads. Anything superfluous to the message was cut right out.

Right across the design industry too, the need for more simplicity and impact was apparent. Brand owners of packaged goods, for example, responded to the rise of popular own-label packaging in supermarkets, which threatened their market share, with some singular creative responses of their own.

One of the best of these featured in the 1985 D&AD Annual: Smith & Milton's pack design for the Cuisine Française label from Sharwood's set a new trend in the sector with its white background, Matisse-style brushstroke illustration (by Brian Grimwood) and absence of a standard food packshot. It showed a

Photo: David Bailey

It takes up to 40 dumb animals to make a fur coat.

But only one to wear it.

GREENPEACE

If you don't want animals to be gassed, electrocuted, trapped or strangled, don't buy a fur coat. 36 Graham Street London N1 8LL. Tel: 01-251 3020

Title It Takes Up to 40 Dumb Animals to Make a Fur Coat
Client Greenpeace
Agency Yellowhammer

"The sharpest knives in the drawer left an overriding impression of 1985 giving a countercultural two fingers to the relentless promotion of a winner-takes-all approach.

brand breaking the rules and behaving like an own-label product – and its loose, hand-drawn, brushstroke style encouraged designers everywhere to abandon all those scientifically geometric logos of the 60s and 70s in favour of a more liberated, artist-like approach.

If the Sharwood's design was radical in the creative sense, Boase Massimi Pollitt's (BMP) defiantly brilliant press and poster campaign to save the Greater London Council – "If you want me out, you should have the right to vote me out" set beneath a low-key image of Ken Livingstone – crystallised one of the great political confrontations of the 80s.

BMP even wrapped yards of red tape around a giant billboard to show how Whitehall bureaucracy would strangle London without the GLC, and this masterstroke, combining creative flair with cutting satirical edge provides perhaps my lasting memory of 1985. The battle was lost – the GLC was abolished – but that is not what is remembered.

If you had told creative directors back in 1985 that Ken Livingstone would still be politically active and run for London Mayor in 2012, on the 50th anniversary of D&AD, they would have been amazed. But that's a different story. ●

"
There was an inescapable
paradox in the creative
industry advancing image-
making techniques to deal
in ever more alluring dreams,
while simultaneously telling
it how it really was.

Title Sharwood's
Client J A Sharwood

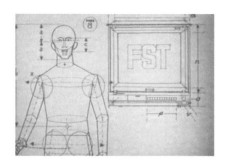
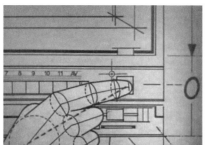
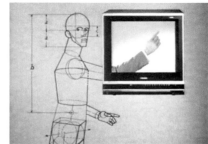

Toshiba FST – 'Hello Tosh'

SUNG: Hello, hello…
Hello Tosh, gotta Toshiba?
Hello Tosh, gotta Toshiba?

That's an FST. (CHORUS: Right?)
That's an FST. (CHORUS: Right?)

It's the flattest, squarest, tube.
It's the flattest, squarest, tube.

They ain't half built well.
They ain't half built well.

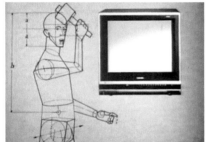

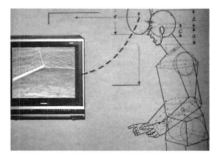

SPOKEN: 'Course, every Toshiba
component is built strong to last
longer narmean?

SUNG: That's good.
(CHORUS: Ennit?)
That's good. (CHORUS: Ennit?)

Hello Tosh, gotta Toshiba?
Hello Tosh, gotta Toshiba?

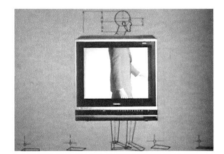

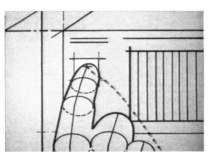
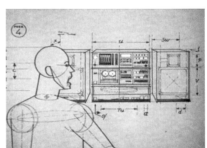

Toshiba Hi-Fi – 'Hello Tosh'

SUNG: Hello, hello…
Hello Tosh, gotta Toshiba?
Hello Tosh, gotta Toshiba?

Like your hi-fi system.
Like your hi-fi system.

It's got a fair-old bit of power.
It's got a fair-old bit of power.

We are talking quality.
We are talking quality.

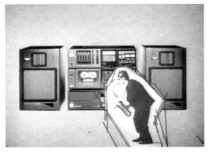

SPOKEN: 'Course, every Toshiba
component is built strong to last
longer narmean?

SUNG: Get your ears round that.
(CHORUS: Wallop!)
Get your ears round that.
(CHORUS: Wallop!)

Hello Tosh, gotta Toshiba?
Hello Tosh, gotta Toshiba?

Title Hello Tosh
Client Toshiba UK
Agency Gold Greenlees Trott

1986
John McConnell

John McConnell was a Director of Pentagram for 31 years before re-establishing McConnell Design in 2005. McConnell is involved in all areas of graphic design, including corporate identity, packaging and signage programmes, posters, books and print.

From 1983 to 1990, he was a board Director responsible for design at Faber & Faber. He has been a non-executive Director of Cosalt and is a member of the Royal Mail Stamp Advisory Committee.

McConnell has won Black and Yellow Pencils, the D&AD President's Award, an American Art Directors Club award and a Gold Biennale (Warsaw). He served as President of D&AD in 1986, and is a member of the Alliance Graphique Internationale, a Fellow of the Chartered Society of Designers and a Royal Designer for Industry. In December 2002 John was awarded one of two special commendations for the Prince Philip Designers Prize.

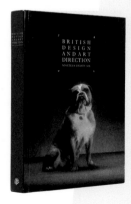

1986 Annual

Annual Design Mike Dempsey, Michael Lindley; Carroll Dempsey & Thirkell
Cover Photography Peter Lavery

Youth declining to pay any regard to what happened previously is pretty silly – it's like a brain surgeon saying, "Oh, I can't be bothered to read about that. I'll start from scratch and learn as I go." When I was young, I felt the same about the people before me. I was going to screw them and be better than they were. Now I've become old and sensible, I realise how great they were – so, when the youth wake up and get over their acne and anxiety, they'll work that out themselves. Us old fuckers weren't that bad.

I don't remember with any pride at all that in the mid-80s we were still having the dos at the Hilton – that was the biggest single room you could get at the time without going to Earls Court. Agencies would buy tables for 15 and 20 people, load them up with booze – and when they got the Award, the tables stood up and applauded, and screamed and shouted.

But there would be graphic designers like John Gorham who would get a Yellow Pencil for a letterhead, and have one person – probably his wife or his mum –

with him, and was of course at the back. He had this long walk with this slow applause, and they couldn't keep it up, so by the time he got to the stage it petered out. As such, I stupidly made the mistake of sticking the Graphic Design and the Advertising on separate nights. At the time, I thought it was the right thing to do. There were no ramifications, but the designers wanted to be there – they felt separated and isolated.

When you look through this year, it wasn't a high point in my view. All industries are cyclical, the system goes up and down. I have picked one of the ads for Punch magazine. I just think it's a lovely line – "They asked me to contribute to Punch. Isn't 80p a week enough?" And this book cover for 'The Iron Man' is iconic – I was then Design Director for Faber & Faber, though I simply commissioned it.

Nicholas Thirkell's book for the V&A Museum on fabrics – what I like is that if you look at the other stuff at the time, which was all trying to be something else, this was just very well crafted

Title Royal Mail stamps
Client Royal Mail
Design Group Newell & Sorrell Design

"THEY ASKED ME TO CONTRIBUTE TO PUNCH. ISN'T 80p A WEEK ENOUGH?"

David Puttnam is a very busy man.

A fact confirmed by his secretary who, fresh from the Margaret Thatcher Charm School, treats a simple request for a minute of his time as a personal affront.

Perhaps on the basis that opposites attract, her boss is the opposite.

Fresh from the David Puttnam Charm School, he accommodates his many roles, from one man saviour of the British film industry to TV company director to working producer with all the youthful self-effacement of someone who is middle aged and supremely confident.

What, you may ask, does someone as addicted to work as Mr Puttnam is, do to relax?

A highly personal question, the answer to which might well contravene certain clauses of the Advertising Standards Authority rules.

However, this much is known.

He derives great pleasure from arguing with Alan Parker, the film director. Enjoys Beethoven's Violin Concerto in D (Source: Desert Island Discs). And regularly hurls tactical advice at Tottenham Hotspur. He also reads Punch.

Punch?

Does David Puttnam really part with 80p for Simon Hoggart's acidic interpretation of the goings-on in the Mother of All Parliaments?

Not really.

Or Clement Freud's cultivated obsession with oral gratification?

Certainly not.

How about Alan Coren's pyrotechnic elaborations of the week's headlines?

No thank you.

David Puttnam

Is there even a passing interest in what Roy Hattersley, Melvyn Bragg, Benny Green or Hunter Davies have to say every week?

Passing just about sums it up.

Week after week, David Puttnam is able to resist the spikey contributions of these formidable talents and those of Punch's legendary cartoonists.

Instead, his antidote to a capricious and dangerous film world is to be found in the unerring accuracy of Dilys Powell's cinema reviews.

'Local Hero' she predicted would be prevented from being a smash because it '...ends on the withdrawal rather than the climax of emotion... leaving the spectator with the feeling that he has missed something, been cheated of something.

After so much pleasure, one needs a tiny explosion of triumph.'

'She is seldom wrong' concedes Mr Puttnam.

Her Punch review of 'Chariots of Fire' explained the key role played by the legs.

Then took the time (and column inches) to add '...that it is pleasing to see the Prince of Wales, later the exiled Duke of Windsor, presented as an honoured and honourable figure'.

And her critique of 'Killing Fields' signed off with comments from the co-star that actually criticized the film.

This mixture of irreverence, idiosyncrasy and wit are not, of course, unknown at Punch.

Indeed, for many people it offers a necessary respite from the narrowness of their business lives.

If you haven't read it lately, perhaps you should. After all, as David Puttnam freely admits, all film producing and no play makes one an awfully dull boy.

Punch
Every Wednesday

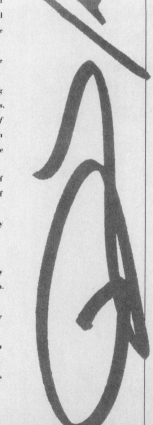

Title Punch
Client Punch Publications
Agency Leagas Delaney

Title V&A Museum books
Client Victoria & Albert Museum
Design Group Cooper Thirkell

"Real creativity comes from engineers. For example, I was given the Prince Philip Designers Prize and came second... but I came second to the designer of the Rolls-Royce engine.

and elegantly done, and not at all embarrassed about having a traditional appearance. It was fit for purpose.

I enjoyed the Royal Mail stamps. I like stamps that are full of lots of graphic information. And I remember Martin Lambie-Nairn's Smarties commercial. That was the other thing in D&AD – the commercials get all the interest, because they move!

I remember very early on, someone from London Business School told me he wanted to be in the creative business because it seemed to be more "g-strings and champagne". And I once said: "In the end 'creativity' f***s up. I usually slide over that word quickly, and I use it very rarely and if I do it's disparagingly." I'm pretty sure it comes from art education, which is on the whole braindead. It's fed into you to be creative – injected into you from whenever you go to art school. And you spend every second of your life following this and then you realise that it's all junk. It's intelligence that is actually important; being clever is better.

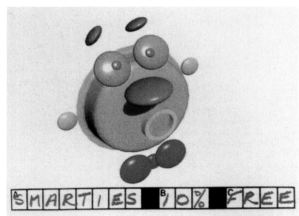

Smarties – '10% More'

SFX: Music.

VO: What's got more than it had before?

KIDS: Smarties!

SFX: Cheers.

VO: How much more than it had before? 10%.

SFX: Whooping, clapping.

VO: What do you call the extra you get for nothing?

KIDS: Fred – NO! FREE!

SFX: Hooray!

VO: Where can you put a whole lot more?

SFX: Clapping.

VO: Only Smarties have the answer.

Title Smarties – 10% More
Client Rowntree Mackintosh York
Agency J Walter Thompson

Real creativity comes from engineers. For example, I was given the Prince Philip Designers Prize and I came second… but I came second to the designer of the Rolls-Royce engine. I thought: well, I can come second to him. That seemed to me to be really serious work, and I was just piddling around.

I'm hoping that we can become more intelligent, and bring some enlightenment to what a graphic designer does. All you are doing is taking words, the form of communication in our society, and either making them mean more or – if you do your job badly – less. You can't do it in a way that denies the original message, and once you get that clear and get over it, then you get down to doing decent work and being intelligent about it.

I do a lot of work with in-house designers now, and I make them work hard. I ask why they have done things. I want to make sure that the work is intelligent and logical. Don't even dare say, "Well, because I thought pink was lovely," because I'll string you up.

Now and again, a magazine will pop up and say, "Would you pick the next six guys coming up?" And I say no, because it would screw their life up. Poor sod, they're trying to struggle their way up, and then you do that to them! My advice to the young generation is to dodge getting picked like that at all costs, because it's deadly. The real thing, and I always keep going back to this, is to do with intelligence. The industry's Achilles' heel is that so many people think it's creative – they don't understand that it's about common sense and intelligence. If I ever wanted a memorial, I would like it to say, "At least he was intelligent." Avoid creativity at all costs. ●

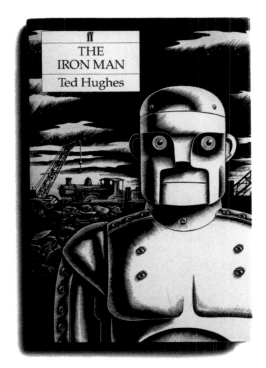

"All you are doing is taking words, the form of communication in our society, and either making them mean more or – if you do your job badly – less.

Title The Iron Man
Client Faber & Faber
Design Group Faber & Faber

1987
Jeremy Sinclair

Jeremy Sinclair was born in 1946. He
joined CramerSaatchi in 1968. He helped
found Saatchi & Saatchi in 1970, and
M&C Saatchi in 1995.

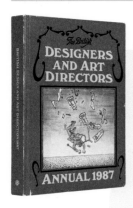

1987 Annual

Annual Design **Cinamon & Kitzinger**
Cover Design **Dave Horry**
Cover Art **Glen Baxter**
Typography **Len Cheeseman**
Art Direction **Dave Horry**

Title Lanson Champagne
Client JR Phillips
Agency Saatchi & Saatchi

As President of D&AD, you can't claim any credit for the quality of the work, but you do have an influence over the juries. And in 1987 the jury picked some cracking ads. In fact, the jury was so well-picked that it picked 60 of our pieces of work at Saatchi & Saatchi, compared to 13 by Abbott Mead Vickers, 13 by Boase Massimi Pollitt (BMP), 12 by Collett Dickenson Pearce and ten by WCRS. Well done, team!

Looking back, the jurors weren't quite so surefooted with the Awards. The only Black Pencil they gave that year was to Gert Dumbar for his signage programme for the Rijksmuseum in Amsterdam, which looks okay now. But there was a film that the jury only gave a Yellow Pencil to and I guarantee when I tell what it was, you'll a) remember it and b) agree it should have won a Black Pencil. It was written by John Webster and Frank Budgen for The Guardian, and was called 'Points of View'. If you don't know it, look at it now on YouTube and see what you can do in black and white in 30 seconds.

The next ad that should have won a Black Pencil was Hamlet's 'Photo Booth'. It was

a 60-second spot during which a bald man with a combover attempts to take a photo-booth passport photo of himself with his hair in the right place. As always with Hamlet, the reward for failure is a satisfying Hamlet cigar. Again, if you have never seen it or haven't seen it recently, look at it now – I know you'll laugh.

For Gold Greenlees Trott's outstanding Holsten ad, the agency raided classic film for shots and re-edited them to make a story about Holsten Pils. This was GGT in its heyday. Incidentally, note that back then every agency was known by its initials – there were no Mothers or Nakeds or Red Brick Roads. But there was a Yellowhammer, which produced a personal favourite and won a Yellow Pencil. It was for Cancer Research, and featured the late Patricia Phoenix aka Elsie Tanner of 'Coronation Street'. The ad showed her waving goodbye, with the copy simply reproducing the standard funeral message, "No flowers but donations to the Cancer Research Campaign." She had been a famously heavy smoker.

In those days, Bartle Bogle Hegarty was hardly born, but it did have a sweet entry

Title Pilkington Glass – Bullet Proof
Client Pilkington Brothers
Agency Saatchi & Saatchi

Pilkington Glass – 'Bullet Proof'

Open on a presenter addressing camera.

During the commercial we cut back and forth between the presenter and a man some distance away, who is assembling a rifle.

PRESENTER: There aren't many things today in which Britain leads the world. Our motorcycle industry has vanished, our shipbuilding industry is not what it used to be, but there is one area in which Britain not only leads the world, but is actually getting stronger every day. You may not have noticed it because the product is often invisible. You're looking at it right now. Glass. In recent years Pilkington, Britain's leading glass company, has risen from number four in the world to number one. Today Pilkington is the biggest, most successful glass company in the world, with products like fibre optics, ophthalmics, camera lenses and even more…

We see the presenter through the sight of the gun, the man shoots and the bullet is stopped by a glass screen we had not noticed before.

PRESENTER: …bullet-resistant glass. Pilkington. The world's leading glass company.

> " Incidentally, note that back then every agency was known by its initials – there were no Mothers or Nakeds or Red Brick Roads.

Title Points of View
Client The Guardian
Agency Boase Massimi Pollitt

The Guardian – 'Points of View'

VO: An event seen from one point of view gives one impression.

Seen from another point of view it gives quite a different impression.

It's only when you see the whole picture that you fully understand what's going on.

with a Levi's film called 'Parting', backed by Percy Sledge singing 'When a Man Loves a Woman'. A young WCRS was producing lovely double-page spreads for BMW, aka 'The Ultimate Driving Machine'. And elsewhere, David Abbott was turning out Volvo classics, such as the man wrapped in a roll of cotton wool against a headline that says simply, "Or buy a Volvo".

By now, you must be wondering about the 60 Saatchi ads in the book. Well, there were some that announced that Australians wouldn't give a Castlemaine XXXX for any other lager. Another launched The Independent with the line, "It is. Are you?" We had our share of pro bono entries – our work for Guide Dogs for the Blind won a Yellow Pencil with its image of a blind man with a dog's eyes and the headline: "No surgeon in the world can help this man see. But a dog can."

Title Holsten Pils – Cooper
Client Watney Mann & Truman Brewers
Agency Gold Greenlees Trott

Holsten Pils – 'Cooper'

GRIFF RHYS JONES: Oh, look out, it's Gaz come to rustle our Holsten Pils again.

GARY COOPER: That's why I'm here, how about it?

GRIFF: Don't you know draught lager's half price until high noon?

COOPER: It so happens I didn't know and it doesn't mean anything to me one way or the other.

GRIFF: No, you like the sugar turning to alcohol in Holsten Pils, you just don't like paying for it.

SFX: Smack!

GRIFF: And why should you when you can have mine?

SFX: Ha ha ha!

MVO: A Holsten Pils Production.

"A bald man with a combover attempts to take a photo-booth passport photo of himself with his hair in the right place... If you have never seen it or haven't seen it recently, look at it now – I know you'll laugh.

Hamlet Cigars – 'Photo Booth'

EVO: Happiness is a cigar called Hamlet. The Mild Cigar.

Title Hamlet Cigars – Photo Booth
Client Gallaher
Agency Collett Dickenson Pearce

We had campaigns for Cunard, British Rail, British Airways and Campbell's soups, but perhaps my favourite was a corporate demonstration for Pilkington Glass starring Timothy West. The film cuts between the actor giving the corporate spiel and a marksman assembling, loading and aiming a rifle at him. He fires. The presenter is nervous but is saved thanks to a single sheet of Pilkington's bullet-resistant glass through which we have been watching.

Finally, 1987 was the year in which we managed to afford the first ever full-colour Annual by selling adverts at the back of the book. Some were against it, but we felt adverts had a place in the D&AD Annual. We changed the accountants and the auditors, and finally managed to get the Association to break even. ●

1988
Gert Dumbar

Gert Dumbar studied Painting and Graphic Design at the Royal Academy of Fine Arts (now the Royal Academy of Art) in The Hague. He later studied on the postgraduate Graphic Design programme at the Royal College of Art in London.

In 1977, Dumbar established Studio Dumbar. With his team he has completed extensive corporate identity programmes for numerous major national and international clients, including PTT (the publicly owned former operator of the Netherlands' postal and telecom services), the ANWB (a Dutch motoring association), railway operator Nederlandse Spoorwegan, the Dutch police, Danish postal service Post Danmark (with Kontrapunkt) and Czech fixed-line operator Ceský Telecom. Studio Dumbar's many awards include two D&AD Black Pencils.

Since 2003, Gert Dumbar has taught at the Royal Academy of Art in The Hague. He frequently lectures at art schools and international design conferences.

1988 Annual

Annual Design **Mary Lewis, Ann Marshall; Lewis Moberly**
Cover Design **Judy Veal, Mary Lewis, Ann Marshall**
Cover Photography **Laurie Evans**
Typography **Mary Lewis, Ann Marshall**
Illustration **Geoffrey Appleton**
Art Direction **Mary Lewis**

Title Channel 4 promo
Client Channel 4
Production Company Simon Broom Associates

I'm a great admirer of British graphic design; partly, this is because the English language is very flexible. There are also many examples of what I call "stylistic durability" in British design. To name a couple: the London Underground map, designed by Harry Beck in 1931, and the Gill Sans typeface, by Eric Gill.

British designers are the only ones who really bring their sense of humour into the visual image. I can't think of any other cultures who do this – maybe the French, certainly not the Germans. It's a very powerful method of communication, because British humour is very human. It works on an international level, and therefore a lot of other places try to copy it, and that is where things fall apart.

Much of the work looks dated in the 1988 D&AD Annual, and that is a pity, because in those days there was enough talent to make things that were not necessarily eternal, but which had stylistic durability.

I have been on the D&AD jury several times. Once, when we didn't have much time to judge, I said to my fellow jury members, "Suppose this building is suddenly on fire. Which three pieces of work would you like to take outside?" It saved a lot of time, because there were very few selections!

When I was President, it was the first year that we made a little bit of profit, a dirty word at D&AD. I'm from abroad, however, and the Dutch can handle money very well, so I said to them, "Let's make a profit." I also wanted to change the D&AD identity to make it much more European – I am the only President who has come in from abroad.

There was a huge D&AD exhibition in Los Angeles at the Pacific Design Center, and Prince Andrew insisted that I show him around and talk about D&AD. It was quite an experience, and showed that the Royal Family had an interest in visual communication as well. It's a bit strange that a foreigner was selling British design abroad, but it was a great pleasure.

I have been awarded two D&AD Black Pencils. One was for corporate identity design for the Westeinde Hospital in The Hague in 1987; it was sort of an optimistic design, because in a hospital everybody is down, so the design needed some humour. It is still in use by the hospital, which brings us again to stylistic durability.

Title Whisky bottles
Client Arthur Bell & Sons
Design Group Michael Peters & Partners

"
It is becoming increasingly important to make young designers aware that they should have some sort of engagement with social issues. That is where the future of design lies.

Title Wine bottles
Client ASDA Stores
Design Group Lewis Moberly

The other was for the signage system for the Rijksmuseum Amsterdam in 1982, which was also very successful. Because it was a magnetic system, you could change the direction of the signs, which lay behind a Perspex plate.

When I was young, the sky was the limit. Today, however, there are very big problems in the world, from the environment to the economy and beyond. In terms of what D&AD should do next, it is becoming increasingly important to make young designers aware that they should have some sort of engagement with social issues. That is where the future of design lies. ●

Title Issey Miyake store
Client Issey Miyake UK
Design Group Stanton Williams

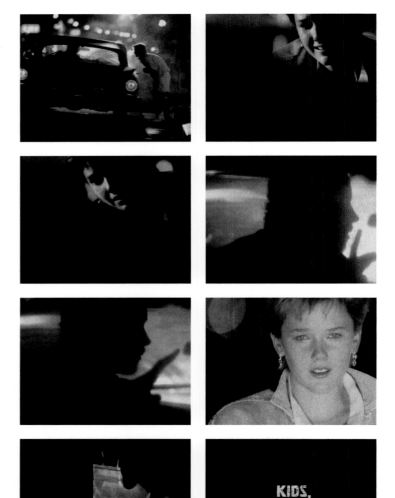

Drug Free – 'Interview'

Dealer 1 slams roof of car with teenagers inside.

DEALER 1: Creeps! I don't believe it! Driving in from the suburbs in their daddy's car to score and then trying to beat me down on the 'price'… I don't cut my price for nobody. (screams) Specially for these rich creeps. I got good stuff – you want good stuff, you gonna pay for it.

DEALER 2: They'll be back.

DEALER 1: Trying to tell me they take it or leave it. Did you see those little punks, man?

DEALER 2: You're gonna be the first one to take it or leave it.

DEALER 1: Yeah, drivin' their daddy's big car. You know what I'd like to do to them? I'd like to rub their faces…

DEALER 2: You know they're so stupid, they deserve to be burned.

DEALER 1: They're good for nothing, man…

DEALER 2: They're good for something… They're good for taking money off of.

DEALER 3: (waves crack in car of kids) Hey man, got some good crack… what do you need?

MVO: Kids, it's you against them.

Drug Free – 'Girl and Dealer'

GIRL: Hi Richie, I really need to talk to you.

RICHIE: Yeah, yeah, I got you covered.

GIRL: I only want a little – come on.

RICHIE: Sure, I understand.

GIRL: Just a couple of hits. I don't have any money – please.

RICHIE: You mean you bring me out here for nothing! That's a no-no you understand? What are you stupid? What do I look like…

GIRL: Richie, I just gave you a hundred dollars!

RICHIE: That's got nothin' to do with now!

GIRL: Richie, please!

RICHIE: Listen to me: no money, no candy, no crack, you understand? Now dissolve, lose yourself.

GIRL: Richie, come on, don't leave please!

RICHIE: Listen, shh, shh – that girl you're gonna get – that little red-headed girl and both of yous are gonna come over to my crib…

GIRL: Charlotte?

RICHIE: That's right. Go to a nice little party understand me? Then I'll take care of ya.

MVO: Kids, it's you against them.

Title Interview
Client Media Advertising Partnership for a Drug Free America
Agency Ogilvy & Mather

Title Girl and Dealer
Client Media Advertising Partnership for a Drug Free America
Agency Ogilvy & Mather

1963   1964   1965   1966   1967   1968   1969   1970   1971   1972   1973   1974   1975   1976   1977   1978   1979   1980   1981   1982   1983   1984   1985   1986   1987

Drug Free – 'Tricks of the Trade'

SFX: Traffic noise.

MAN: You know kid, all you gotta do is be cool. You just give the stuff to your best buddies. You take it to a party. Tell your friends it's a great high. They should just try it. Tell them it can't hurt them.

BILLY: I can do that.

MAN: Yeah, it's easy. Those kids are going to be a pushover, 'cause they like you. You're a hot shot, right? They'll love you for it.

BILLY: How much do I charge?

MAN: Right now, nothing.

BILLY: Nothing?

MAN: Just give it away. Let 'em have a free taste. Then you watch. You watch and you see who comes back for more.

BILLY: And then I start charging.

MAN: You're a smart kid. You have a good day at school, Billy-boy.

SFX: Traffic noise.

MVO: Kids, it's you against them.

Drug Free – 'Candy Store'

SFX: Traffic noise.

JOEY: This place is a dump, man. You ain't gonna make no money in here.

CARLOS: You don't know nothing.

JOEY: I don't know nothing? I know that this is rotten. I know that I don't see no people in here. So where's your gold mine?

CARLOS: It's down the street, man. The school.

JOEY: The school? Oh, I see, you're gonna get rich on selling gum to school kids.

CARLOS: Not gum, man. This. For ten dollars, the little snotnoses can blow their heads off. The little brats are dying to fry their brains. And I'm only too happy to help them.

JOEY: So where do they get the money?

CARLOS: Who cares where they get it? As long as they get it.

SFX: Traffic noise.

MVO: Kids, it's you against them.

Title Tricks of the Trade
Client Media Advertising Partnership for a Drug Free America
Agency Ogilvy & Mather

Title Candy Store
Client Media Advertising Partnership for a Drug Free America
Agency Ogilvy & Mather

1989
John Hegarty

Sir John Hegarty is Founder of Bartle Bogle Hegarty (BBH). He started in advertising as a Junior Art Director at Benton & Bowles, London, in 1965. He almost finished in advertising 18 months later, when they fired him.

In 1967 he joined the CramerSaatchi consultancy. It became Saatchi & Saatchi in 1970, with Hegarty as a founding shareholder. He left in 1973 to co-found TBWA London as Creative Director.

In 1982 he left to start BBH, which was soon one of the most talked about and awarded advertising agencies in the world. The agency has won every Agency of the Year accolade and every creative award possible, and has been at the forefront of the industry for 27 years.

In 1996, he was appointed to the Board of Trustees of the Design Museum, and in 2006 he was awarded honorary doctorates by Buckinghamshire Chilterns University College and Middlesex University. Hegarty was awarded a knighthood by The Queen in 2007 in recognition of his services to the advertising and creative industries.

1989 Annual

Annual Design Ray Carpenter
Cover Design Nigel Rose
Cover Model Matthew Wurr
Cover Photography Kevin Summer

"I never read The Economist."

Management trainee. Aged 42.

Title I Never Read The Economist
Client The Economist
Agency Abbott Mead Vickers SMS

To borrow Churchill's famous quote on democracy, D&AD is the worst form of award scheme, apart from all the others that have been tried. Having finally been elevated to the Presidency in 1989, I left a year later feeling inadequate, frustrated and disappointed. More so because I wholeheartedly supported the association, and still do – but in your year of office, you come to terms with the impossibility of judging creativity.

Mine was the year we failed to give a Black Pencil to anyone. The brilliant Economist poster 'I Never Read The Economist' only got In Book in the Copy section. From the mould-breaking Guardian redesign to the Metropolitan Police and innovative British Rail TV ads, the juries failed to recognise creative brilliance at work. In my own inadequacy in the Annual's foreword, I defended the lack of Black Pencils, rambling on about the severity of D&AD juries and the need to uphold standards.

As the Berlin Wall collapsed and the Tiananmen Square rallies got underway, we were turning our backs and failing to recognise work that would influence and change the way creativity worked. Such is the failure of instant assessment and the jury system.

Title Relax
Client British Rail
Agency Saatchi & Saatchi

British Rail – 'Relax'

SFX: Music.

SUNG: Anytime you choose

Kick off your shoes

Rest your weary eyes

Catch up with the news

Her favourite book will be

The perfect company

Relax

Forget about the blues

You're doing fine

Leave your cares and worries

Down the line

Loosen up your tie

Watch the world speed by

Relax

> "To borrow Churchill's famous quote on democracy, D&AD is the worst form of award scheme, apart from all the others that have been tried.

Title Next store
Client Next Retail
Design Group Din Associates

Despite its failings, D&AD remains a
beacon of brilliance in a compromised
world, ploughing money back into student
education, promoting the creative
message and exhorting its practitioners
to do better.

Looking back is a dangerous and
sobering business. Apart from wondering
why you were wearing a Hugo Boss
suit and defending creative juries
who lacked perspective, it does have
one main appeal. You can right some
of the wrongs that were committed
under your Presidency. So, to all those
responsible for the work I've selected,
congratulations – in my book, you would
have received Black Pencils.

Perhaps I shouldn't have been so harsh.
It was also the year 'The T-Factor Diet'
became a bestseller, Phil Collins got into
the charts with 'Two Hearts' and people
flocked to see 'Crocodile Dundee II'.

COULD YOU TURN THE OTHER CHEEK?

COOL CUSTOMER, are you? Okay, let's see how far you can get before you blow your stack.

You are walking down a street. Some youths start jeering at you: "'Ello, 'ello, 'ello." Smile. You've heard it all before, every name a copper can be called: rozzer, old bill, pig, fuzz, peeler, flatfoot, the filth. And some less complimentary. Shrug it off.

You're out in the patrol car when you see a car without lights weaving through the traffic. You flash your headlights at him to stop. Instead, he accelerates away.

Siren on. Ahead your target, still without lights, narrowly misses a woman on a pedestrian crossing and then goes the wrong way round a roundabout, while a youth leaning out of the passenger window showers you with empty beer cans and two-finger salutes.

The car skids round another corner and slides into a brick wall, but the youths inside are out and running. You chase, abandoning your car with its engine still on and door left wide open. As you grab the driver, he mouths obscenities at you.

"You can't go on the attack, whatever the provocation."

Still in control of your temper? Okay, try this.

A demonstration is turning into a riot. You're bussed in, nervous and not sure what to expect. It's frightening. The crowd, in ugly mood, surges against the frail police line.

Suddenly a lone voice calls your number "EF203, EF203." The others take it up. "EF203, EF203." They're all staring at you, trying to psyche you out. Why you?

It gets worse. Bottles arc down and burst in showers of flame. Stones and half bricks drop out of the air and threaten to brain you. You cannot leave the line.

At last the crowd starts drifting away. As the tension ebbs, you see a man step forward and deliberately stub out his cigarette on the flank of a police horse.

This all sounds a bit melodramatic, but we've made none of it up. Each of the details we've described really happened. How would you have reacted?

Strangely, people often find that in a real emergency they stay calm. But stress builds up in the body like static and can earth itself without warning.

Three days after a riot like the one

As a police officer, sooner or later you're bound to encounter abuse, threats, provocation, even physical violence. Be careful how you respond. Lose your temper and you could lose your job. **Photograph by Don McCullin**

above you may arrest a well dressed drunk. "Look here," he drawls, "do you realise who you're talking to?" And jabs you in the chest.

Careful. This trivial annoyance may become the lightning rod for all that pent up stress and rage.

If, in any of the situations we have described above, you were to lose your temper, you might also lose your job.

It doesn't seem fair, does it? But then being a police officer is no ordinary job. As someone sworn to uphold the law, you of all people cannot break it.

So what should you do? Should you say: "Are you going to come quietly or do

I have to use earplugs?" In fact, a bit of humour can often defuse a potentially ugly situation. As can tact, restraint and good common sense.

Of course, it's a strain being on best behaviour 24 hours a day. Never switching off. With the very highest standards to set and live up to. Sometimes, all that bottled up stress can make us difficult to live with.

An officer on motorway patrol raced to an accident. A car was on fire. The heat was ferocious. He had to watch, helpless, as a child the same age as his own daughter burned to death before his eyes.

When he got home, his wife produced supper. Without a word, he picked up his plate of food and flung it through the window. Until then he had kept control of his emotions. But that night of all nights he could not face a cooked meal.

As a police officer you will inevitably endure your share of unpleasantness and you'll have to evolve your own way of dealing with it.

But why are we dwelling on these

traumatic subjects? Isn't this supposed to be a recruitment advertisement? Are we trying to put you off?

Actually, yes.

If you're put off by an advertisement, you'd never be able to cope with the reality.

"It gets worse. Bottles arc down and burst in showers of flame."

And we need people who can cope. People who are tough, tender, sensitive, strong and disciplined, all at the same time. They aren't easy to find. At present we take only one in five applicants. We'd rather look at fewer, better candidates.

Seeing you've got this far, we'll now admit that a career in the Met isn't all grief. Few jobs are as rewarding.

Ask the much loved Streatham home beat officer who, helmet under arm, cigar stuck firmly in mouth in flagrant disregard of regulations, can tell you the name of every child in his manor.

Ask the constable who, while patiently unravelling the intricacies of gang warfare in, of all places, Southall, has been invited to six Indian weddings in the last year.

Ask the sergeant who now runs what is virtually a Bengali advice centre in Whitechapel.

We can offer 28,000 more examples. If you don't believe us, stop any police officer in the street and ask.

When you've learned what they get out of the job, ask how they got in. They'll tell you about our twenty week

basic training course at Hendon. And life on the beat at one of London's 187 police stations where, under the tutelage of a sergeant, you will learn the art of handling people. And yourself.

Right now, your next step is to fill in and post the coupon below.

We're looking for mature, fit people aged between 18½ and 45, especially from the ethnic minorities. You should be at least 172cms tall if you're a man, 162cms if you're a woman.

Ideally, you'll have some 'O' level passes or their equivalents, but we value your personal qualities more.

To find out more please telephone: 01-725 4492 (Ansaphone: 01-725 4575) or fill in the coupon or write to: The Recruiting Officer, The Metropolitan Police Selection Centre, Department MD 960, Freepost, London W2 1BR.

Name

Address

Postcode   Age

Title Could You Turn the Other Cheek?
Client Metropolitan Police
Agency Collett Dickenson Pearce

Title The Guardian redesign
Client The Guardian
Design Group Pentagram Design

"

D&AD remains a
beacon of brilliance in
a compromised world,
ploughing money back
into student education,
promoting the creative
message and exhorting its
practitioners to do better.

1990
Ron Brown

Ron Brown obtained a scholarship to Twickenham College of Art, after which he worked in several small agencies. In 1970 he joined Doyle Dane Bernbach as Senior Art Director. In 1972, he spent two and a half years with BBDO as Group Head.

After that came an 18-month spell at Young & Rubicam, followed by a return to BBDO. He joined Abbott Mead Vickers when the agency was founded as a director and Head of Art, in order to work with David Abbott. The partnership lasted 20 years, at which point Abbott retired. Brown continued as Executive Head of Art for a further seven years.

1990 Annual

Annual Design **John McConnell**
Cover Design **John McConnell, Jason Godfrey**
Book Design **David Lum**

"

The tougher jurors' decisions are, the more likely next year's entrants will strive to produce greater work.

In 1990, as D&AD President for that year, I wrote these words as introduction to the Annual:

"That should have been in the book"

Yes, many of us were disappointed again when work we thought worthy of getting into the Annual, didn't.

As those of you who have sat on a Design and Art Direction jury will know, the demands on the quality of the work increases every year.

This is not surprising, the Association was originally set up, 28 years ago, to inspire creative people and encourage innovation. It has always aimed to promote excellence in Advertising and Design and represent only the best work.

When judging, a D&AD juror is looking for greatness and originality, which is why it's so difficult to get even one piece of work accepted, let alone win a 'pencil'.

One jury this year only voted in one item. The jury members saw nothing new and inspiring, and innovation cannot rise through imitation.

These exacting principles have helped establish Design and Art Direction as 'elitist' and we should be proud of it.

The 'Book' is the one you most want to get your work into.

The 'Awards' are the most prestigious, the ones you'd like to win above all others.

And it will remain that way, providing we don't expect Design and Art Direction to lower its standards.

What we must do, is raise ours.

There were three pieces of work in particular which stood out for me, namely the ads for Le Creuset, the Royal Mail stamps, and, in the TV and Cinema section, the 'Dambusters' Carling Black Label commercial. This work embraced the innovation and principles that D&AD stand for.

Envy and admiration swept through me when I saw the first of the Le Creuset ads appear in the press. Three others followed, all immaculately executed, producing an outstanding campaign that deservedly won two D&AD Yellow Pencils.

It's faultless work. It's a wonderful concept, beautifully written with wit and charm. It's art direction that hits you in the eye, simple and powerful. The first responsibility for a creative team is to make sure the ad gets noticed, and the use of strong gritty photography and the colour orange does this masterfully.

Le Creuset kitchenware enjoys the same reputation as the Aga cooker. Made of iron, it's durable, and the design is sophisticated – a classic for the kitchen. With products that look so good, it's a brave client who doesn't insist they're featured in the advertising, but here was a client who understood that this was advertising that entertained, with all the ingredients to make its products desirable.

Title Royal Mail stamps
Client Royal Mail
Design Group Michael Peters & Partners

Title Our Shoes Outlast the Men Who Make Them
Client Timberland
Agency Leagas Delaney

THEY USED TO SAY MASTURBATION WAS BAD FOR YOU. NOW IT COULD SAVE YOUR LIFE.

Title Department of Health AIDS information ad
Client Health Education Authority
Agency BMP DDP Needham Worldwide

When the Government killed the dog licence they left us to kill the dogs.

Title When the Government Killed the Dog Licence They Left Us to Kill the Dogs
Client RSPCA
Agency Abbott Mead Vickers SMS

Designer Mark Pearce at Michael Peters & Partners produced the concept for the Royal Mail stamps. Using ten artists' work to illustrate 'Smile', he produced a beautiful set of ten 20p stamps. Stamps have featured in many D&AD Annuals as it's a medium that allows artists and designers a free hand, and the standard is always extremely high. These, however, surpassed any I had seen before, and were worthy winners of a Yellow Pencil.

The big prize of the year went to the Carling commercial. It deservedly won a Black Pencil, the highest award available, and two Yellows. It's a spoof on the World War II bombing of a German dam portrayed in the classic movie 'The Dam Busters', and was conceived as part of the ongoing 'I Bet He Drinks Carling Black Label' campaign.

Directed by Roger Woodburn, it's an example of outstanding craftsmanship.

He reproduces the film's dramatic bombing sequence with perfection. It's gripping. Then, to the surprise of the viewer, the sombre mood changes to brilliant comedy, as a German soldier on the dam deflects the bombs with a demonstration of world-class goalkeeping. At that point the pilot removes his mask and utters the famous line: "I bet he drinks Carling Black Label." As an added twist the co-pilot pulls his mask off, and mumbles his reply exactly as it would be if he had his mask on. Stupendous! A beautifully crafted script, superbly targeted at the drinking man's market.

The 1990 juries were as tough as ever. D&AD Chairman Edward Booth-Clibborn said of the advertising jury: "This was, without doubt, an uncompromising jury, who rejected many passable advertisements and ultimately chose only those which were outstanding."

As jury member Adrian Holmes stated, "It was ever thus," and he's right. The tougher jurors' decisions are, the more likely next year's entrants will strive to produce greater work.

D&AD Annuals are only part of how the Association helps to inspire coming generations of creative talent. In 1991, the programme of workshops continued. Professionals working within the business gave their time to run them, and we were extremely grateful. Briefs were set to send to art school courses throughout the country as part of the longstanding Royal Mail Student Awards Scheme, which has produced an excellent standard of work that many students use as part of their portfolios.

Those of us fortunate enough to enjoy a career in advertising and design have been able to indulge ourselves

Title Le Creuset campaign
Client Kitchenware Merchants
Agency Saatchi & Saatchi

in a world of creativity. Clients trust us with large budgets and they naturally expect us to deliver the best work possible. In return we have to push the limits of our talents to improve their businesses, be it selling their products, raising funds for charities, helping in the fight against smoking, obesity, cancer or AIDS, or improving the environment we live in. No piece of work in this Annual happened overnight – it would generally mean "burning the midnight oil" to produce something unique, compelling and original.

The D&AD Annuals give us the opportunity to showcase exceptional ideas and craftsmanship, and challenge others who work in our industry to do better. ●

Title Dog Wearing Trainers
Client Reebok UK
Agency Lowe Howard-Spink

Carling Black Label – 'Dambusters'

SFX: Drone of aeroplane.

Open on pilot in mask and goggles sitting at the controls of a Lancaster bomber. He's speaking through his mask, although his mask makes him unintelligible.

We cut to the rear of the plane, where another pilot is fixing his sights on the target ahead. Cut to dam wall. A German sentry emerges from a hut; he stops dead in his tracks, his attention caught by the sound of the incoming aeroplane. Cut to view of the Lancaster's bomb doors opening. A perfectly round bomb drops through the hatch and plummets towards the reservoir below. It lands on the water, and begins to bounce. The bomb whistles towards the dam wall. The sentry saves it, goalkeeper-fashion.

PILOT 1: (muffled blurb)

PILOT 2: (indiscernible muffled reply)

Cut back to the sentry, who's in a panic. Rolling the bomb to one side, he heaves off his overcoat, bobs down and prepares for the next. Cut to an avalanche of bombs dropping from the bomb doors. They all bounce towards the dam. Cut to the two pilots looking out of their windows. One pulls the mask off his face. It's Steve.

STEVE: I bet he drinks Carling Black Label.

Cut to co-pilot. He pulls the mask off his face. It's Mark. He acknowledges. However, his reply is exactly as it would be if he still had his mask on. We cut to packshot: five pints of Carling Black Label, with a little round ball bouncing across the top of them in time to the jingle.

Title Carling Black Label – Dambusters
Client Bass
Agency WCRS Matthews Marcantonio

"No piece of work in this Annual happened overnight – it would generally mean 'burning the midnight oil' to produce something unique, compelling and original.

Title Bottles
Client D'Amico & Partners
Design Group Michael Peters & Partners

Carling Black Label – 'Squirrel'

SFX: Theme from 'Mission: Impossible'.

Open on a garden assault course, at the end of which lies a saucer of hazelnuts. At the beginning sits a squirrel.

With breathtaking agility the squirrel leaps into action, clambering up a six-foot pole, scurrying along a length of chain, leaping across a see-saw, up a shoot, across another hurdle, and with a gigantic leap, over to where the hazelnuts await.

We cut to two owls who have been casually observing.

OWL: I bet he drinks Carling Black Label.

SUPER: Carling Black Label.

Title Carling Black Label – Squirrel
Client Bass
Agency WCRS Matthews Marcantonio

Title Binoculars
Client UAD Company
Design Group Rodd Industrial Design

1991
Martin Lambie-Nairn

After beginning his career as a graphic designer in television, Martin Lambie-Nairn formed his first design agency in 1976. He is now recognised as one of the foremost designers of his generation in broadcast branding. His rebranding of the BBC won every prestigious award in design and broadcasting in the UK and the USA.

Over the 20 years following his agency's creation, Lambie-Nairn diversified into a number of different sectors, from banking and insurance to retail and telecoms.

Martin is a Royal Designer for Industry, a Fellow of the Royal Television Society and an Honorary Doctor of Art at the University of Lincoln.

1991 Annual

Annual Design **Peartree Design**
Cover Design **Graham Watson**
Cover Photography **John Parker**
Art Direction **Graham Watson**

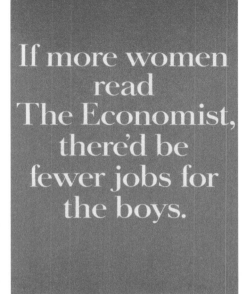

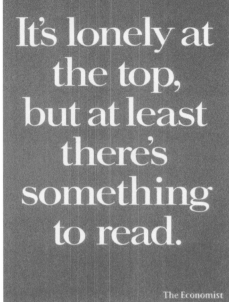

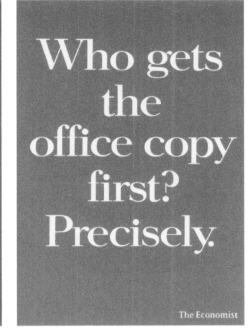

Title The Economist campaign
Client The Economist
Agency Abbott Mead Vickers BBDO

I can barely remember what happened
last Tuesday, let alone in 1991.
But it became clear that I was not
going to slip out of this one easily
when the 1991 D&AD Annual arrived
on my desk with a thud.

Having resigned myself to oblige,
I thumbed through the Annual and
was quickly taken aback by its contents.
I was looking at some great work.

It was not of a particular era: almost all of
it could have been created yesterday. Not
only that but some of it was quite simply
wittier, cleverer and better crafted than a
lot of work produced today.

I had not expected this. After all, we work
in an industry that embraces the new.
Could it be that we had not moved on,
or that creativity, like Rip Van Winkle,
had remained asleep for 22 years? Or
was there another answer?

I have a theory – not held in 1991 but
developed since – that provides the
answer. The first part of which is this:
Great work lasts and becomes the
foundation for more great work. And
the second: Great work is not created
by companies but by great people, both
clients and creatives.

The 1991 Annual confirmed this theory,
and provides two neat examples in
the Economist and Silk Cut advertising
campaigns, both of which I regard as
great work.

Neither of these campaigns could have
been an easy sell. What David Abbott
and Marcantonio initially proposed to The
Economist was unlike any other creative
solution. It was clever, exceptionally
simple, crafted and completely original.
The meeting with the client must have
been scary for all concerned. But the
client took the risk and as we all know
now, this one idea ran for about 30
years. We did not tire of it, but rather
looked forward to every new version.
The result? The Economist became
famous and successful and the creative
work a reference point for years to come.

The similarities between Silk Cut and
The Economist are very close.

It just so happened that I was in a
meeting with Paul Arden (Saatchi &
Saatchi's Creative Director at the time)
just before he was about to present the
final work to his client. He showed it to
me. It was a piece of purple silk with a
horizontal cut in it – and nothing else. It
certainly ticked the original box, but as
Paul left the room for the meeting he
made the comment that he had no idea
whether it was great work or rubbish. He
presented it, the client bought it, and the
Silk Cut work deservedly became one of
the most famous and effective long-
running campaigns.

These two campaigns were my inspiration
for the BBC2 identity. Until then, TV
channel identities were animated logos
– temporary affairs that would often be

"

1991 was one of many exceptional years that we've had since the late 60s and continue to have today. All of which fits my theory that great work lasts.

redesigned when either fashions or Channel Controller changed. There was no understanding of the value of brand consistency.

I wanted to devise a scheme that would take a theme and create dozens of versions, thus remaining fresh and surprising for years, while building a consistent brand – the exact strategy adopted by the Economist and Silk Cut campaigns.

The key for this to be realised was my client, Pam Masters, Head of BBC Presentation. If we were to do this, it would be unlike any other channel branding scheme seen before. If we failed, her professional judgment and future career would be jeopardised.

At the point of delivering the first BBC2 idents to the client, I suffered the same lack of confidence that Paul Arden had experienced with his Silk Cut work. So convinced was I that the work was not good enough that I suggested to my colleagues that we reshot it all at our expense. Luckily I was talked out of it. But I was not the only one who thought they were not good enough. The Channel Controller hated them and was going to air them for two weeks and then dump them. During the two weeks the "apoplectic" Channel Controller happened to have dinner with Richard Rogers and Charles Saatchi, who introduced the subject of the "brilliant" new branding sequences. The next day Pam Masters received a note saying that the new sequences would remain on screen after all. So, it is thanks to Richard and Charles that the work remained on our screens.

Pam took the risk. The identity for BBC2 not only achieved the objectives for the channel but also raised the creative reputation of the BBC globally… and Pam kept her job. Today, 22 years later, the brilliant Channel 4 branding sequences (which I had nothing to do with) continue to inspire the nation, and they are based on the BBC2 creative strategy.

I do not think that 1991 was the exceptional year for creativity. I do think it was one of many exceptional years we've had since the late 60s and continue to have today. All of which fits my theory that great work lasts.

Finally, that year I gave the President's Award to Abram Games. He was over 90 years old. During World War II he designed the posters that became part of our culture and history. He designed the first ever BBC channel identity in this country. In 1950 he designed the graphics for the Festival of Britain. Later, he produced the logos for the Queen's Award to Industry as well as countless organisations and companies. Between 1940 and 1960 he was *the* graphic designer in this country. It was a pleasure to recognise him.

He was a single-minded and uncompromising character who believed that simplicity applied with visual wit would communicate more effectively than the work of his contemporaries. He was right, and we aspire to do the same: create great work for great clients that lasts and inspires other to do better. ⬡

LOW TAR As defined by H.M. Government **Warning: SMOKING CAN CAUSE FATAL DISEASES** Health Departments' Chief Medical Officers

Title Silk Cut
Client Gallaher
Agency Saatchi & Saatchi

LOW TAR As defined by H.M. Government **STOPPING SMOKING** **REDUCES THE RISK OF SERIOUS DISEASES** Health Departments' Chief Medical Officers

Title Grow Your Own Food
Design Abram Games

Title BBC 2 identity
Client BBC Television
Production Company Lambie-Nairn & Company

"I gave my President's Award to Abram Games. He was over 90 years old. During World War II he designed the posters that became part of our culture and history.

1992
Tim Delaney

Tim Delaney started his career in advertising in the mailroom. He worked as a copywriter at Young & Rubicam and Boase Massimi Pollitt before joining BBDO London, where he became Creative Director at 27 and Managing Director at 31.

He founded Leagas Delaney in 1980, and over the years has won awards for his work in all the major awards schemes, notably Britain's D&AD, America's One Show and the Cannes International Advertising Festival.

He was President of D&AD in 1992, and received the D&AD President's Award three years later. The Creative Circle President's Award and the British Television Awards' Lifetime Achievement Award have also been bestowed on him in recognition of his contribution to the communications industry. He was inducted into the One Show Advertising Hall of Fame in America in 2007 and Campaign's British Advertising Hall of Fame in 2008. Delaney remains a working copywriter.

1992 Annual

Annual Design **Peartree Design**
Cover Design **Nick Bell**
Cover Photography **Andy Rumball**
Section Dividers **Nick Bell**

Title Age Doesn't Improve Everything
Client Levi Strauss UK
Agency Bartle Bogle Hegarty

It is impossible to write about my year as President without reference to the changes at the top of the organisation.

I held a series of meetings with the design community to ascertain why they were so unhappy with their lot. They wanted a different Dinner. Design Awards were always less respected by the rowdy crowds at the Awards evening, apparently. They wanted new categories. Secession was in the air.

In our meetings, I reminded the rebels that approximately 75 per cent of all of D&AD's activities were paid for by the advertising community in one way or another, and that if they did, for instance, organise a separate Dinner for the Design Awards, it would most likely take place in a B&B off Praed Street.

It was during this process that one of the staff at D&AD divulged the misdeeds that led eventually, via an evenhanded and formal hearing, to the suspension and exit of the Executive Chairman and the Financial Director.

Despite these shenanigans, the actual business of D&AD proceeded uncharacteristically smoothly. The judging and Dinner were organised in exemplary fashion – the customary issues with the sound system were finally resolved, and as I recall there was even a pot of flowers on every table. Sweet.

The judging took a leaf from the One Show and was conducted outside London in order that last-minute no-shows were kept to a minimum, and to allow the design and advertising communities to mingle and enjoy each other's shared ideals.

The resulting Awards and Book were deemed of an appropriately high standard. The President's Award was bestowed upon Neil Godfrey for being one of those art directors who, for 30 years, not only made all his campaigns look immaculate, but also always sported a tan.

Another interesting highlight of the year saw the best of the work from across the UK's art colleges come to one venue in London. This came about after a particularly plaintive plea from Falmouth College of Arts in Cornwall asking me to attend their Dip show. It occurred to us that very few people from London went to any of these end-of-year art college shows, which was not only sad but mildly shocking. Hence the now annual Student Expo.

Also, it would be remiss if I didn't mention the contribution of Anthony Simonds-Gooding, who became Chairman in my year. One of life's great human beings, he brought with him integrity and common sense, and determined that D&AD should attend to its business with professionalism. He also hired the indefatigable David Kester as Director. A formidable team, they were the architects of the D&AD we know and admire today. ●

Title Cages Save Lives
Client Volvo Concessionaires
Agency Abbott Mead Vickers BBDO

"The President's Award was bestowed upon Neil Godfrey for being one of those art directors who, for 30 years, not only made all his campaigns look immaculate, but also always sported a tan.

Title Keyhole
Client The Economist
Agency Abbott Mead Vickers BBDO

Nike – '180 by Alex Proyas, Australia'

Music and SFX up and throughout.

TITLE CARD: 180.

Title card scrolls from right to reveal: "by Alex Proyas Australia".

Cut to medium close-up of moving fans.

Cut to close-up of individual wearing goggles and tight cap.

Cut to medium close-up side view of person running with fans in background.

Shot of person passing behind post.

Cut to medium close-up of fan with rings around stands.

Side close-up of person with cap on.

Cut to moving shot of person running on pillows in background.

In foreground: circle with swirl on it on stand.

Person running toward camera.

Medium close-up of person running away from camera on pillows.

Stakes with 1, 2, 3 on them in background.

Cut to close-up of moving fans.

Overhead shot of person running on pillows in foreground, a stake with the number six on it and power lines.

Cut to moving fans.

Cut to person running towards camera with line of pillows in background.

Back shot of person standing looking to their left, right, left and right again at Y in pillow formation. Fan in foreground on right.

Cut to close-up of Nike shoe as heel is lifting off the floor.

TITLE CARD: Orange Nike 180 logo.

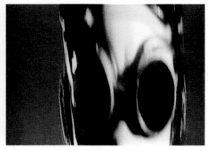

Title **180 by Alex Proyas, Australia**
Client **Nike**
Agency **Wieden+Kennedy**

"A highlight of the year saw the best of the work from across the UK's art colleges come to one venue in London. This came about after a particularly plaintive plea from Falmouth College of Arts in Cornwall asking me to attend their Dip show.

Nike – 'Air by Bo Jackson'

VO: A-one, two, three, four!

CHORUS: (singing) Bo knows it's got the air thing!

BO: (singing) Nice shoes!

CHORUS: Bo knows it works!

BO: Bo knows it's got the air thing!

CHORUS: Bo knows they…

BO: Stop! This is ridiculous. I'm an athlete, not an actor.

BO: (from TV) Let me out of this thing. I've got rehab to do. Gimme those shoes.

GUY: Bo?

BO: (to the family) Excuse me. You watch too much TV, kid.

(music up)

Cuts to Bo working out.

CHORUS: Bo knows it's got… the air thing.

BO: Hey! Where's that music coming from?

CHORUS: Bo knows it's…

BO: You know I don't have time for this!

GEORGE FOREMAN: But I do! Hit it!

(Music up)

CHORUS: George knows it's got the air thing!

Title Air by Bo Jackson
Client Nike
Agency Wieden+Kennedy

1993
Aziz Cami

Aziz Cami was one of the founding
partners of The Partners, which has
established a reputation within the
design industry for creative and
commercial excellence.

He has over 40 years' experience in
design and corporate branding, and is
known for the powerful identities he
has created for such leading luxury and
premium sector clients as Asprey, De
Beers LV, Diageo's Reserve Brands Group,
Harrods, Jaguar, McLaren, Saks Fifth
Avenue, Vertu and Wedgwood.

Cami was President of D&AD in 1993.
He has won over 200 creative awards,
including D&AD Yellow Pencils, DBA
Design Effectiveness Awards and awards
from the Art Directors Club of New York
and Communication Arts.

1993 Annual

Annual Design **Peartree Design**
Cover Design **Neil Godfrey**
Cover Photography **Neil Barstow**
Typography **Jeff Merrells**
Art Direction **Neil Godfrey**
Modelmaker **Simon Lunn**

Marco Pierre White, from the safety of Table 3.

"Come and see my new restaurant," he said, "but don't ask me to pose for a bloody picture."

Marco's cooking being rivalled only by his temper, I didn't protest.

On the other hand, we're about to start work on his new cookbook, 'White Heat II' and here was a chance to capture the maestro in a moment of spontaneous combustion. So I pocketed the Olympus 110 Superzoom.

The smallest 3 x zoom camera in the world, it'll sit under a napkin without attracting the attention of even the most

attentive maître d'. And with a range of 35-110mm it can pick out a wild mushroom at 30 paces, let alone a wild chef at 20.

Tuesday lunchtime arrives. So do I, and am whisked to table 3, with a river view. Marco sends greetings from the kitchen and a bottle of Krug.

I check the menu.

Automatic film loading, winding, speed setting, exposure control and exclusive 'thinking' flash. Followed by a highly recommended multi-beam auto focus. For 'weatherproof' I also optimis-

tically assume 'sauce proof'. (A ladle-full of bouillon goes a long way.)

Superzoom at the ready, I keep an eye on the kitchen door.

My starter appears (baked sea scallops with lemon and cinnamon - heaven).

Then the gastronomic tornado himself. A tiff over a taste tatin, it seems. As Marco explodes, I snap. The result, you see above.

A few days later I show him.

'Harvey's Canteen' is being heaped with praise from all quarters, and Marco is in ebullient mood.

"Crafty sod," he beams, "my compliments to Olympus."

OLYMPUS 110 SUPERZOOM.

Title Marco Pierre White
Client Olympus Optical Company UK
Agency Collett Dickenson Pearce

Having been the first President-Elect of D&AD during 1991, I had no excuses for thinking 1992 was going to be an easy ride, and it wasn't. 1992 was about rebuilding and renewing D&AD among all this turbulence.

Our first challenge was surviving an investigation by the Charity Commission. At risk was the essential charitable status of D&AD – without that, we were sunk.

Next, we had to stave off bankruptcy. To buy time, we needed money until our main source of income arrived in the form of entry fees for the annual Awards. In one week, we raised a total of £40,000 in short-term loans from four of our leading advertising agencies. Without that loan and the favourable ruling by the Charity Commission, D&AD would have gone bust. And what none of the members knew at the time was that the constitution then in place committed all of them to paying, equally, any shortfall in funds. All current members will be relieved to know that we quickly changed that pernicious clause!

With disaster averted, we turned our attention to growth, both in revenue and in reputation – although we knew that growth in such a recessionary climate wouldn't be easy. Firstly, we added a new category of membership, Associate Membership. This included international, student and, importantly, client members, all of whom shared the Association's beliefs and values.

Secondly, we embarked on a communications programme to articulate the benefits of membership to D&AD, and introduced a range of new discounts on associated products and services. We also introduced the concept of President's Lectures and subsidised the ticket price. In our first year, we had lectures from Tibor Kalman, Tony Brignull, Steve Henry, Paul Rand, Bob Levenson and Johnny Meszaros. These activities boosted the membership to over 1,000 for the first time in 31 years of D&AD's history, a 25 per cent increase on the previous year.

Thirdly, we abolished hanging fees. It had always seemed to me an absurd tax on success to charge people to have their winning work showcased in our exhibitions. They had, after all, already paid a generous fee to enter the Awards. It did, however, mean an income gap of £100,000 at a very difficult time. I was delighted and relieved when extra entry fees more than compensated for that shortfall.

Fourthly, we chose to broaden the remit of D&AD and include Product Design as a vibrant new category within the annual Awards.

Fifthly, in a major attempt to boost our reputation and relevance, we launched a massively ambitious new concept to engage clients and the general public with creativity: the Festival of Excellence in Design and Advertising. This involved exhibitions of the best work from the previous year's D&AD Awards; exhibits of great advertising and design from around the world; and lectures and workshops every breakfast, lunchtime and evening. It was all held in a specially constructed pavilion in the centre of London. The funding came from industry donations (the vast majority from advertising agencies) and supplier and client sponsorship. Our plan was to expand this into a Creative Festival of London, but we were held back from that goal by the lack of support from other advertising and design organisations. Despite this, the Festival of Excellence attracted a remarkable attendance of 4,000 people over seven days in May.

Finally, we stepped up support for our core activity – the student education programme. This was greatly expanded, despite our limited funds and resources. Ben Casey created the D&AD Education Scheme, which was established as our central educational plank. More than 30 colleges immediately enrolled, and the concept culminated in the D&AD Student Expo, held at the Royal Horticultural Halls in London. This proved to be a fantastic showcase for young talent and resulted in many students being given job opportunities despite a shrinking economy.

Client Nike UK
Agency Simons Palmer Denton Clemmow & Johnson

Client Nike UK
Agency Simons Palmer Denton Clemmow & Johnson

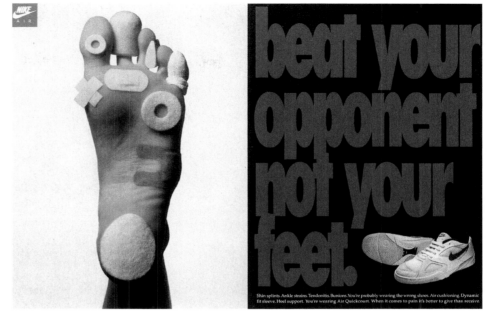

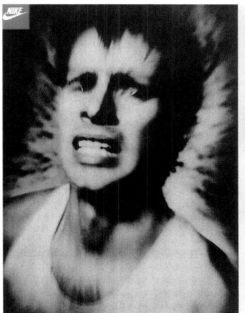

"
The Festival of Excellence attracted a remarkable attendance of 4,000 people over seven days in May.

We also laid the plans for the merger between D&AD and John Gillard's School of Communication Arts, which initially took space at our headquarters in Vauxhall and eventually moved to its own premises in Smithfield.

Given all this activity, it would be easy to forget to mention the work. Flicking back through the 1993 Annual is a real delight. Hats off to the still-fresh Nike campaign and Olympus ads. In Design, who wouldn't be inspired by the stylish and innovative elegance of the Harvey Nichols packaging and BIS publications? From our new Product Design category, the Bisque radiators also caught my eye as having more than stood the test of time.

Looking back on this turbulent year, it seems appropriate that the President's Award went to John Gorham, an outstandingly talented, honest and hardworking person who always did the right thing. God bless you John, we all miss you.

So, my Presidential year ended with both relief and pride. D&AD had not only survived but had grown and flourished in almost every area. None of this would have been possible without the wisdom and steady hand of Executive Chairman Anthony Simonds-Gooding, and the tireless and positive support of the D&AD staff and Executive Committee, who had endured a year of turmoil and worry. Thank you all, again. ●

Title **Harvey Nichols packaging**
Client **Harvey Nichols**
Design Group **Michael Nash Associates**

"1992 was about rebuilding and renewing D&AD among all this turbulence."

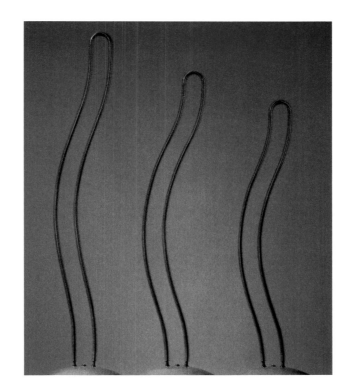

Title Bisque radiators
Client Bisque Radiators
Design Group Priestman Associates

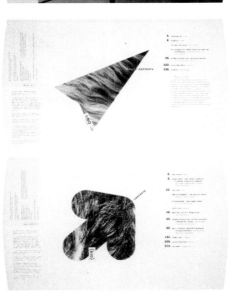

Title BIS publications
Client BIS Publishers
Design Group Koeweiden Postma

1994
Adrian Holmes

Adrian Holmes graduated in Film and Photographic Arts at the Polytechnic of Central London. Soon realising he was actually happier behind a typewriter than a tripod, he took a job as a junior copywriter at Grey in 1976.

After working his way through a frankly alarming number of agencies – including Leo Burnett, Abbott Mead Vickers, Foote Cone & Belding, Cogent Elliott, Colman & Partners, Saatchi & Saatchi, Collett Dickenson Pearce and WCRS – he finally settled down as joint Creative Director of Lowe Howard-Spink in 1989.

In 1999 he became worldwide Chief Creative Officer at Lowe, and in 2005 he moved to Young & Rubicam, where he spent five years as Executive Creative Director of its Europe, Middle East and Africa region.

Now no longer required to remove his shoes every morning at Heathrow Terminal 5, he is back writing advertising for various clients and agencies in London – and suddenly remembers why he came into this business in the first place.

1994 Annual

Annual Design **Lewis Moberly**
Cover Design **Michael Johnson**

Title We've Corrected Our Mistakes
Client D&AD
Agency Lowe Howard-Spink

Title Industrial Secrets for Sale
Client The Economist
Agency Abbott Mead Vickers BBDO

As I arrived as President-Elect in 1993 under Aziz Cami, there was what I can only describe as a thin haze of smoke still hanging in the air – the aftermath of Tim Delaney's explosive 1992 putsch. But without Tim's courageous one-man storming of the Bastille, I'm really not sure D&AD would be around today.

Our agency, Lowe Howard-Spink, wrote an ad for D&AD which neatly summed up the story so far. The visual showed the famous Yellow Pencil with the addition of an eraser on the end, and a headline which read: "We've corrected our mistakes."

There was indeed quite a lot to correct: the jury system was completely overhauled to make it more democratic and less susceptible to manipulation. The President-Elect system was introduced, so every future President spent a year getting to know the ropes before actually taking over – thus avoiding abrupt changes of policy every year. As a result of these and other changes, the Association's membership recovered from its disastrous low of 650 in 1992 to 1,387 in 1994 – an extraordinary turnaround.

Of course, the man who should really be credited with this recovery came in the towering form of Anthony Simonds-Gooding, brought in by Tim Delaney as D&AD's Chairman in a masterstroke of executive casting. He was the former Whitbread MD who had famously approved the 'Heineken Refreshes the Parts' campaign in the face of highly critical research, thus securing his impeccable creative credentials for all time. Just as crucially, his business savvy and reassuring "commander on the bridge" presence was exactly what D&AD needed to help steady the ship. When Anthony was deservedly awarded the CBE for services to the creative industries in 2010, I described him as "the giant maypole around whom we in the creative community have danced and frolicked".

Another key figure at this time was David Kester, who was appointed Chief Executive in 1994. His sheer energy and buttoned-down efficiency propelled D&AD ever forward for the next nine years. Lest we forget, D&AD will naturally revert to a state of organisational entropy and chaos given half the chance. It may be there to celebrate the finest flowering of creativity, but it will always need a stout trellis in order to do so.

The 1994 Annual itself is something I'm very proud of. It had a wonderfully executed cover designed by Michael Johnson, who turned the entire Book into an oversized zipped pencil-case, with just the word "pencils" blind-embossed on the shiny yellow plastic – very Beatles 'White Album'. The internal design and layout were also beautifully done, the work of Lewis Moberly: nothing tricksy, just elegant typography that you could actually read (compare please with the 1983 Annual, set in miniscule Eurostile Extended and the palest of pale greys – the whole thing could have been sponsored by Specsavers as far as I'm concerned).

More to the point was the actual work that year, and a very fine crop it was too. A Design Black Pencil went to the lovely BBC2 idents, while my favourite Advertising Yellow Pencil winner was AMV BBDO's 'Industrial Secrets for Sale' print ad for The Economist – I genuflect before its perfection. Also worthy of special mention are Levi's 'Creek', the Tony Kaye-directed 'Tested for the Unexpected' for Dunlop and the US 'Got Milk?' campaign – particularly the uproarious 'Aaron Burr' one. But I could easily add to that list the Boddingtons 'Cream of Manchester' print campaign, 'Supermarket Trolleys' for Heineken and 'Slow-Motion Crash' for Volvo.

"
Lest we forget, D&AD will naturally revert to a state of organisational entropy and chaos given half the chance.

Title **BBC2 idents**
Client **BBC Presentation**
Design Group **BBC Graphic Design Department**

Notice how old-school that list looks today: all were pieces executed in the classic mainstream media of television, press and poster. Back in 1994, the word "digital" had little if anything to do with our world; oh, how blissfully unaware we all were of Things to Come. There was also still a huge amount of creative snobbery surrounding the area of direct marketing. I once heard a so-called "above the line" agency refer to their direct marketing arm as follows: "Yes, well, we do the actual ideas. Those chaps downstairs fold them for us."

Looking back at my time as D&AD President, I now realise what a huge privilege it was to do the job, and I would like to underline my thanks to all those people who made the experience so much fun. I think the only aspect I really didn't enjoy was the incessant tin-rattling for sponsorship money – and I bet that hasn't changed.

Oh, and just one other thing: if anyone out there has got a 1963, 1971 or 1973 Annual they'd like to sell, let me know. Those three gaps on my D&AD bookshelf are really bugging me. ●

Title Dunlop – Tested for the Unexpected
Client SP Tyres UK
Agency Abbott Mead Vickers BBDO
Production Company Tony Kaye Films

Dunlop – 'Tested for the Unexpected'

MUSIC: The Velvet Underground's 'Venus in Furs'.

VIDEO: Strange demons orchestrate a series of attacks against a car equipped with Dunlop tyres.

The car has to dodge motorised pianos, forge flooded roads, avoid exploding bombs and grip to the road through a river of marbles.

It is evil versus the tyres, but the latter are more than a match for these bizarre hazards.

Dunlop. Tested for the unexpected.

Title Got Milk? – Aaron Burr
Client California Milk Processor Advisory Board
Agency Goodby Berlin & Silverstein

Got Milk? – 'Aaron Burr'

SFX: Radio playing Viennese classical music.

Open on large studio as camera slowly pans across several antique collections.

Cut to close-up of man spreading peanut butter on piece of bread.

Cut to large bookcase titled 'Hamilton's Memoirs', on which sits a large, framed painting of Alexander Hamilton.

RADIO DJ: And that was the Vienna Wood Dance… in B, one of my all time… favourites. Now let's make that… random call with today's $10,000 question.

Cut to man stuffing the folded, peanut butter piece of bread into his mouth.

RADIO DJ: …Who shot Alexander Hamilton in that famous duel?

Cut to two antique guns, presumably used in the famous duel.

Cut back to man, still with mouth full, sitting in front of phone and carton of milk. Camera moves around room, from statue of Hamilton, to famous bullet in showcase.

Cut to painting of duel between Aaron Burr and Alexander Hamilton.

SFX: Phone ringing.

MAN: Hewo?!

RADIO DJ: Hello, for $10,000… who shot...

MAN: Arwoon Boor!

RADIO DJ: Excuse me?

MAN: Arwoon Burr. Whai, hold on, lemme… dring some milk.

Cut to man as he pours a splash of milk form the carton. It's virtually empty.

RADIO DJ: I'm afraid your time is almost up.

MAN: Arwoon Boor!

RADIO DJ: I'm sorry. Maybe next time.

SFX: Phone hang-up. Dial tone.

MAN: (pathetically mumbles to himself) Arwoon Boor.

TITLE/SUPER: Got Milk?

Title **Creek**
Client **Levi's**
Agency **Bartle Bogle Hegarty**
Production Company **Lewin & Watson**

Levi's – 'Creek'

MUSIC: Classic choral music.

We see a middle-class family taking an excursion into the country in their horse-drawn cart, in 1866. Judging by their dress and demeanour, the two daughters have had a very strict and sheltered upbringing.

We see the family laying out a picnic. After the picnic, the two daughters wander off towards a creek. As they approach the creek, they see a young man in the water.

MUSIC: Changes suddenly to heavy guitar-led rock track.

We see the older girl's eyes as she stares, spellbound by the young man. We cut to her mouth as her lips slowly part, in awe. We pan down the young man's body as water laps over his torso… He appears to be naked. Her sister has found a pair of trousers by the edge of the water. She runs with the trouser, and hides behind a tree with her sister.

They wait, with a mixture of fear and excitement, as his body comes out of the water. He's wearing 501s. The girls look confused and glance down at the trousers they are holding. They look towards the creek. An old, bearded man is swimming towards them. The trousers clearly belong to him. The girls turn to watch the young man from behind the tree as he walks off through the forest.

SUPER: In 1873, Levi's jeans only came shrink-to-fit.

SUPER: (batwing logo) 501. The original jean.

> Back in 1994, the term 'digital' had little if anything to do with our world; oh, how blissfully unaware we all were of Things to Come.

1995
Mary Lewis

Mary Lewis is Creative Director at
Lewis Moberly, which she founded
in 1984 with Robert Moberly.

Her numerous awards include a
D&AD Black Pencil, three D&AD
Yellow Pencils and the D&AD
President's Award.

In 1995, she became the first female
President of D&AD.

Clients of her diverse, award-winning
brand design work include Waitrose,
Selfridges, La Grande Epicerie de
Paris, Grand Hyatt, Moët & Chandon
and Johnnie Walker.

Mary has been profiled in The
Sunday Times and the Financial
Times and is a contributing author
of 'Understanding Brands'.

1995 Annual

Annual Design Lewis Moberly
Cover Design John Gorham

Title Kaliber – Hello Girls
Client Guinness Brewing GB
Agency Euro RSCG WNEK Gosper

I am inevitably asked how it was to be D&AD's first female President. It was special, but as with my work as a designer, I have never had to think about it. However, there was a memorable aspect I used to enjoy. At the Presidents' Dinner, a gathering of the best boys in the industry, Anthony Simonds-Gooding would say, "Lady and gentlemen, please raise your glasses…"

1995 was the year we gave a new Award, the D&AD Special Award for Outstanding Contribution to Education, to somebody who was very special. The late John Gillard was a revered and inspirational tutor who ran the School of Communication Arts, and his contribution to education was phenomenal. Among the guests on Awards night were many of his former students. One by one they came up on stage, until a quarter of the room was emptied. Sam Cooke's 'Wonderful World' burst into sound and the great and good of design and advertising sang their hearts out to John.

I gave the first President's Award for Product Design. It went to Seymourpowell, a consultancy whose team were then best known for their work on motorbikes – they rode and designed them, and were known affectionately as "the bikers". Before I announced the

Award, the sound of roaring engines filled the room. All in all, it was a noisy night.

The President's Lectures were gathering momentum, attracting record audiences. Saul Bass lived his legend, Tony Kaye sang a song and Maurice Saatchi, whom I had never heard speak, told a story. Saatchi politics were rife then and it was an absolutely packed house. People expected some industry laundering, but he went out on stage in surprisingly beautiful suede shoes, and said, "I'm going to tell you all a story." The tension visibly went out of the room. He started telling the fable about the frog and the scorpion, and the whole audience just curled up.

As a designer President, I got charged with the "look" of D&AD. It had become sloppy and ad hoc – Committee meetings were productively (and sometimes dramatically) spent debating the merits of our equities! So we got the house in order – typefaces, colour, the Awards logo. We set our standards as high as those we expected of our members.

Not only was I President, but Lewis Moberly was nominated for a Yellow Pencil that year, so there was something of a dilemma as to how I would accept and present the Pencil simultaneously. I had an amusing time on stage with Ruby Wax swapping Pencils.

FedEx

Federal Express ®

Title FedEx logo
Client Federal Express
Design Group Landor Associates San Francisco

Title Snopake
Client Sternstat
Design Group Halpin Grey Vermeir

This was a year of firsts, not just for me and for D&AD, but for public engagement with design – the first public exhibition of 'The Cream of British Design & Advertising' was held at the Saatchi Gallery. Against this backdrop I have chosen five pieces of work, no easy decision. When I consider them collectively, the link is the power of poignant ideas.

Wonderbra's 'Hello Boys' set the tone of the year, politely cheeky and perfectly pitched. And cleverly bounced back by Kaliber's 'Hello Girls'! Guinness rode the crest of the wave, bravely, boldly and brilliantly.

On to D&AD, and its call for entries. This is my favourite. Our famous logo is beautifully observed to contain a powerful message. The creative team must have sat back and smiled.

One of the Yellow Pencils went to the Queen Elizabeth's Foundation for Disabled People. The message hits home with a thunderclap of poignancy and relevance.

Another nomination to get my vote is the Florida Coalition to Stop Gun Violence poster. The tension in this image is magnetic. It draws you in and then hits back hard. Love it.

I had a tough choice with symbols and typography, so I decided to go for two. Snopake's hidden delete sign is typical of Geoff Halpin's clever observation and masterful play with type. And FedEx is an all-time favourite. I like looking at it and writing it. There aren't many logos you can write as they are. Its simplicity is its power. ⬡

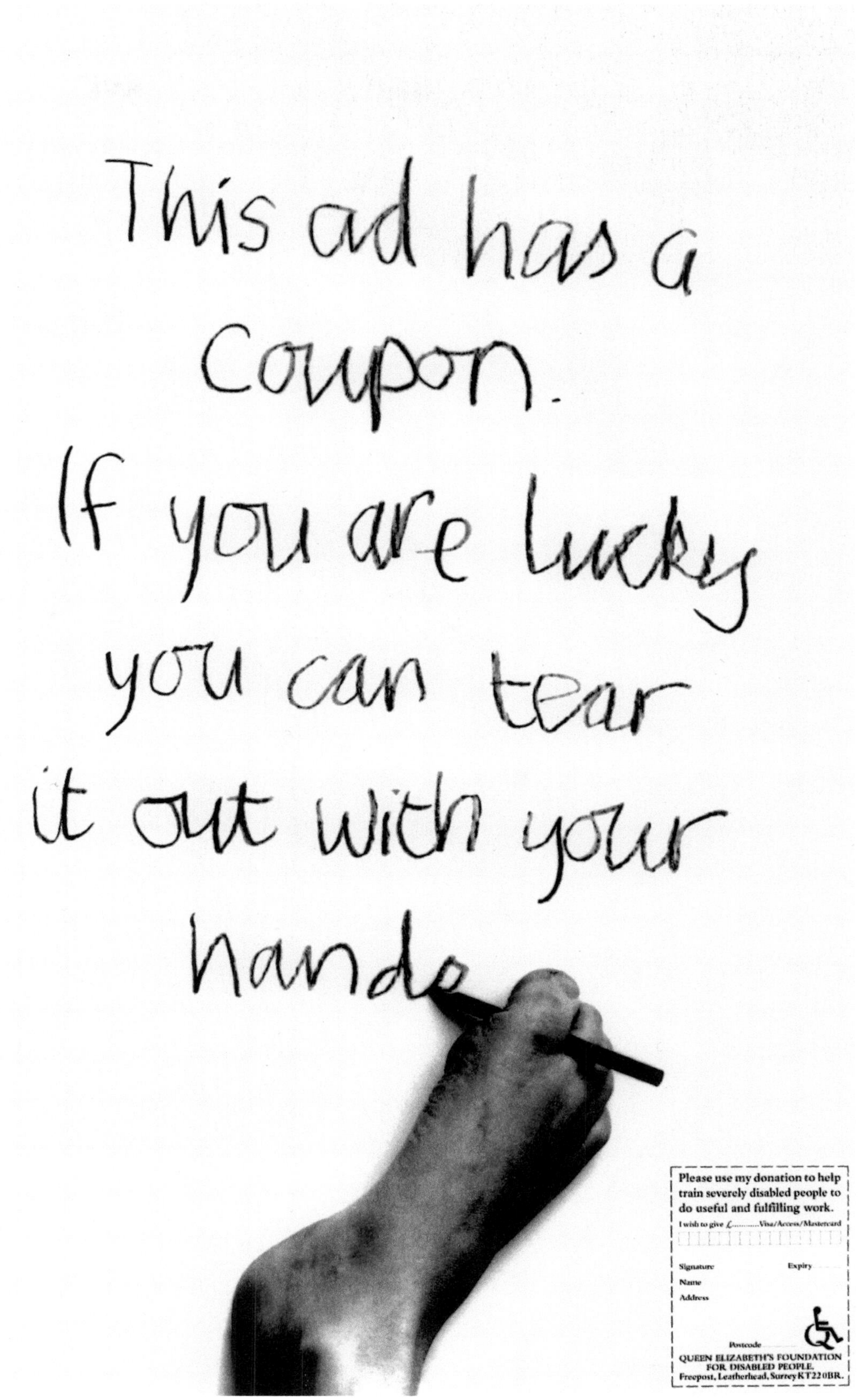

This ad has a coupon.
If you are lucky
you can tear
it out with your
hands

Please use my donation to help
train severely disabled people to
do useful and fulfilling work.

I wish to give £............Visa/Access/Mastercard

Signature   Expiry
Name
Address

Postcode
QUEEN ELIZABETH'S FOUNDATION
FOR DISABLED PEOPLE,
Freepost, Leatherhead, Surrey KT22 0BR.

Title Queen Elizabeth's Foundation for Disabled People
Client Queen Elizabeth's Foundation for Disabled People
Agency Abbott Mead Vickers BBDO

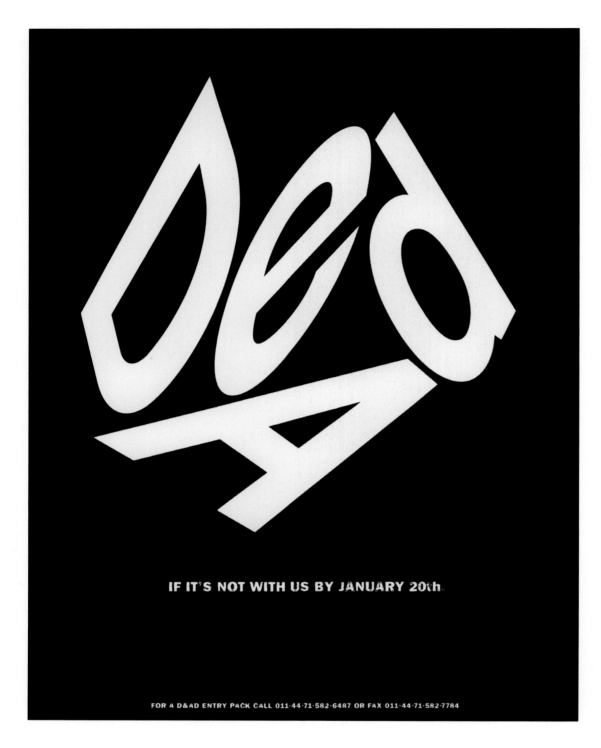

Title Dead
Client British Design & Art Direction
Agency Abbott Mead Vickers BBDO

" We got the house in
order – typefaces, colour,
the Awards logo. We set
our standards as high as
those we expected of
our members.

Title Florida Coalition to Stop Gun Violence
Client Florida Coalition to Stop Gun Violence
Agency Crispin & Porter

"It was a year of firsts, not just for me and for D&AD, but for public engagement with design – the first public exhibition of 'The Cream of British Design & Advertising' was held at the Saatchi Gallery.

1996
Graham Fink

Graham Fink's awarded work includes the British Airways 'Face' commercial, voted one of the 100 best commercials of all time, and work for Land Rover, Red Rock Cider, the Metropolitan Police, Hamlet cigars, Dixons and Transport for London. After landing his first job in 1981, he worked at Butler Dennis Garland, before moving to Collett Dickenson Pearce, then WCRS, Saatchi & Saatchi and Gold Greenlees Trott.

In 2001 he founded thefinktank, a conceptual production company.

In 2002 he set up The Art School, which some have called Britain's most radical art school.

In 2005 he became Creative Director at M&C Saatchi.

In 2011 he moved to Shanghai to be Chief Creative Officer for Ogilvy China.

1996 Annual

Annual Design **Peartree Design**
Cover Design **Tony Kaye**
Thanks to **CDT Design, Lewis Moberly**

1996 was, thank God, a vintage year for D&AD. Why the relief? Well, we had committed heresy and invited people from outside "the business" to sit on juries. Not just any old people, either. Gilbert & George and Damien Hirst on Illustration. Martin Amis and Will Self for Copywriting. Mel Smith and Griff Rhys Jones on Radio. Many will remember the controversy that raged around this decision. I still have a newspaper cutting from The Times debating the idea, and it was the "water-cooler conversation" of the year (although most places didn't actually have water coolers then, of course).

In the end, most of these "outsiders" didn't actually turn up, but it did have the desired effect of making D&AD famous in the real world and helped secure the sponsorship money we needed.

Three people dominated advertising in 1996: Tony Kaye, Walter Campbell and Tom Carty. That's not to say no one else got a look-in, but these guys were in the midst of their purple patch. The stories that came back from their shoots together were jaw-dropping. If social media had been around then, these guys would have been the Twitterati.

Amidst rumours of going massively over budget and Tony shooting 1,000 miles of film, their 'Twister' TV spot for Volvo took most of the Pencils that year (including the elusive Black for Direction). It is interesting to note that after the first round of judging, it actually failed to get into the Annual. Thankfully, after much debate, it was brought back, and the rest is history. There's a lesson to be learned there, somewhere.

Guess? was the other big winner, with an epic spot starring Harry Dean Stanton, Juliette Lewis and Traci Lords. Stunning filmmaking by Andy Morahan ensured it won a clutch of Pencils too. Bastards!

Another one of my favourites was Bartle Bogle Hegarty's Audi ad. You know, the one where an arrogant city boy boasts about his lifestyle while behind the wheel of a shiny new Audi. Only at the end do we realise he's actually on a test drive, as he throws back the keys back to the bemused salesmen with a "Nah, not really my style, know what I mean?" Frank Budgen directed this one, helping him notch up an amazing 15 entries in the Book (the same number as Tom and Walt).

A ten-second Peperami Mini ad was another popular winner, with an edgy piece of animation featuring a Peperami stick grating his own head off. The endline "A Little Bit of an Animal" was a classic.

Meanwhile, with faster computers and shiny new buttons, some amazing things were being done in the land of Pop Promos. A whole bunch of us would regularly sit glued to a monitor trying to work out how something had been done, especially on Mark Romanek's film for Michael and Janet Jackson ('Scream'). Rumoured to have cost over $6million, their double act in a spaceship dazzled us with its technological brilliance.

Michel Gondry was a name on everyone's lips. The quietly spoken but very demanding French fella had by this time invented dozens of new techniques and half of adland were queuing around the block to work with him. His video for the Rolling Stones was sublime: morphing 7,500 photographs together to mesmerising effect, Gondry gave the world a technique that has been copied a million times since, but never bettered.

Meanwhile, Spike Jonze fashioned another memorable Björk video, and young genius Jonathan Glazer created a classic film for Radiohead's 'Street Spirit (Fade Out)' that made "speed-ramping" all the rage.

> "Michel Gondry was a name on everyone's lips... Half of adland were queuing up around the block to work with him.

Title Clockwork radio
Client Baygen Power International
Design Group TKO Product Design

Title Lamppost
Client Adidas
Agency Leagas Delaney

Sadly, while new legends were being born, one legend died this year. His name was Helmut Krone. If you're a young art director and have never heard of him, hang your head in shame. Remember those great Volkswagen ads – 'Lemon'? 'Think Small'? They were by Helmut Krone, and with them he changed the way that press ads looked forever. I'll always remember one thing he said: "Show me a page I've never seen before." In 1996, Dave Dye and Adidas showed us that page with 'Lamppost'. It's one of my all-time favourite ads.

In Hollywood, David Fincher made a much talked-about film, 'Se7en'. Talked about not simply because of – spoiler alert – Gwyneth Paltrow's head in a box, but because of the title sequence, which rightly won a Pencil in Graphic Design and spawned a plethora of lookalikes. The other important film of the year was 'Trainspotting', directed by Danny Boyle. The iconic film poster got into the Book for Design and on to bedroom walls everywhere.

Talking of walls, that master of typography Len Cheeseman designed a series of "graffitied" ones in Auckland for the Red Cross. Le Grande Fromage was given the freedom to the city as a result. They look as fresh today as they did back then.

Closer to home, the trendiest girl on the block, Miss Tiger Savage, was making a big name for herself with some of the freshest art direction around. This was especially evident in her Levi's 'Cut in the 60s' campaign, created with the equally talented Paul Silburn.

In the design world, Alan Fletcher, as always, dominated. His iconic book covers were especially strong. Alan always had a mischievous glint in his eye and a visit to his studio gave you a clue as to why he was such a brilliant creative. Whether making animals out of cardboard or gluing together thousands of tiny nails and painting them into faces, evidence of the childlike enthusiasm that shone through his work was everywhere. I always thought the advertising world could learn a lot from him.

1996 was also the year that Trevor Bayliss devised his now classic clockwork radio. I could go on and on... so much talent this year and a fantastic Book. Looking back, it makes me want to grab my layout pad and do something better, which is what D&AD is all about, isn't it? ●

> "In Hollywood, David Fincher made a much talked-about film, 'Se7en'. Talked about not simply because of – spoiler alert – Gwyneth Paltrow's head in a box, but because of the title sequence.

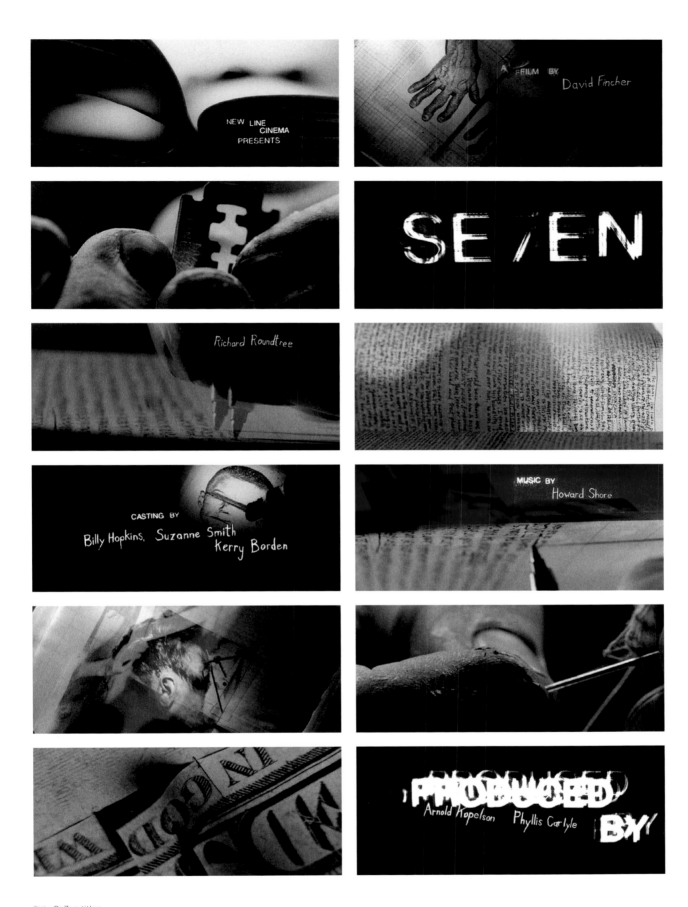

Title Se7en titles
Client: New Line Cinema/David Fincher Design
Agency: R/Greenberg Associates

Title Twister
Client Volvo Cars UK
Agency Abbott Mead Vickers BBDO

Volvo UK – 'Twister'

METEOROLOGIST VO:
A tornado is a rapidly rotating
column of air in contact with
the ground. It comes from
thunderstorms.

You've got to get yourself
there in the exact spot that
the tornado forms.

Sometimes rain and hail wrap
around this region and envelop it,
and we call that 'The Bear's Cage'
and that's a very, very dangerous
area to be in.

We drop probes into the paths of
tornadoes, trying to get an idea
of what kind of force is contained
within these vortices.

We hope to be able to forecast
these storms better... to save lives.

Manoeuvrability is very important.

It handles the road like it's on rails.

We have to depend on the vehicle
for our lives.

Title Cheat
Client Guess?
Agency Paul Marciano Advertising

Guess? – 'Cheat'

A seedy private investigator in Los Angeles takes a brief from a new client.

This rich young woman wants her fiancé's fidelity put to the test.

The private eye puts Julie, one of his decoys, on to the case. His girls know how to dress for and talk to men.

He tells us that Julie is trying to get through college. She admits that she gets into scary situations, but it's a job and the money is great.

Later, clothed in Guess?, she's picked up in a bar while the PI records the meeting from his car outside.

Given a few chances to clear himself her quarry denies his relationship. Three times.

"Bingo," says the PI.

Julie walks out of the bar, the job complete.

"My girls look so good, people ask me, 'Is it fair?'" he says. "And I have to tell them, quite frankly… no."

And he gives a wry chuckle.

1997
Mike Dempsey

Mike Dempsey has been a graphic designer for over 40 years. He spent the first decade in publishing, then founded design consultancy CDT Design in 1979.

He has created everything from stamps for Royal Mail and feature-film title sequences for Ridley Scott, Louis Malle, Dennis Potter, David Hare and Bruce Beresford to visual identities for English National Opera, the Southbank Centre, the Design Museum and the London Chamber Orchestra.

Dempsey has won ten D&AD Yellow Pencils and a Black Pencil, as well as the Chartered Society of Designers' Minerva award. He is a member of Alliance Graphique Internationale and a past Master of the Royal Designers for Industry, and was President of D&AD in 1997. He set up Studio Dempsey in 2008.

1997 Annual

Annual Design Peartree Design
Cover Design Fernando Gutiérrez
Art Direction Mike Dempsey

1997 was a dramatic year of change for Britain. A beaming Tony Blair swept into power with a landslide victory for New Labour. Channel 5 was launched. We won the Eurovision Song Contest for the first time in 18 years with Katrina & the Waves' 'Love Shine a Light', and 'The English Patient' received nine Oscars, including Best Picture. We said farewell to Hong Kong, and the public was outraged by the Royal Academy's 'Sensation' exhibition. NASA landed a probe on the surface of Mars, and the whole world was stunned by the sudden death of Princess Diana.

In that same year, D&AD celebrated its 35th birthday, and, as President, I presided over some major changes too. After decades of rowdy behaviour at the Grosvenor House Hotel, we moved the annual Awards to two new venues. The first was the Empire Leicester Square where, for the first time, we were able to accommodate students. After that, it was a leisurely stroll (admittedly in the rain) to the Café Royal for the Dinner.

In 1997 we introduced the D&AD Education Council, ring-fencing £500,000 for it and making possible the first Student Awards Annual. All past Presidents were given free life membership in recognition for the time and effort donated over the years. And we introduced the Presidents' Dinner, giving me the great pleasure of entertaining 18 past Presidents, all squeezed into a private room at the Groucho Club. It remains an annual event 15 years on – happily, at a bigger venue.

Title Muzik Masters
Client Deconstruction/Muzik
Design Group Farrow Design

"

1997 was a dramatic year of change
for Britain. A beaming Tony Blair swept
into power with a landslide victory for
New Labour. Channel 5 was launched.
We won the Eurovision Song Contest
for the first time in 18 years...

Fifteen years ago, D&AD was relatively
buoyant, in a large part due to the
enthusiastic and passionate David Kester
at the helm (a man who could generate
sponsorship coffers at the drop of a hat),
along with the guiding hand of Anthony
Simonds-Gooding as Chairman. During
the year, D&AD increased its turnover by
28 per cent. Things were looking rosy.

Interactive Media, as it was then called,
was introduced as a category, and this
change was signalled on the front of the
elegant D&AD Annual cover, designed by
Fernando Gutiérrez. It featured a single
computer button. On the back there was
a lone pencil-sharpener and a beautifully
written appreciation of the humble pencil,
crafted by the extemporary talent of Will
Awdry. I gave the President's Award to
that brilliant master of television branding,
Martin Lambie-Nairn, for his outstanding
contribution to our industry.

So, what of the work in that year?
It is often de rigueur for the old guard
to lament the passing of the so-called
"golden days", when they felt work was
"exceptional". But it is only when you
take the time to look back that you can
really assess the quality of the work.
More often than not, it doesn't live up
to an often overinflated memory.

Title Eurostar train
Client Eurostar UK
Design Group Jones Garrard

"You don't have to wait, as you used to do, for a D&AD Annual to show you the way. Now, great work is floating around the ether 24/7 for all to view, admire and be inspired by.

Flipping through that 1997 Annual now, it is easy to spot the special pieces – work that still stands up, despite the prevailing style of the time.

In Graphics, Mark Farrow's beautiful CD packaging for 'Muzik Masters' by the Deconstruction/Muzik label is as beguiling as when I first saw it 15 years ago.

From Posters, it was the great idea and wit of Bates Dorland's startling poster for the Discovery Channel's 'Shark Week' that is still a winner for me, even though it didn't actually win anything.

Meanwhile, Advertising that year saw a rare airing of beauty and craft in the shape of a campaign for English Heritage from Leagas Delaney. Wonderful long-form writing, typography and art direction, and supreme execution.

A Product Design highlight came in the shape of the sleek front-end of Eurostar. I still love watching it as it cuts through the countryside. It combines a lovely sense of movement and elegance, perfectly realised by Jones Garrard.

Title Shark Week is Back
Client Discovery Channel
Agency Bates Dorland

Title John 2 Yuri
Client one 2 one
Agency Bartle Bogle Hegarty

one 2 one – 'John 2 Yuri'

JOHN MCCARTHY: Who would I most like to have a one 2 one with? An astronaut. It would have to be the first: Yuri Gagarin. I'd want to know what drove him to sit in that tiny cockpit, on top of what was little more than a giant firework.

He chose to risk everything. He really did go where no man had gone before, not knowing if he'd ever come back. He was up there for only 108 minutes. It must have seemed like years – if not to him, to his family.

If I could have a one 2 one with Yuri Gagarin I'd want to ask how he felt about being unknown one day, and next morning being the most famous man on the planet. When you've seen the world totally at peace as he did, how do you come to terms with the fact that it isn't?

SUPER: McCarthy 2 Gagarin.

VO: Who would you most like to have a one 2 one with?

TITLE/SUPER: one 2 one. the people to have a one 2 one with.

In TV & Cinema Advertising, the one 2 one commercial from Bartle Bogle Hegarty, directed by Mehdi Norowzian, epitomises the collaborative process of filmmaking. All of the creative disciplines have to work seamlessly together to deliver the whole, from direction, cinematography, art direction and sound design to the equally important post-production areas.

I bought my first D&AD Annual in 1964. A rather slim, humble, black and white affair. But it inspired the hell out of me and I was determined to be eventually included in its pages. I wanted to be part of that creative elite. And that is what D&AD continues to do. It is about inspiring everyone to be better.

Who would have thought that from its beginnings back in 1962, D&AD would have evolved to the international big-shot it is today? For me, the international dimension has somewhat diminished our individual creative identity. But we are now exposed to so many world influences via the internet, that would have happened anyway. We can now see what everyone is doing at the click of a mouse. To an extent, that is the real danger for D&AD. You don't have to wait, as you used to do, for a D&AD Annual to show you the way. Now great work is floating around the ether 24/7 for all to view, admire and be inspired by.

Also, there are the ever-increasing "global awards" popping up every year. The design industry has expanded vastly, with many solo practitioners working in a fiercely competitive market. Many of those young designers consider D&AD as both expensive and irrelevant in this digital age, and have found new and more immediate ways to share and celebrate work.

As it reaches its 50th anniversary, let's hope that D&AD can keep up the standards it set all those years ago and keep those stubby little Yellow and Black Pencils rapier-sharp. As for the White Pencil, well, time will tell.

IN 1092 William Rufus, angered that Carlisle was *proclaimed* part of Scotland, went north, drove the Scots out and ordered the building of a stronghold in the borderlands. Thus *Carlisle Castle* was constructed just half a mile outside the city. And ever since it has been the scene of numerous battles with different factions fighting for ownership. It was besieged by parliamentarians in the Civil War, then by Bonnie Prince Charlie during the Jacobite Rising. In order to repel such attacks, the castle defences have been extensively remodelled over the centuries. Perhaps the most notable 'guest' at Carlisle Castle was *Mary Queen of Scots*, a prisoner there back in 1568. You can see Queen Mary's Tower and take the very route she took during her daily walks around the grounds.

THIS year marks the 250th anniversary of the imprisonment of *Jacobites* inside Carlisle Castle following the 1745 Rising. Led by Bonnie Prince Charlie, they succeeded in taking Carlisle Castle before marching southwards to claim the throne for Charlie's father, James Stuart. An *exhibition* within the castle tells the dramatic story of the Jacobites' movements. *How* they returned north in defeat with the Duke of Cumberland's men hot on their heels. *How* they were captured and imprisoned, many of them later to be hanged, drawn and quartered on the nearby *Gallows Hill*. In a dungeon, you will see the famous *Licking Stones*. A permanently moist wall which provided a little water for the Jacobites in this overcrowded prison.

Located in the small village of Belsay, 14 miles north-west of Newcastle, *Belsay Hall* consists of a well-preserved fourteenth-century castle, the ruins of a seventeenth-century mansion and one of the most important *neo-classical* houses in Britain. But the real jewels in the crown are the 30 acres of magnificent formal gardens, exotic quarry gardens and woodland that surround the buildings. A stroll through the grounds at Belsay

reveals sycamore, oak and ash trees, the Magnolia Terrace, the Rhododendron Garden, the lovely Meadow Garden. Much of what you see there reflects the eccentric character of *Sir Charles Monck*. He returned from his 19-month European honeymoon, 1804–1806, full of ideas to build a *new home* at Belsay in beautiful neo-Greek style. And to have it set in an equally beautiful landscape.

TO celebrate the 1996 Year of Visual Arts, Belsay Hall will come alive again from 9th May until 26th October. The '*Living at Belsay*' exhibition will feature the work of selected craftsmakers and artists who'll be refurbishing the entrance and the three main reception rooms. It's a novel idea which will see the normally bare rooms equipped with magnificent furniture, fine ceramics, glassware and wall hangings. A rare chance to see contemporary artistry in an historical setting.

WHEN
YOU BUILD A CASTLE FOR A KING WHO'S RENOWNED FOR CHOPPING PEOPLE'S HEADS OFF, YOU BUILD A REALLY NICE CASTLE.

WHEN Osborne House was completed in 1851 to provide a country residence for Queen Victoria, it was considered by Her Majesty to be 'small and snug'. However, to humble subjects such as you and I, it is anything but. *Osborne*, on the Isle of Wight, served as a peaceful seaside retreat where Queen Victoria and Prince Albert could escape the strict confines of ceremony. And a *magnificent* retreat it is too. Albert's passion for the Italian *Renaissance* is clearly evident, what with the Italianate terrace, the Andromeda fountain and the cement copies of the fine Medici Lions from the *Loggia de' Lanzi*, Florence. Inside you will see a classical Roman statue, the *Marine Venus*, a lovely fresco painting by William Dyce and lots of extravagant grotesque decoration. In the Durbar Room there's a change of country, this state banqueting hall having been designed in the Indian style. Other rooms worth visiting are the Royal Apartments, the Billiards Room and the Nursery Suite. And the perfect way to *finish your day* at Osborne House is to take a Victorian horse and carriage ride from the main building to the delightful Swiss Cottage, a present from the Queen to her children in 1854.

HENRY VIII aside, many other royals have spent time at WALMER CASTLE. Amongst them Queen Victoria and the current Lord Warden, HRH *the Queen Mother*. Indeed, this delightful residence, just a mile from Deal in Kent, boasts an extremely impressive list of distinguished visitors. Like William Pitt the Younger, who was Lord Warden until his death in 1806. He would try and visit whenever his official duties would allow. A later Lord Warden, the *Duke of Wellington*, was equally taken with his 'charming marine residence'. His room is arranged just as it was during his stay, its plain, modest furnishings bearing testimony to the Iron Duke's preference for unsophisticated surroundings. You can see the very armchair where he died in 1852, his campaign-bed which still retains its original horsehair mattress and, in the WELLINGTON MUSEUM just along the corridor, the boots worn by the celebrated British war hero.

Walmer Castle, Kent.

D URABILITY, not beauty, was the main requirement in the construction of *Walmer Castle*. However, the architects, not wishing to take any chances with the notoriously hard to please Henry VIII, wisely decided to address both issues. One of a chain of coastal artillery forts, Walmer was built to thwart any invasions by Spain or France. This was a real possibility as Henry's split with the Roman Catholic Church and destruction of many monasteries had infuriated the papacy. The castle differed from earlier mediæval defences in that it had no high walls or lofty towers. In fact, so *attractive* was Walmer that only minor modifications were needed to make it the comfortable residence it is today. For more information on English Heritage and our role in preserving the nation's significant buildings please *call* 0171 973 3434 or *visit* any one of our 400 sites.   It's yours. Why not visit it.

ENGLISH HERITAGE

WHILST
WINSTON CHURCHILL WAS INVOLVED IN OPERATION DYNAMO AT DOVER CASTLE, DOCTOR JENKINS WAS INVOLVED IN OPERATION BERT'S LEFT LEG 60 FEET BELOW.

DURING World War II, when many British women and children found refuge in London's tube stations, many British soldiers were hiding in an underground system too: *The Secret Wartime Tunnels* beneath Dover Castle. A maze of passages, offices and hospital dormitories which served as a military base for Churchill's troops. It was here that one Vice-Admiral Ramsay masterminded the evacuation of Dunkirk. And here that hundreds of casualties of war received the finest of medical attention. You can experience their sights, sounds and even smells at Dover Castle. To find out more information on English Heritage and our role in preserving the nation's significant buildings, please *call* 0171 973 3434 or visit any one of our 400 sites.   It's yours. Why not visit it.

ENGLISH HERITAGE

HADRIAN'S WALL
IS MUCH MORE PLEASANT THESE DAYS. EVERYBODY LEAVES WITH EXACTLY THE SAME NUMBER OF LIMBS THEY CAME WITH.

A TRIP to the northernmost parts of England during Emperor Hadrian's reign wasn't quite the delightful day out it is today. Marauding local tribes, hostile to the foreign presence of Rome, were often involved in brutal conflicts with Hadrian's troops. In AD 122, to keep these bloodthirsty northern 'savages' away from the Roman's 'civilised' world, the emperor ordered the construction of a 73-mile *wall* which would run from coast to coast along the north of England. Each mile punctuated by a small fort. So *outstanding* is this piece of Roman military engineering that Hadrian's Wall has since been designated a World Heritage Site. For more information on English Heritage and our role in preserving the nation's significant buildings, please *call* 0171 973 3434 or *visit* any one of our 400 sites.   It's yours. Why not visit it.

ENGLISH HERITAGE

Title English Heritage campaign
Client English Heritage
Agency Leagas Delaney

1998
Tim Mellors

Tim Mellors is based in New York and
is the Worldwide Creative Director of
Grey Group. He has been a magazine
journalist, a commercial film director and
the host of a TV series, and is a trained
psychotherapist. He has been Creative
Director for Publicis, Saatchi & Saatchi,
Gold Greenlees Trott and his own agency,
Mellors Reay.

He has been President of D&AD,
President of the Jury at Cannes, and
President of the Creative Circle. Tim's
awards include five D&AD Pencils and
15 Lions (three of them Gold). In 2002,
Tim was awarded a doctorate in the arts
by the university of his home city, Derby.

1998 Annual

Annual Design **Peartree Design**
Cover Design **Paul Pickersgill**
Cover Photography **Paul Zak**
Typography **Andy Dymock; Typeworks**

'Parklife'. 60 seconds. One minute. 1997 in a nutshell. Brash, colourful, exciting, crude, populist and annoyingly watchable.

Is it Blur's track? Jonathan Glazer's pop art direction? Rick Lawley's splintered editing? Or simply the schoolboy antics of Eric Cantona, Ian Wright and Robbie Fowler? No, it's all of it. It's Nike bringing the Premiership to Hackney Marshes.

Nobody in the world can hold a candle to what was happening on TV and in the cinema in the England of 1997.

Before every man and his dog were directing, before you could make an internet film for the price of a sandwich, real directors were making real scripts that were as modern and cool as anything today, but also skilfully crafted masterpieces, true works of art.

Watch the calm way Gregory Rood assembles the galaxy of stars at his disposal to each sing a line of Lou Reed's 'Perfect Day' for the BBC. It's a masterpiece of restraint, a collection of faultless cameos that perfectly demonstrates how eclectic and influential the Beeb has been in the world of music.

Behold The Mill's Pierre Ruffin's magically dark effects for Michel Gondry's Smirnoff commercials. It's a brilliantly simple idea from Lowe Howard-Spink that dances dangerously on the edge of the unspoken promise of vodka – that it will make you hallucinatingly drunk. No wonder the client looked sheepish.

Those on-the-knuckle, hair-bristlingly uncomfortable, dead-eyed observations seem to characterise all the best work of this period.

Glazer again with a seminal black and white reportage piece for Volkswagen. Riots, petrol bombs, snarling alsatians and a punch in the gut. But not a single frame of the car going round an Alpine hairpin bend. Instead we've got Jeremy Craigen's spare, gloriously understated endline about the safety of the little Polo: "Have you ever noticed how protected you feel when you make yourself small?"

If you think that's minimalist, have a marvel at the pared-down simplicity of the work for London Underground done by the creative directors on that VW job, Richard Flintham and Andy McLeod. It's a poster of the Thames from above, the Piccadilly Circus statue of Anteros at one end, a house at the other.

Title The Power of Books
Client Waterstone's Booksellers
Agency BDDP GGT

"Before you could make an internet film for the price of a sandwich, real directors were making real scripts that were as modern and cool as anything today.

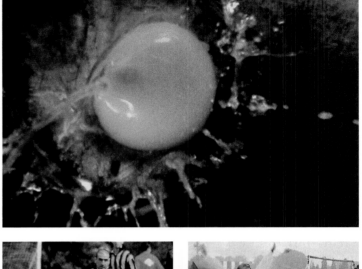

BBC – 'Perfect Day'

The film demonstrates the diversity of the BBC's musical output.

Throughout, we see a series of moving 'slides', depicting various international musical artists interpreting Lou Reed's 'Perfect Day'. These are intercut with slides of a beautiful English garden, photographed from dawn to sunset.

The impression is that we are sharing someone's musical memories.

The performers range from Lou Reed to Tom Jones, David Bowie to Boyzone, Lesley Garrett to Heather Small, Shane MacGowan to Tammy Wynette. We also see the Brodsky Quartet, Courtney Pine and Andrew Davies conducting the BBC Symphony Orchestra. Finally, as the sun sets in the garden, we see a series of titles.

TITLE: Whatever your musical taste, BBC radio and television caters for it.

TITLE: This is only possible thanks to the unique way the BBC is paid for by you.

Fade up BBC logo.

TITLE: You make it what it is.

Nike – 'Parklife'

WOMAN: Football, football, football. We get nothing but football morning, noon and night.

MAN: Shut up.

(Music starts: 'Parklife' by Blur.)

Confidence is a preference for the habitual voyeur of what is known as (Parklife)

And morning soup can be avoided if you take a route straight through what is known as (Parklife)

John's got brewers droop he gets intimidated by the dirty pigeons, they love a bit of it (Parklife)

Who's that gut lord marching? You should cut down on your porklife mate, get some exercise

CHORUS: All the people
So many people
They all go hand in hand
Hand in hand through their parklife

Know what I mean?

NIKE LOGO & CAPTION: Whatever league you're in...

Just do it.

Title Perfect Day
Client BBC
Agency Leagas Delaney

Title Parklife
Client Nike
Agency TBWA Simons Palmer

Smirnoff – 'Smarienberg'

This commercial is an exciting chase through time and space. It takes place by means of the Smirnoff bottle which magically transforms one scene to the next.

The adventure begins with our heroine who sits waiting in a bar. Through the Smirnoff bottle she sees her boyfriend rush in. She pulls out a gun and shoots at him. But when we see through the bottle the scene transforms, her bullet changing into a bee that is attacking an evil warlord with the girl now lying on a bed behind. Suddenly her boyfriend smashes through the window and snatches her up before diving out again, pursued by the enraged warlord.

The chase continues through a storm-tossed boat, a Transcontinental Express and a rugged desert pursued by a menacing UFO, until finally the boyfriend is cornered in an alley in Chinatown.

Just as the warlord's men close in, our hero escapes through a rusty door. From the other side and through the bottle we see him reappear in the bar – as in the beginning of the commercial – except this time we can see his pursuers too. Bang! The heroine's bullet shatters the bottle. The villains vanish and the hero escapes into the arms of the heroine.

Title Smarienberg
Client Pierre Smirnoff Company
Agency Lowe Howard-Spink

VW Polo – 'Protection'

We see rioters being repelled by water cannons, a fallen jockey in danger of being trampled by other horses, a man attacked by dogs, a boxer taking repeated blows from his opponent and firemen being engulfed by a backdraft of fire.

TITLE: Have you ever noticed how protected you feel when you make yourself small?

We fade up on a Polo.

TITLE: Polo.

TITLE: VW.

Title Protection
Client Volkswagen
Agency BMP DDB

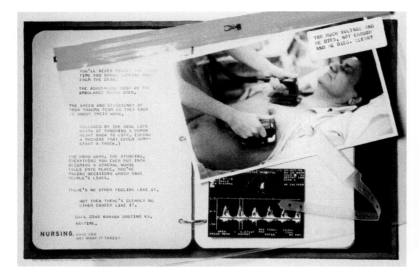
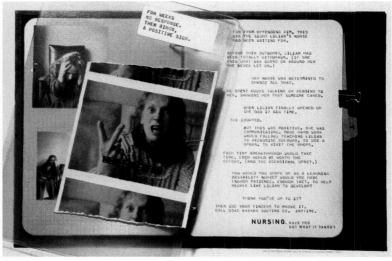
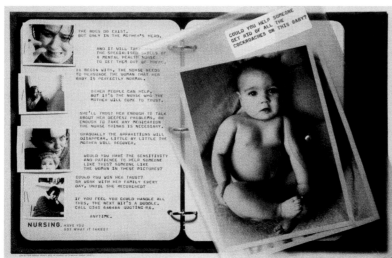
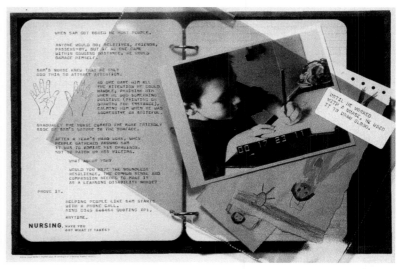

Title Nursing campaign
Client Department of Health/COI
Agency Saatchi & Saatchi

> **Delightfully underwritten by Mike McKenna, it's a series of open casefiles that ask if you have what it takes to deal with them.**

That's it, except for the line: "Making London simple." Not exactly door-to-door brush-selling, but so evocative and elegant it's in the Annual six times.

Saatchi & Saatchi's nursing campaign is the heavyweight in Press, another whispering wonder that grabs your attention in the sneakiest of ways. Delightfully underwritten by Mike McKenna, it's a series of open casefiles that ask if you have what it takes to deal with them. Roger Kennedy's impeccable typography. John Messum and Colin Jones's deceptively unassuming art direction and Graham Cornthwaite's truthful pictures are as about as 90s realism as it gets.

Paul Belford and Nigel Roberts's Waterstone's campaign for GGT summed

up the decade with a charred volume by Hitler, Pol Pot and Mao Tse-Tung alongside the line, "...were right about one thing. The Power of Books." Somehow it just wouldn't be the same with a melted Kindle.

Of course, some things change and some just seem to go on forever. David Bailey, who was my choice for the President's Award in 1998, is enjoying an umpteenth reinvention this year. He's got a new exhibition – this time it's his paintings – and there's a drama doc on the telly about his first Vogue shoot in New York with Jean Shrimpton. I've been working in Manhattan myself for the past eight years. Looking back at London, looking back at my time as D&AD President... it's a bittersweet experience. But as Bailey would say, "Screw that, mate. What's next?"

1963 1964 1965 1966 1967 1968 1969 1970 1971 1972 1973 1974 1975 1976 1977 1978 1979 1980 1981 1982 1983 1984 1985 1986 1987

Title Making London Simple
Client London Transport
Agency BMP DDB

1999
Richard Seymour

Richard Seymour is co-Founder and
Design Director of Seymourpowell.

Having initially trained as a graphic
designer and illustrator, Richard moved
quickly through advertising and film
production design before setting up
Seymourpowell with Dick Powell in 1984.

Since then, the consultancy has risen to
the forefront of product and innovation
design, with a string of world firsts to its
credit, including the first cordless kettle,
the first pocket mobile phone and the first
private spaceship (for Virgin).

He is a formidable public speaker,
Creative Director (a role he undertakes
for several of Unilever's global brands),
futurist, foodie and occasional musician.

He has been awarded the D&AD Award
for Outstanding Contribution to Design,
the FX Lifetime Achievement Award
and Senior Fellowship of the
Royal College of Art.

1999 Annual

Annual Design **Peartree Design**
Cover Design **Farrow Design**
Section Dividers **Farrow Design**

It was a great time to be President, and it was an even better time to be a Product Design President. As the millennium hurtled towards its otherwise rather feeble conclusion (remember the river of fire and how our computers were all going to blow up?), the Book saw Product Design rise like Prometheus.

The iMac, in all its candy-coated glory, served notice upon an ad-drenched membership that the product wasn't something you just wrote a campaign about, but something that propagated itself by dint of its own infectious excellence. It was something so astounding that it jumped the species barrier from mushroom-coloured office equipment to domestic interior decor in a single, athletic leap. At this stage of its development (easy to say now), Apple was transitioning from early-adopter techie through gumball domestic to New Modernism, its universal aesthetic for global dominance. Nobody, even during this glorious moment, could possibly imagine that, 13 years later, this company would be the most valuable brand on the planet; its brilliant progenitor, Steve Jobs, would be dead; and its focused and deferential design wizard would have become Sir Jonathan Ive. Or that its stock value would virtually double after Jobs's death, for that matter.

The sobering truth is that the iMac was already in the minds of Apple's high presidium years before we got to see it. It's possible that the iPad was already on their roadmap by the time the 1999 Annual went to print.

Jobs once reflected that the great thing about the future was that there were no competitors there. The further into the future your thinking went, the more you could shape it. He didn't believe that the future was something that just happened to you.

Audi's submission, the TT, was another gobsmacking example of how a technically competent but otherwise somewhat dull auto brand could deliver a heart-stopping confection into the overstocked hot hatch market. It re-wrote the book on German visual language. Was it a car or a low-flying Me 109? Was it a Bang & Olufsen-pimped buzz bomb or an underpowered piece of curb candy?

Whatever. It was cool, impudent and, yes, emotional.

Audi got to New Modernism before Apple in the pantheon of millennial product design, then lost it in the subsequent decade, whereas Apple just kept on going.

TBWA's 'Double Life' TV commercial for Sony was an absolute stonker this year too, not just for its indelible visual imagery (try looking at this mad kid's face and not hear the words "…and conquered worlds" ringing in your ears), but for the prescience it demonstrated as to where digital technology was actually heading. It would be four more years before Second Life and Facebook were launched, but already the democracy and etiquette of a virtual existence were being prototyped and played out in the gaming world.

You need to read this script to remind yourself what it felt like to be released from your humdrum yadda-yadda existence and pitched into a world where you could relinquish your inadequacies and physical disabilities to become a Master of the Universe on a low-res colour LCD.

Much has changed since then, yet much has stayed the same. The anthropology is identical but the toys are a little shinier.

Massive Attack's pop video for 'Teardrop' raised some eyebrows by portraying what appeared to be a living human foetus in vivo, until the little rascal started singing along to Liz Frazer's eerie lyrics. Great close-ups of a consummate piece of animatronic model-making really had you believing it, until the camera pulled out to reveal the whole thing. At the time, we didn't know that we were witnessing the beginning of the end of the art of physical movie model-making, so it is a significant marker of when we began to go, "Yeah… it's not real," in the realms of the moving image.

Title **Audi TT**
Client **Audi**
Design Team **Audi AG**

Title iMac
Client Apple Computer
Design Group Apple Design Team

> **"**
> Steve Jobs once reflected that the great thing about the future was that there were no competitors there. The further into the future your thinking went, the more you could shape it.

Funny, isn't it, how we've got to the point now where we sort of believe everything and nothing that we see onscreen? I love the competence of the technology, but I hate the fact that it's robbed me of the "How the hell did they do that?" feeling. I worked in movie production design in the early 80s, when effects were predominantly physical, and it still makes me wonder how a cardboard cut-out of a spaceship shot from a moving Land Rover in a blacked-out studio in '2001: A Space Odyssey' still aces a full-house digital representation today. But 'Rabbit in Your Headlights' for UNKLE really pulled it off. Great shooting, great casting. Great effects (several "stunt and cut") and a great, unexpected climax, with plenty of well-integrated digi going on. Even now, I enjoy watching it. Because it still feels real, even though it's not… damn it.

For me, 1999 represented a high-water mark for many design and communications disciplines. Idea-based graphic design still held craft in great reverence. Illustration hadn't yet overindulged in digital post-effects. TV ads were still great; Guinness's absorbing and wacky 'Swimmer' ad would only be beaten by 2000's 'Drummer', in my estimation.

Pop videos brought wit and skill to bear on often quite humdrum musical material, and the art of the single, powerful image (as represented by the giant beetle sculpture on the cover of Massive Attack's 'Mezzanine') was still honoured.

The disciplines were still separate and discernible, although their rapid, convergence-driven mutation was on the march – disciplines that were decades if not centuries old were giving way to a new world order.

I remember thinking as I stepped down from the Presidency, "So what the fuck happens next?" I guess we're finding out, but it's a brave man that can speak with authority on where the creative disciplines will be 13 years from now. ⬡

Title Rabbit in Your Headlights
Artist UNKLE
Production Company Academy Plus

"

The disciplines were still
separate and discernible,
although their rapid,
convergence-driven
mutation was on the
march – disciplines that
were decades if not
centuries old were giving
way to a new world order.

Title PlayStation – Double Life
Client Sony Computer Entertainment
Agency TBWA

PlayStation – 'Double Life'

A diverse series of characters deliver separate lines of a monologue describing their other lives playing PlayStation.

MONOLOGUE:

For years I've lived a double life.

In the day I do my job,

I ride the bus,

Roll up my sleeves with the hoi polloi.

But at night I live a life of exhilaration,

Of missed heartbeats and adrenaline,

And, if the truth be known,

A life of dubious virtue.

I won't deny I've been engaged in violence,

Even indulged in it.

I have maimed and killed adversaries,

And not merely in self-defence.

I have exhibited disregard for life,

Limb

And property,

And savoured every moment.

You may not think it to look at me,

But I have commanded armies,

And conquered worlds.

And though in achieving these things

I have set morality aside,

I have no regrets.

For though I've led a double life

At least I can say,

I have lived.

TITLE: Do not underestimate the power of PlayStation.

2000
Larry Barker

Larry Barker started his advertising
career in the early 80s, doing odd jobs
at Aalders & Marchant. He then moved
into the creative department, where he
worked with Paul Leeves and, later,
with Rooney Carruthers.

He progressed, with Carruthers, to Boase
Massimi Pollitt (BMP), after which there
followed spells at Doyle Dane Bernbach
(DDB) and Abbott Mead Vickers. Things
began getting serious at Bartle Bogle
Hegarty with the iconic Häagen-Dazs
campaign and the 'Swimmer' ad for
Levi's. A move to Creative Directorship
at WCRS was followed by the creation of
Orange and its 'Future's Bright' campaign,
as well as award-winning advertising
for Worthington and the launch of the
Caffrey's brand.

Finally, Barker returned to BMP DDB
to take up Creative and, eventually,
Executive Creative Directorship. He now
works full-time as a screenwriter.

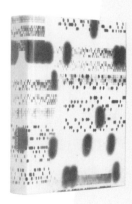

2000 Annual

Annual Design **Peartree Design**
Cover Design **Vince Frost; Frost Design**
Section Dividers **Vince Frost; Frost Design**

Title Pathé
Client Pathé
Design Group Landor Associates

Ten years is a long time in advertising.

It's an even longer time out of it.
Believe it or not, however, this year it
has been the best part of ten years since
I darkened the doors of an advertising
agency (apart from a few years' half-
hearted freelance, over which we'll draw
a veil). Imagine that – ten years of having
to buy your own lunch.

Not that there appears to be a lot of
lunch-buying going on these days – I can't
help feeling that those of us working in
the 80s and 90s had the best of it.

Tough luck, suckers.

Some things, though, never change.
I guess D&AD is one of them.

Not the way it's organised or run,
you understand. I well remember the

constant need to adapt to a rapidly
changing landscape, to stay relevant.
I also remember the "breakfast" meetings
where such matters were discussed at
length – though who has breakfast at
that time of the morning is beyond me.

I'm talking more of its sheer "importance"
– the fact that it matters so damn much.
It always did – from the moment the
impossibly weighty package of Annuals
arrived in reception to be torn apart
by otherwise, let's be honest, quite
wimpy creatives.

Within seconds, the first shout of "How
did that get in?" would go up, closely
followed by: "Well, that never bloody ran."

It mattered so much that, at the time,
there were vast budgets set aside for
Awards proofs. You know the ones –
tiny logo, no fly-shit across the bottom

All the sounds you are about
to hear are made by a real bird.

The Lyrebird.

It can mimic any sound it hears in
its home, the rain forest.

The Kookaburra

A Sulphur Crested Cockatoo

Even a camera shutter

and a car alarm

and this

Only buy wood products approved by
The Forest Stewardship Council

WWF – 'Lyrebird'

A lyrebird imitates perfectly a
series of sounds: other rain-forest
birds, a camera shutter, a car
alarm and, finally, chainsaws.
Viewers are asked to only buy
wood products approved by the
Forest Stewardship Council.

Title Lyrebird
Client World Wildlife Fund
Agency Saatchi & Saatchi

and a completely different shot. Or the
90-second cut that "ran" once in a small
cinema in Wales. If I'm honest, this was
part of the "game" that I was less than
enamoured with – I'm sure that, in
these straightened times, such budgets
and practices have evaporated.
Good thing, too.

Advertising and design are not art – there
is no purity. It's the place where art and
commerce meet, and it's a battle zone.

After a battle, there must be medals for
the winners – but not the cheats. Love it
or loathe it, these were the lengths that
people were willing to go to get into the
sainted Book.

My first entry was way back in the early
80s – "through the back door" as Paul
Leeves so generously put it (the ad was
in for Type – I wrote the copy). The last
was in the year of my Presidency of
D&AD (barring Creative Director entries,
which I always felt were a little spurious
and, frankly, unearned) for a commercial
that, in part, began the process of me
reconsidering how exactly I wanted to
wield my pen.

I remember we spent a lot of time trying
to get to the heart of why there were so
few women in creative departments.
I know later Presidents took up this work,
and it would be interesting to look at the
figures now. I also waved the flag for my
own profession – the writers.

The word "copywriting" was banned
under my stewardship; a misleading
word, it implied that we only filled in the
grey squiggles of C4 Magic Marker at
the bottom of press ads. Also, it was a
nightmare when you tried to explain to

Marmite – 'Apartment'

(Man and woman enter apartment laughing.)

WOMAN: Would you like to sit? Coffee?

MAN: Please.

(Woman goes to get coffee. When she returns, they kiss. He recoils, coughs and looks horrified. The last shot reveals the Marmite bagels she's been eating.)

SUPER: You either love it or hate it.

Title Marmite – Apartment
Client Best Foods
Agency BMP DDB

your mum exactly what it was that you did. ("So, you're the one who puts the little 'c' in the circle? And they pay you for this?")

It was also the year I learned that D&AD was so much more than the Book. It was fast becoming a truly international brand; entries from abroad had vastly increased. There are still some who bemoan this broadening of the Awards remit, but it cannot be denied that the funding this brought in was put to good use here at home.

New Blood was born, forever enshrining D&AD's fervent belief in education. The website became a go-to address for creatives of every persuasion, and the Awards show itself was elevated to a whole new level, freeing itself from dowdy silver-service roots that made it more a masonic Ladies Night than a celebration of all that was brilliant about the industry.

On the night itself I was seated between Stephen Fry and Malcolm McLaren. I spoke only once, but with these kind of names willing to lend theirs to our cause, I knew that things were going in the right direction.

As for the ads, I knew 'Surfer' would win from the second I first saw it – it still gives me the shivers. However, the most ironic and, in retrospect, iconic moment was when the Yellow Pencil for Interactive was collected by none other than the legendary and much missed John Webster, advertising's Mr TV – the man who used to consider a 48-sheet poster campaign "below the line". How things have changed. ●

NEW **GUINNESS** EXTRA COLD

FIRE

NEW **GUINNESS** EXTRA COLD

NEW **GUINNESS** EXTRA COLD

"

The word 'copywriting' was
banned under my stewardship;
a misleading word, it implied
that we only filled in the grey
squiggles of C4 Magic Marker
at the bottom of press ads.
Also, it was a nightmare when
you tried to explain to your mum
exactly what it was that you did.

Title Guinness Extra Cold
Client Guinness
Agency Abbott Mead Vickers BBDO

"Within seconds, the first shout of 'How did that get in?' would go up, closely followed by: 'Well, that never bloody ran.'

Guinness – 'Surfer'

NARRATOR: He waits.

That's what he does.

And I'll tell you what.

Tick followed tock followed tick followed tock followed tick.

Ahab says, 'I don't care who you are, here's to your dream.'

The old sailors returned to the bar... 'Here's to you, Ahab.'

And the fat drummer hit the beat with all his heart.

Here's to waiting.

GOOD THINGS COME TO THOSE WHO...

GUINNESS DRAUGHT

Title Surfer
Client Guinness
Agency Abbott Mead Vickers BBDO

2001
David Stuart

David Stuart was a founding partner and Creative Director of The Partners, which has topped the Design Week Creative Survey for most of its existence.

He has nearly 40 years' experience in both design and branding, and advises companies on how best to express themselves.

Stuart is particularly keen on encouraging more creative collaboration within the industry and promoting a greater use of wit and humour in design. He is the co-author of the design bestseller 'A Smile in the Mind'.

2001 Annual

Annual Design Esterson Lackersteen
Cover Design GBH

Title British Museum Great Court
Client British Museum
Architects Foster & Partners

One thing that shines clearly through the haze of memory is that 2001 was a vintage year for the D&AD Awards, with a wonderful crop of entries and lots of Black Pencils. These include one for the London Eye, which has gone on to become as iconic a representation of London as Big Ben – and a much better place from which to enjoy a magnificent view of the city.

There were also quite a few entries to a new category called Interactive. Now, whatever became of that? I jest – entries have increased 152 per cent over the last ten years and will no doubt quadruple over the next fortnight, given the ever-accelerating pace of digitally related change.

My strongest memory, however, is of a disappointment. Encouraged by having previously been successful in introducing one much-needed new category into the Awards – Writing for Design – I had made it a Presidential priority to get another adopted. I very much wanted to see D&AD start recognising outstanding examples of Collaboration. That is to say, projects where multiple agencies representing different disciplines – advertising, design, online, PR, sales promotion and so on – had worked together in a truly cooperative fashion, for the benefit of the client and the brand.

That may not sound particularly controversial or noteworthy. Yet my observation – then and now – is that it very rarely happens. Somehow the good-heartedness and generosity so often on display within our business abruptly goes missing when a client asks two or three creative businesses to come together, put aside their ancient rivalries, and create a campaign that none of them individually would be capable of delivering. Too often, small-mindedness, insecurity and a desire to snatch as big a slice of the cake as possible make genuine collaboration impossible.

In any case, I did not succeed (partly for reasons very much out of my hands, which I'll come on to) but personal frustrations aside, the result is that, ten years on, I look back on recent Annuals and see a lot of work that looks small to me: work lacking the impact, ambition and wholeness that is only achieved when we pool our talents and resources, and freely share our best ideas.

The external event that caused my year as President to end in a distinctly minor key was 9/11; in the days and weeks that followed, it was as if someone had pressed the "pause" button. As governments huddled, and the world waited to see what would happen next, business largely stopped in its tracks. Suddenly, advertising and design didn't seem hugely important. If this D&AD President had ever been seduced by a sense of the prestige and importance bestowed on him by the role, he would have very quickly regained a sense of perspective. Luckily, he didn't need to.

More than a decade later, the world is still turning. While nothing has diminished the significance of those terrible events, we are able to believe once more that what we do in our business is, in its relatively small way, important and valuable; that we owe it to ourselves and each other to do it as well as we are able. And – at the risk of making you heave a sigh of relief that such a repetitive old fart is no longer at the helm of D&AD – I would say that means embracing collaboration. ◖

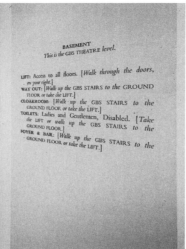

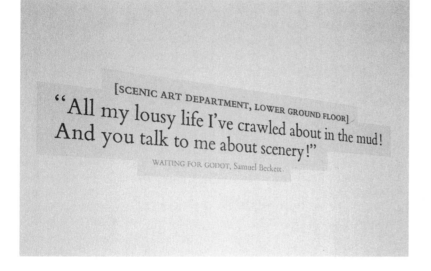

Title RADA signage
Client Royal Academy of Dramatic Arts
Designers Lea Jagendorf & Andrea Speide

"Somehow the good-
heartedness and generosity
so often on display within
our business abruptly goes
missing when a client
asks two or three creative
businesses to come together.

The external event that caused my year as President to end in a distinctly minor key was 9/11... Suddenly, advertising and design didn't seem hugely important.

Title Raymond Chandler: The Complete Novels
Client The Folio Society
Illustrator Geoff Grandfield
Design Director Joe Whitlock-Blundell

Title London Eye
Client The London Eye Company
Architectural Design Marks Barfield

Title Sports Illustrated
Client Sports Illustrated
Agency Fallon Minneapolis

2002
Peter Souter

Peter Souter worked at Abbott Mead
Vickers BBDO for nearly 20 years
and was Executive Creative Director
for nearly ten of them. In 2009 he
left to write other things.

2002 Annual

Annual Design Esterson Lackersteen
Cover Design Mother

Title Consumer poster specials
Client Radio Times
Agency Miles Calcraft Briginshaw Duffy

"

'Don't watch the wrong side' on the wrong side of a grubby 48-sheet poster is the kind of idea that made me want to get into the ideas business in the first place.

Advertising bought me a nice present – a cute, fake New England lighthouse perched, rather precariously, on the edge of the only proper cliff in Kent. I like it because the view always changes, every minute of every day. I'm sitting typing this in the observation tower, which offers 180-degree views of the North Sea. Views that change with each twinkle of the sun and breath of wind.

I am telling you all this not to show off (okay, maybe to show off a little bit – isn't advertising a brilliant way to make a living?), but because I've been asked to look at the 2002 D&AD Annual again and pick the five things I like best.

The only thing is, every time I look at a D&AD Annual, my year or any year... the view changes. You find new things to love, new talents to marvel at, new ideas that have grown in stature since the last time you looked. I flipped 2002 open for the first time in an embarrassingly long time (these last few years I've been writing things that are a bit longer than ads and pay much, much less) looking for five things I liked, and failed.

I actually found 37. I tried narrowing it down from a first harvest in the hundreds, but 37 was as low as my Post-it notes got. Then I realised that it didn't matter. If you are holding this celebration of D&AD's first 50 years in your hand, you already love ideas and are more than capable of picking your own favourites. The view keeps changing. So, here are five of the 37 things I liked today.

Go to page 164 and look at Mike Straznickas's Heinz Ketchup bottles. I'm sure Mike would be the first to call them Jim Bosiljevac's ketchup bottles, because the writing is wonderful too. Mike and Jim won the 2002 Yellow Pencil for Outstanding Brand Labels by realising that the brand that they were labelling was already so famous you didn't need to tell people it had ketchup inside. They could, instead, use the space on the front to tell us that it was "Not new and improved". And that it was "On a first name basis with onion rings". And, my favourite, the hugely helpful "Instructions: Put on food". This work won its shiny prize because it was brave and human and funny. Three excellent things to be. Heinz marketing executives Brian Hansberry and Justin Lambeth deserve praise for being those three things themselves the day they bought this fabulous idea.

Now flip, if you will, to page 40. Bottom right you'll see a magnificent backside. Paul Briginshaw and Malcolm Duffy were busy launching their own agency ten years ago with this wonderfully simple guerrilla ad for the Radio Times. See if you can find a spare letter in this idea. No? Me neither. "Don't watch the wrong side" on the wrong side of a grubby 48-sheet poster is the kind of idea that made me want to get into the ideas business in the first place. It wouldn't look out of place in any of the 50 Annuals we've all had a hand in making so far.

Jump to page 380 and you'll find a Mexican bed ad that is as funny and sweet as any episode of 'Outnumbered',

"
Cute kid in cute PJs bounces on the left of two
beds in a classic split-screen comparison...
Then he bounces clean across the split-screen
divide on to the right-hand bed and falls
instantly asleep. Cue Sealy logo. Utterly brilliant.

Budweiser – 'Mr Horse-Drawn Carriage Driver'

ANNOUNCER: Bud Light Presents... Real Men of Genius.

SINGER: Real Men of Genius!

ANNOUNCER: Today we salute you... Mr Horse-Drawn Carriage Driver.

SINGER: Mr Horse-Drawn Carriage Driver!

ANNOUNCER: You start your day with a 'tip, tip' and a 'cheerio!', which is odd because you're from Brooklyn.

SINGER: Jolly old Brooklyn!

ANNOUNCER: While most people sit behind a desk, you proudly sit two feet behind a four-legged manure factory.

SINGER: Oooh!

ANNOUNCER: No one knows the guts it takes to ride the subway to work dressed as a foppish dandy from the 18th century.

SINGER: Hey foppish dandy!

ANNOUNCER: Blaring horns, profanity, vicious insults all met with a courtly tip of your stovepipe hat.

SINGER: Cheerio!

ANNOUNCER: So crack open an ice-cold Bud Light, buggy boy. (SFX: bottle opening) Because the way you say 'giddy-up' makes us say 'whoa'.

SINGER: Whoa! Whoa! Whoa!

ANNOUNCER: Bud Light Beer. Anheuser-Busch. St Louis, Missouri.

Title Budweiser – Real Men of Genius
Client Labatt Breweries
Agency DDB Chicago

Title Heinz Ketchup
Client HJ Heinz Company
Design Group Leo Burnett Chicago

'Modern Family' or 'Two and a Half Men'. My friend Walter Campbell always used to say he was trying to create the best thing on television. Not the best ad on television, mind; the best thing on television. Funnier than the comedies, more moving than the movies, more compelling than the news. Are you trying to do that? You really should. Anyway, back to those talented Mexicans: Tony Hidalgo, Jorge Aguilar and Ruben Bross. These fine young North Americans made the rest of us look bad back at the turn of the century with the greatest ever side-by-side demo, I think. Cute kid in cute PJs bounces on the left of two beds in a classic split-screen comparison. Bounce, bounce, bounce, bounce. Hyperactivity personified. Then he bounces clean across the split-screen divide on to the right-hand bed and falls instantly asleep. Cue Sealy logo. Utterly brilliant.

Have you ever been to page 302 of any D&AD Annual? That's where Radio Commercials generally lurk, and my guess is it's the least-thumbed area of any Book. Which is a shame, because some very clever people live there, Bob Winter and John Immesoete for example. It isn't often that a campaign titles itself after its creators but the Bud Light 'Real Men of Genius' series did just that. You really have to track them down and listen for yourself, but I'll just point up the 'Ice Skater' execution and its glorious dénouement, "You may never wear a medal, but sequins are shiny too." Oddly, now that I make my living in the horrifically tough world of screenwriting, I have come to appreciate even more just how brilliant advertising creatives can be when they try.

Will you let me have one Abbott Mead ad before I go? The reason to pick the Economist 'Missing Piece' poster on page 34 is that it comes with such a delightful back story that if you made it up and stuck it in a movie nobody would believe you. David Abbott, the greatest British copywriter by some considerable margin, had written the first Economist poster – 'Management Trainee' – 15 years earlier, beginning AMV's greatest campaign. Eventually it became so universally loved and understood we were able to run a poster where the logo wasn't even necessary. Pretty cool. But the coolest part of the story is that 'Missing Piece' was written by David's son Matthew. The circle of life doesn't get much more satisfyingly circular than that. ●

Sealy – 'Boy'

A superb parody of the side-by-side demo format. We see a split-screen view of two identical bedrooms. A little boy is bouncing energetically on a mattress on the left side of the picture. A super tells us that this represents rival brands. On the right side, the mattress is a Sealy. Suddenly the boy jumps from one bed to the other, making a mockery of the split-screen rule. As soon as he lands on the Sealy mattress, he falls asleep. The comic timing is immaculate.

SUPER: Your rest deserves a Sealy.

Title **Boy**
Client **Sealy Mattress Company**
Agency **Amy Kagan**

Title Missing Piece
Client The Economist
Agency Abbott Mead Vickers BBDO

2003
Michael Johnson

Designer/writer/thinker Michael Johnson
runs johnson banks, a London-based
design consultancy with a global reputation.

The company works on design projects
as varied as The Science Museum and
a space observatory in Japan. The firm's
experimental typography in Japanese and
Chinese has been exhibited in Shanghai,
and its recent 3D typography, Arkitypo,
quickly became an internet phenomenon.

Johnson writes for many design journals
and lectures worldwide on branding,
identity issues and design history. He
has won most of the design world's most
prestigious awards (including eight D&AD
Pencils), has dozens of designs in the
Victoria & Albert Museum's permanent
collection and, in 2003, was one of
D&AD's youngest ever Presidents. In his
spare moments, he edits the design blog
Thought for the Week.

2003 Annual

Annual Design **Esterson Lackersteen**
Cover Design **Inflate**

Having not studied at a "name" design college, my awareness of those Yellow Pencils lagged a bit behind. But I had, over the course of the 90s, become a strange "student" of D&AD by virtue of the fact that I had borrowed a big pile of cash to buy a complete set of Annuals. I hadn't done this because I was cramming for an MPhil on post-war British commercial art – I was just a slightly undertrained designer trying to learn from the history of the business, and it had become obvious that this was where I should start.

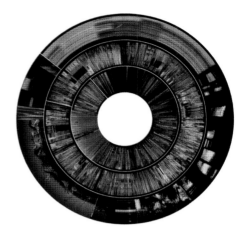

Given the then paucity of decent historical material on the history of the business, D&AD Annuals for all their flaws and odd curatorial glitches provided a unique insight into multiple zeitgeists. The 60s Annuals offer a fascinating window into the emerging skills of the industry figures – then junior – who would go on to dominate design and advertising for the next three decades.

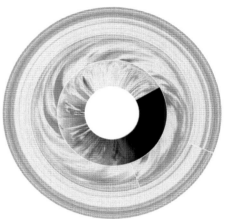

If I pick up an Annual from the mid-70s, I'm transported back to a humdrum Derbyshire childhood where the only glimpse of another life seemed to be hinted at through the pages of The Sunday Times Magazine. The late-80s Annuals then illustrate a curatorial "gap" that D&AD has sometimes struggled with ever since – a solid body of commercial work holding sway over anything experimental or groundbreaking.

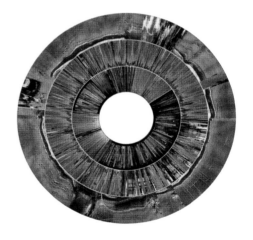

Anyway, the point of this contextual rambling is that, at the end of the 90s, when asked to put a few slides together on what it could do next, as the organisation's unofficial archivist I simply pointed out that its 40th birthday was approaching (in 2002) and it would be great to celebrate that. A book. Maybe an exhibition? That kind of thing.

Looking back, that was a fairly pivotal moment. As I threw myself into researching the idea, making presentations to the V&A and starting conversations with co-curators, I still hadn't really thought this through. When my three years were up on the committee, I stayed on another 12 months to get the 'Rewind: 40 Years of Design & Advertising' project up, running, published and exhibited. Then a few people approached me about staying on for an unprecedented fifth year. As I thought about that five-year journey, it began to dawn that maybe, just maybe, it would be fun to be Mr President.

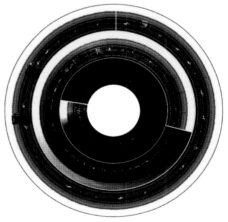

Title Last Clock
Client Digital Hub Interactive
Designers Ross Cooper, Jussi Ängeslevä

Title Blue Carpet
Client Newscastle City Council
Designer Thomas Heatherwick

My recollections of the Presidential year itself, as I'm sure is the case for others, are of a lot of fun, a huge amount learned and a massive amount of work. When the then Chief Executive of D&AD departed midway through my term, the workload promptly doubled. For some reason, as I busied myself with the 'Rewind' project, I was also midway through a book of my own, and at a critical point I lifted my head from a set of proofs to see my accountant hovering ominously by my desk, ashen-faced, clutching a piece of paper that informed me we were down to our last 30 grand in the bank. This is not really up there in my great memories of all time, but is a useful lesson in being aware of how much extracurricular activity you can and can't do while running a small company.

Other memories of that year? Some bright spark decided that the Awards would be held at Earls Court, in the round. A fine idea in theory, but the practice of walking out to a "cold" audience of 2,000 people clutching a very heavy loudspeaker designed to look like the tip of a pencil? Awful.

I was at least able to redress a bit of historical balance by awarding Michael Wolff and Wally Olins the President's Award. Despite their 30 years of groundbreaking work, together and apart, D&AD had been a bit lax in actually acknowledging their pioneering thinking.

Dig a little into the winners of 2003 and you spot a few early sightings of names destined to feature in our future creative consciousness (such as David Droga, then working at Saatchi & Saatchi UK, and Thomas Heatherwick). This was only the second year Innocent got in the book – oddly, it wasn't to win for another decade but the firm's influence has remained undeniable. One of my favourite pieces of the year was one

> " There was perhaps no standout piece in the year – no 'Surfer', iMac or London Eye. Hence no Black Pencil.

of those "close but no cigar" nominated pieces – a set of hand-illustrated wardrobes for Howies retail stores. Beautiful.

I'm sure Apple won a hatful as its glory decade gathered pace, and oddly I was involved (more by accident than design) in one of the great advertising campaigns that year, by Campbell Doyle Dye for Merrydown Cider, which played neatly with the duality of the merry/down name. But there was perhaps no standout piece in the year – no 'Surfer', iMac or London Eye. Hence no Black Pencil, and I fear history won't view this as a killer year for the creative work.

Luckily, the experience didn't kill me. I emerged older, wiser and greyer, blinking into daylight. Had I been President a bit too early? Perhaps. Do I miss it? Sometimes. Do I regret it? Not one tiny bit. ●

Title **Cartoons**
Client **NSPCC**
Agency **Saatchi & Saatchi**

Title **Wardrobes**
Client **Howies**
Design Group **Carter Wong Tomlin**

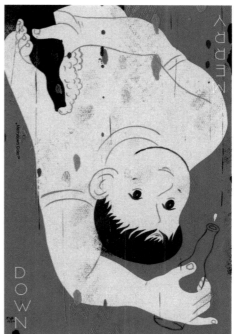

Title Merrydown Cider
Client Merrydown
Agency Campbell Doyle Dye

2004
Nick Bell

Nick Bell started his career at
Abbott Mead Vickers BBDO, before
becoming Executive Creative Director
of first, Leo Burnett, then JWT.

At Leo Burnett, Bell helped transform
the London agency into the most
successful in film at Cannes in 2001.

At JWT, he took the London
office from being outside the
Gunn Report's top 100 to being
the seventh most awarded agency
in the world in 2006.

He is now Global Creative Director at
DDB. Bell's many personal awards
include two D&AD Yellow Pencils, the
Cannes Grand Prix and four Cannes
Gold Lions.

In 2003, he was elected D&AD
President by his peers.

2004 Annual

Concept and Creative Director Dave Dye; Campbell Doyle Dye
Design Tonic
Illustration Sean Rodwell; Aeriform

I remember getting a phone call from David Kester, who was the Chief Executive before I became President. He said he would like to take me for lunch, which was surprising because the previous year, when we'd been judging down in Brighton, I had been very exacting about something or other, and I thought he had found me to be a monumental pain in the arse. But David took me out to a very nice restaurant and blew me away by saying, "We'd like you to run for President of D&AD."

Every President is asked to select and pursue a Manifesto. I wanted to choose something that is at the very heart of what we do. Because clients predominantly have an inclination to compromise and play safe, they tend not to get the standard of work they could from their agencies. I said I'd like to work with D&AD's existing programme – Creativity Works – to help both clients and agencies in this respect.

Before I actually became President, a couple of things happened. First, I left Leo Burnett to become Executive Creative Director of JWT. Though JWT was extremely supportive and proud that its new Creative Director was in this prestigious role, JWT was a huge job and my priority had to be with the agency.

Then David Kester resigned as CEO of D&AD and Michael Hockney took over. There was so much Michael wanted to do when he came in. He wanted to truly internationalise the Awards, and built

a two-week programme of lectures, seminars and viewings around an Awards night at a new venue, Old Billingsgate. With the focus on all of this, we weren't able to put as much energy and focus as we would have liked into the Manifesto. Consequently, though I was told I was a comparatively hard-working President, I felt I got all the good bits from the D&AD Presidency – introducing the lectures, choosing the recipient of the President's Award and standing up at Billingsgate to introduce the Awards evening – but wasn't able to deliver on the Manifesto.

I will probably be quite controversial in choosing work from my year, as there was work awarded above a couple of the pieces I've picked.

I'll start in the category of Integrated Communications with Honda. I couldn't remember any great Honda advertising in all my time in the business. Then suddenly Tony Davidson and Kim Papworth at Wieden+Kennedy, a great agency but one that had not been strong in London, created 'The Power of Dreams'. Strategy, idea, execution, tone – suddenly, Honda felt like a compelling brand. The Guardian work that year was very good but for me it was Honda.

In the category of Product Design, I have chosen the Apple PowerBook range. I'm in awe of Jonathan Ive's work. My comfort zone – and hopefully my area of expertise – is advertising, and I'm not a techie at all, but even when you're in

> **Because clients predominantly have an inclination to compromise and play safe, they tend not to get the standard of work they could from their agencies.**

Title PowerBook range
Client Apple Computer
Design Group Apple Design Team

Budweiser – 'Mr Way Too Much Cologne Wearer'

ANNOUNCER: Bud Light Presents... Real Men of Genius.

SINGER: Real Men of Genius!

ANNOUNCER: Today we salute you... Mr Way Too Much Cologne Wearer.

SINGER: Mr Way Too Much Cologne Wearer!

ANNOUNCER: Like a bull horn, your cologne announces your every arrival four blocks before you get there.

SINGER: Here he comes now!

ANNOUNCER: Here a splash, there a splash, everywhere a splash-splash. You don't stop till every square inch of manhood is covered.

SINGER: Everywhere a splish-splash!

ANNOUNCER: Overslept and haven't got time to shower? Not to worry, you've got four gallons of cologne and a plan.

SINGER: Pour it on!

ANNOUNCER: So crack open an ice-cold Bud Light, Mr Way Too Much Cologne Wearer. (SFX: bottle opening) Because we think we smell... a winner.

SINGER: Mr Way Too Much Cologne Wearer!

ANNOUNCER: Bud Light Beer. Anheuser-Busch. St. Louis, Missouri.

Title Budweiser – Real Men of Genius
Client Labatt Breweries
Agency DDB Chicago

Budweiser – 'Mr Multicoloured Sweater Wearer'

ANNOUNCER: Bud Light presents... Real Men of Genius.

SINGER: Real Men of Genius!

ANNOUNCER: Today we salute you... Mr Multicoloured Sweater Wearer.

SINGER: Mr Multicoloured Sweater Wearer!

ANNOUNCER: A squiggly, jiggly mish-mash of colours and patterns we wouldn't be caught dead in, but it sure looks good on you.

SINGER: Squiggly! Jiggly!

ANNOUNCER: They say beauty's in the eye of the beholder. We say whoever be holdin' that thing be holdin' one ugly sweater.

SINGER: Keep holding on!

ANNOUNCER: No, I wasn't dragged down the highway and my insides are showing. I'm wearing my new sweater.

SINGER: Someone call a doctor!

ANNOUNCER: So crack open an ice-cold Bud Light, Mr Natty in His Knits. (SFX: bottle opening) It may just be an ugly sweater, but it sure is an ugly sweater.

SINGER: Mr Multicoloured Sweater Wearer!

ANNOUNCER: Bud Light Beer. Anheuser-Busch. St. Louis, Missouri.

Budweiser – 'Mr Really, Really, Really Bad Dancer'

ANNOUNCER: Bud Light presents... Real Men of Genius.

SINGER: Real Men of Genius!

ANNOUNCER: Today we salute you... Mr Really, Really, Really Bad Dancer.

SINGER: Mr Really, Really, Really Bad Dancer!

ANNOUNCER: Arms swinging, knees bending, head bobbing to no particular rhythm. You're either dancing or having a seizure.

SINGER: Call me a doctor!

ANNOUNCER: As soon as you hit the dancefloor the taunts begin. Is that all you got, player? Unfortunately yes, that's all you got.

SINGER: Pour it on now!

ANNOUNCER: Who's in the house? Some guy who can't dance. That's who's in the house.

SINGER: You're a star!

ANNOUNCER: So crack open an ice-cold Bud Light, Mr Happy-Feet. (SFX: bottle opening) Because you really put the 'oogie' in 'boogie'.

SINGER: Mr Really, Really, Really Bad Dancer!

ANNOUNCER: Bud Light Beer. Anheuser-Busch. St Louis, Missouri.

advertising you can be susceptible to the power of brands. It's the form as well as the function, the way everything Apple is designed, that puts it up there with anything I saw in advertising.

Within Radio Advertising I am going for a campaign that didn't get awarded, probably because it had been awarded in previous years. I haven't chosen it because I'm at DDB (the campaign was written some time before I joined), but for years I have loved the 'Real Men of Genius' campaign for Bud Light – not just as an advertising person but also as a bloke. Woody Allen said the greatest pictures are on radio, and I think this is a rare example of a campaign that ran in both TV and radio being stronger on radio.

My fourth pick is in TV and Cinema Advertising. Two spots – 'History' and 'Greetings' – both again for Budweiser. Great ideas that know their audience – great writing, great direction and execution, great acting, and they're just funny.

Also in TV and Cinema Advertising, I've chosen Orange's 'Don't Let a Mobile Phone Ruin Your Movie' campaign by Mother. It was a defining campaign for that agency. I also think it's brave and smart as hell on the client's side to buy a campaign that basically says, "Don't use our product."

There's one last thing that stands out for me from the year of my Presidency. I had to decide on whom I wanted to bestow the President's Award. I started by thinking about my peers, my generation, and then I asked myself who had really inspired me in the business. I thought back to when I was a kid trying to get into a good agency, and I thought about how much I had loved what Dave Trott's agency, Gold Greenlees Trott, was doing. At that time, all the kids wanted to work there and I was no exception. I looked at the D&AD Annuals and what amazed me was that all of the greats of Dave's generation – David Abbott, John Webster, John Hegarty, Tim Delaney, Paul Arden – had received the President's Award and yet his name wasn't there. That was my decision made, and I got a fantastic reaction from the industry for "righting a wrong". Because I got my break not at GGT but AMV, I didn't meet Dave until the moment we shook hands onstage and I handed him the Pencil. I'm not sure who was more honoured that evening, Dave or me. ⬡

Title Budweiser – Greetings
Client Labatt Breweries
Agency Downtown Partners

Budweiser – 'Greetings'

Men are always in trouble. Women love
romantic greetings cards. The Bud Light
Institute has created romantic greetings cards
to get men out of trouble.

Title Budweiser – History
Client Labatt Breweries
Agency Downtown Partners

Budweiser – 'History'

Throughout history, the Bud Light Institute
has invented things to keep women occupied
so men can go out for beers with mates
without feelings of guilt or potential for ending
up in the doghouse.

Do you believe in the power of dreams? When Soichiro
Honda was 8 years old he saw his first motor car. It was an
early edition Model T Ford. Soichiro couldn't help running
after the car. "It leaked oil," he recalled fondly. "I got down
on my hands and knees to smell it. It was like perfume."

There is a place where dreamers go. Where crazy flights of fancy
are valued above all else. Where the only good idea is an idea that's
never been had before. Where dreams can become real. It's called
The Patent Office, Concept House, Newport – M4, junction 28, first
roundabout, fourth exit. Do you believe in the power of dreams?

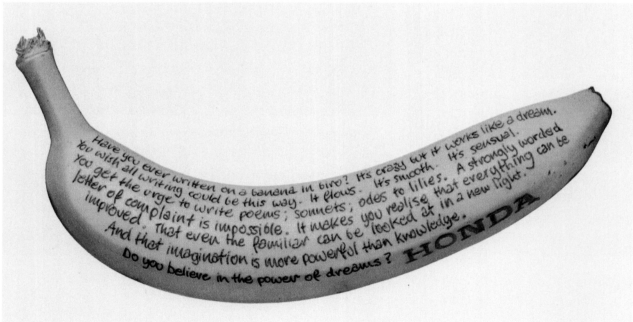

Title The Power of Dreams
Client Honda UK
Agency Wieden+Kennedy UK

Orange – 'Carrie Fisher'

Carrie Fisher pitches her film idea to the Orange Film Commission Board. Her tale of two lovers, who can only correspond by letter, fails to impress. It seems the board are "looking for the magic". In a bit to "make it relevant" they propel the 19th-century period-piece into the 21st century. They get rid of the fog and the horse, and replace them with a car. Perfect. Our lovers can now correspond by... "text"! The board members congratulate themselves, and why not? "The magic is back in!"

DON'T LET A MOBILE PHONE
RUIN YOUR MOVIE.
PLEASE SWITCH IT OFF.

Orange – 'Roy Schneider'

Roy Schneider pitches his film idea ('The Colombian Connection') to the Orange Film Commission Board. All is going well until he reveals it's a black and white film, which confuses the board as this is supposed to be a film about photo messaging, which only comes in colour. Suddenly, they come up with a solution – and poor Roy is left dumbfounded as the board decides to turn his film noir masterpiece into a brilliant example of Film Orange. Unlucky, Roy – you're gonna need a bigger boat!

DON'T LET A MOBILE PHONE
RUIN YOUR MOVIE.
PLEASE SWITCH IT OFF.

Title Don't Let a Mobile Phone Ruin Your Movie
Client Orange
Agency Mother

" Orange's 'Don't Let a Mobile Phone Ruin Your Movie' campaign by Mother was brave, and it was smart as hell on the client's side to buy a campaign that basically says, 'Don't use our product.'

2005
Dick Powell

Dick Powell is co-Founder of design and innovation company Seymourpowell. Founded in 1984, Seymourpowell has produced some of the "milestone" products of the last two decades, for clients as diverse as Unilever, Panasonic, Tefal, LG, Nestlé and Kraft Foods. Powell has sat on the boards of the Design Council, the Design Business Association and the D&AD Executive. He is currently Chairman of D&AD.

2005 Annual

Annual Design **Spin**
Photography **Lee Mawdsley**

Title **Idents**
Client **Channel 4**
Agency **Channel 4**

Towards the end of my first year, D&AD asked me to stay on for a second term, because it wanted to bring the financial year, the constitutional year and the programme year into alignment. Having spent three years as Education Chairman before becoming President, helping D&AD to deliver on its charitable purpose, I felt that D&AD needed to reposition itself more firmly as a not-for-profit charity, especially in the face of other moneymaking awards schemes. Yes, we run the Awards to lionise and evangelise creative excellence, and yes, we make money doing it... but that money is there to support our charitable purpose of helping young people into the creative industries. More than that though, our not-for-profit charitable remit gives D&AD's juries great probity and independence from the financial imperatives of so many other awards schemes – one of the reasons for the very high standards of excellence we consistently uphold. So my first Annual took this as its theme, and we changed our identity to include the words "...and not for profit".

The standout moment of my Presidency was sitting down at the Awards Dinner with Steve Jobs on my right, Stephen Fry on my left and Jonathan Ive next to him, and having the opportunity to honour Ive's great work for Apple with the President's Award. Conspicuously unlike most well-known design divas, he is a modest, self-effacing bloke who is always painstakingly anxious to credit the role of others. Apple's haul of Yellow and Black Pencils over the last ten years highlights its contribution to design and commitment to creative leadership, but what made this Award particularly special was that Jony Ive touches the hearts and minds of creatives around the world, because all of us (in both advertising and design) use his products everyday. I held off the alcohol until the ceremony itself was over and Jony and Steve had left, at which point adrenaline conspired with a few glasses of wine to banjax me completely; I remember very little thereafter, apart from being manhandled on to the floor of a cab by the D&AD team.

Lynx – 'Getting Dressed'

A young man and woman wake up
in bed. They start to get dressed,
but we soon discover that their
clothes are scattered right across
the city. The last shoe sits by two
opposite-facing shopping trolleys
in a supermarket aisle. The couple
met there only hours ago. The man
was wearing Lynx 24/7 body-spray.

Title Lynx – Getting Dressed
Client Lever Fabergé
Agency Bartle Bogle Hegarty

In 2004, I had moaned at the
ad community for dismissing the
effectiveness of Honda's 'Cog' and
choosing instead to get on a high horse
about its originality, thus denying it
the Black Pencil I thought it deserved.
In 2005 justice was done, as the
Wieden+Kennedy (W+K) team pulled
in two Black Pencils and eight Yellow
Pencils for Honda's 'Grrr'. Nothing
gets the creative adrenaline coursing
through the veins more than a real
dislike or hate for the way things are,
married to an anarchic confidence
that you can do it better, and so it
was with the design engineer that
Honda nominated to create a new
diesel engine. He hated the way they
were and vowed to make them better
– a theme that W+K pounced on with
evident glee, asking gruff-voiced author
Garrison Keillor to do the unthinkable
and sing along to a brilliant animation,
bringing some sunshine into our lives
in the process.

The other TV Black Pencil went
to Channel 4's new idents, which
subverted the whole idea of idents
because we just didn't realise what
they were until, for a fleeting moment,
the "4" was momentarily assembled.
They're more like mini-films than
idents. Little essays that eschew
bland and glossy corporate special
effects in favour of slyly engaging
our attention, but which nevertheless
communicate what Channel 4 stands
for. The strategy continues to this day,
a credit to creator Brett Foraker and
his team.

But the favourite ad of my Presidency
was Bartle Bogle Hegarty's (BBH)
'Getting Dressed' for Lynx, one in a long
line of really effective and engaging
ads the agency has done for the brand.
The Unilever/BBH relationship shows
the power of advertising to build,
sustain and re-energise a brand over
a long period of time. This one was
yet another goodie, and garnered four
Yellow Pencils with a hugely engaging
story that takes us from the end – the
result of "the Lynx effect" – back to a
chance encounter in a supermarket.

> Nothing gets the creative adrenaline coursing through the veins more than a real dislike or hate for the way things are, married to an anarchic confidence that you can do it better.

It was set to great music and still looks stunning.

If 2005 seemed a bit weak in design, 2006 yielded two Black Pencils. The first went to the redesign of The Guardian. Of course, it has settled into our consciousness over the last six years, so it's easy to forget how groundbreaking and beautifully conceived it was when it first broke cover. The second went to Leo Burnett's website – the first Black Pencil in Online! It was very dynamic and playful, allowing you to use the firm's pencil to wander and explore its work and point of view in a way none of us had seen before, but without losing sight of the need to inform.

My favourite ad of 2006 was DDB's press campaign for Harvey Nichols, which used a calendar format to suggest that a month's worth of abstinence (eating only beans, or using the phone book instead of loo paper) was required to buy that special thing you lusted after. Like so much great advertising, it made me smile. ⬡

Title **Grrr**
Client **Honda UK**
Agency **Wieden+Kennedy UK**

Honda – 'Grrr'

MVO: Here's a little song for anyone who's ever hated, in the key of grrr.

(Tranquil setting invaded by dirty diesel engines.)

SINGS:
Can hate be good?
Can hate be great?
Can hate be good?
Can hate be great?
Can hate be some-
thing we don't hate?

(Whistling tune)

We'd like to know,
Why it is so,
That certain diesels
Must be slow
And thwack and thrum
And bong and hum
And clatter clat.

(Whistling tune)

Hate something.
Change something.
Hate something,
Change something,
Make something better.

(Whistling tune)

Oh, isn't it just bliss,
When a diesel goes like this?

(Quiet purr)

(Whistling tune)

Sing it like you hate it.

Bababa hate something.
Bababa change something.
Bababa hate something,
Change something,
Make something better.

(Whistling tune)

SUPER: Honda.
The Power of Dreams.

Simon Schama:
America will never
be the same again
G2 Page 8

Lady Macbeth,
four-letter needle-
work and learning
from Cate Blanchett.
Judi Dench in her prime
G2, page 22

Chris Patten:
How the Tories
lost the plot
This Section Page 32

Amy Jenkins:
The me generation
is now in charge
G2 Page 2

£0.60
Monday 12.09.05
Published
in London and
Manchester
guardian.co.uk

theguardian

Backlash over Blair's school revolution

City academy plans condemned by ex-education secretary Morris

An acceleration of plans to reform state education, including the speeding up of the creation of the independently funded city academy schools, will be announced today by Tony Blair.

But the increasingly controversial nature of the policy was highlighted when the former education secretary Estelle Morris accused the government of "serial meddling" in secondary education.

In an article in tomorrow's Education Guardian she writes: "Another round of structural change won't by itself achieve universally high standards. Worse than that it could be a distraction. In five years' time, whose children will be going to these new academies? Will choice and market forces once again squeeze out the children of the disadvantaged?"

Today, the prime minister will say: "It is not government edict that is determining the fate of city academies, but parent power. Parents are choosing city academies, and that is good enough for me."

He will also set out the future of local education authorities as "commissioners of education and champions of standards", rather than direct providers.

The academies replace failing schools, normally on new sites, in challenging inner-city areas. The number of academies will rise to between 40 and 50 by next September. This month 10 city academies started, bringing the total to 27, and Mr Blair will insist the government is on target to reach 200 by 2010. City academies have proved to be among the most hotly debated aspects of his public sector reforms. The Commons education select committee has criticised them as divisive and teaching union leaders have also denounced the expansion of an "unproven" scheme.

However, this will not deter Mr Blair who will point out that in the last academic year the proportion of pupils receiving five good GCSEs **4**» in city academies rose by 8 per cent, four times the national average.
Patrick Wintour and Rebecca Smithers

UK link to terror snatches

The United Nations is investigating the CIA's use of British airports when abducting terrorism suspects and flying them to prisons around the world where they are alleged to have been tortured. The inquiry, led by Martin Scheinin, a special rapporteur from the UN Commission on Human Rights, comes as an investigation by the Guardian reveals the full extent of the British logistical support. Aircraft used in the secret operations have flown into the UK at least 210 times since the September 11 terror attacks. Foreign Office officials have denied all knowledge of the secret flights, telling MPs on the foreign affairs select committee that the ministry has "not granted any permissions for the use of UK territory or air space", and suggested to the Guardian that it was "just a conspiracy theory." Privately, Ministry of Defence officials admit that they are aware of the flights, and that they have decided to turn a blind eye. "It is not a matter for the MoD," said one. "The aircraft use our airfields. We don't ask any questions. They just happen to be behind the wire." **13**»
Ian Cobain and Richard Norton-Taylor

Bad'day mate Aussies lose their grip

Shane Warne at the Oval yesterday. Sport » Photograph: Kieran Doherty/Reuters

Column five
The shape of things to come

Alan Rusbridger

Welcome to the Berliner Guardian. No, we won't go on calling it that for long, and yes, it's an inelegant name.

We tried many alternatives, related either to size or to the European origins of the format. In the end, "the Berliner" stuck. But in a short time we hope we can revert to being simply the Guardian.

Many things about today's paper are different.

Starting with the most obvious, the page size is smaller. We believe the format combines the convenience of a tabloid with the sensibility of a broadsheet. Next most conspicuously, we have changed the paper's titlepiece and headline fonts. Gone is the striking 80s David Hillman design – adapted over the years – which mixed Garamond, Miller and Helvetica fonts. In their place is a new font, Guardian Egyptian, which is, we hope, elegant, intelligent and highly legible.

The next difference you may notice is colour. The paper is printed on state-of-the-art MAN Roland ColorMan presses, which give colour on every page – something that sets us apart from every other national newspaper. The effect will be to give greater emphasis and power to our photography and, we hope, make the whole paper a touch less forbidding than it sometimes may have seemed in the past.

G2 has also shrunk: it is now a full colour, stapled news magazine with newspaper deadlines. Sport has expanded into its own section – at least 12 pages every day, again in full colour.

As the week progresses you'll notice further changes. There are one or two new sections. There will be new columnists, both in G1 and G2 – most notably the pre-eminent commentator Simon Jenkins, who joins us from the Times to write on Wednesdays and Fridays.

Continued on page 2 »

National	**Law**	**International**	**Financial**
Police chief blames Orangemen for riots	**Judges may block deportations**	**Israeli troops leave Gaza after 38 years**	**Sky's Premiership rights under threat**
More than 2,000 police officers and soldiers clashed with loyalists in Belfast in the worst riots for more than a decade. The violence erupted after a small Orange Order parade was rerouted by fewer than 100 metres away from Catholic homes. Hugh Orde, Northern Ireland chief constable, accused Orangemen of taking part in and stoking up the riots, which spread to Ballymena, Antrim, Carrickfergus, Larne, Ballyclare, Glengormley and Ahoghill. More than 30 police and soldiers were injured as rioters used automatic weapons, petrol bombs and blast bombs to attack the security forces, who responded with 450 baton rounds.	The government faces a confrontation with judges over its attempts to deport terrorist suspects to Middle Eastern and north African countries with poor human rights records. Four appeal court judges who may have to decide whether deportations can go ahead have told the Guardian they will refuse to rubber-stamp the UK's human rights deals with countries such as Jordan and Algeria. Despite being urged by the home secretary to respect the country-to-country agreements, the judges say they will demand evidence that the assurances are "worth the paper they're written on".	Israel lowered its flag in the Gaza Strip for the last time yesterday as the government declared an end to 38 years of occupation and troops withdrew from demolished Jewish settlements. The last troops were expected to leave overnight. Palestinian leaders described it as a "liberation", but said Israeli controls on border crossings and other restrictions maintained the occupation. Thousands of Palestinians gathered on roads leading to the settlements, ready to storm the rubble once the last troops were gone. A 12-year-old boy was seriously wounded **17**» by gunfire from an Israeli tank still guarding the settlements.	BSkyB's 13-year monopoly over live broadcasts of Premier League football games is under immediate threat. Media regulator Ofcom has told the European Commission it should force whoever holds the Premiership TV rights to sell a number of games to rival broadcasters. A separate regulatory plan under consideration in Brussels could see individual broadcasters limited to 50% of the live games put up for sale. The League, meanwhile, is resisting all attempts to remove its "exclusivity premium," arguing **26**» that clubs' finances could be undermined. The current rights deal expires in 2007.

15»   **3**»

Bigger isn't always better...

mediaguardian**M**

The danger with
24-hour news is that it
becomes a rolling
service of rumour and
speculation
Helen Boaden Page 2

the**guardian** Monday 12.09.2005

Inside

3   Tony Marchant on TV drama
Birt was wrong about British writers

4   Emily Bell on broadcasting
What's the point of digital switchover

7   Kim Fletcher on the press
Newspapers must embrace the internet

8   Peter Wilby on reports
Where I went wrong at the New Statesman

Jobs index

The story they always feared

Journalists on the Times-Picayune, the New Orleans city newspaper, have defied the destruction to cover the biggest story of their lives. By Duncan Campbell

Celebrating 50 Years of Entertaining

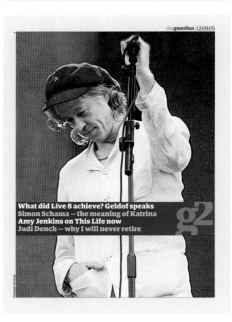

the**guardian** | 12.09.05

What did Live 8 achieve? Geldof speaks
Simon Schama – the meaning of Katrina
Amy Jenkins on This Life now
Judi Dench – why I will never retire

g2

Title **The Guardian redesign**
Client **The Guardian**
Design Group **The Guardian**

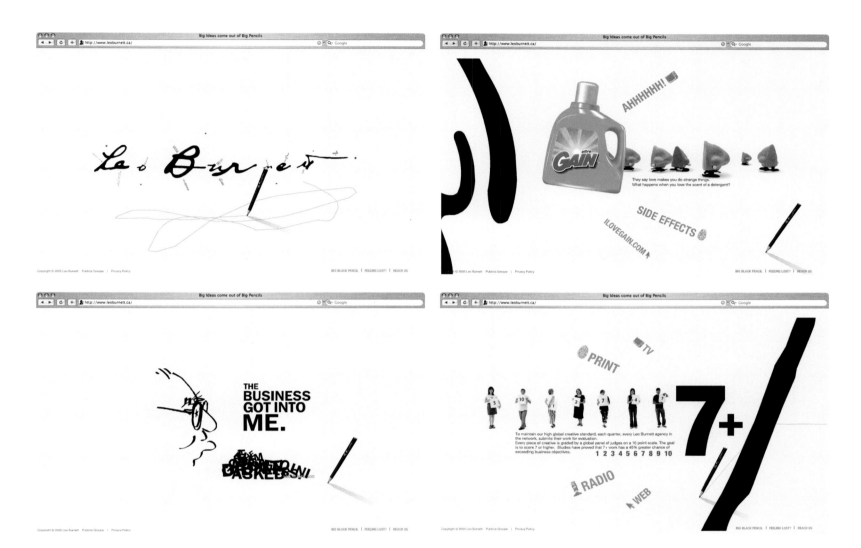

Title Leo Burnett website
Client Leo Burnett Canada
Design Group Leo Burnett & ARC Worldwide Canada

"Our not-for-profit charitable remit
gives D&AD's juries great probity and
independence from the financial imperatives
of so many other awards schemes.

2006
Dave Trott

Born:
Barking, east London

Educated:
1967–70, Art School, New York City

Trained:
1971, Carl Ally, New York City

Work:
1971–80, Boase Massimi Pollitt (BMP)
1980–90, Gold Greenlees Trott
1990–93, Bainsfair Sharkey Trott
1993–2000, Walsh Trott Chick Smith
2000–2009, Chick Smith Trott
2009–date, Chick Smith Trott The Gate

Recognition:
GGT voted Agency of the Year by
Campaign, London, and Most
Creative Agency in the World by
Ad Age, New York. Trott received
D&AD President's Award in 2004.

2006 Annual

Annual Design **Design Project**

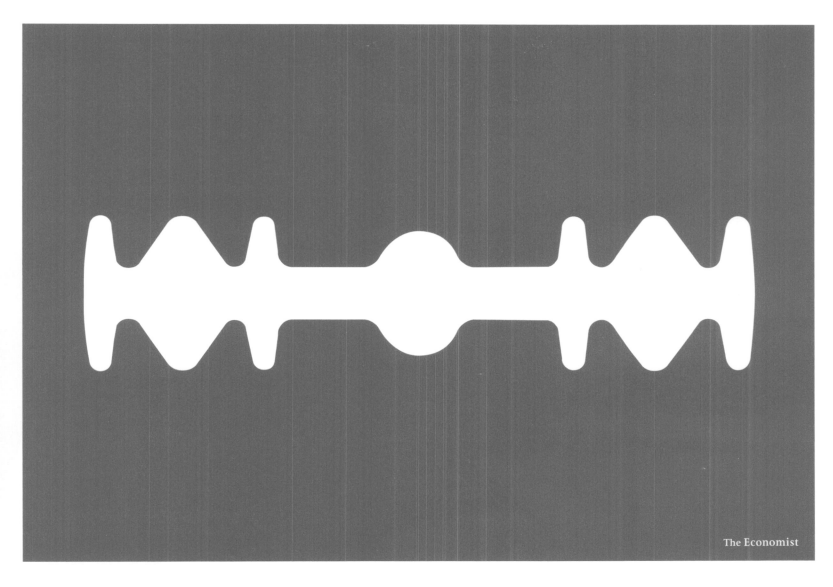

The Economist

Remember the Don McLean song 'American Pie'?

It was about the death of Buddy Holly and the way it affected rock'n'roll.

I feel that way about the D&AD Annual 2006.

It was the year advertising died.

For me, at least.

John Webster (of BMP) died that year.

And for two decades he was half of British advertising.

Collett Dickenson Pearce was the other half. Every year, the D&AD Awards night would be split between John Webster and CDP, both walking up to the podium and carrying back armfuls of Awards.

One man, on his own, doing as much as the entire creative department of the best agency in town.

Usually, John didn't bother going to advertising awards nights.

But he always made an exception in D&AD's case.

Because it was the one he respected.

When I was a young writer at BMP, John told me why he had more time for D&AD.

In the early 60s, it had been set up because writers and art directors wanted their names credited against their work.

And, before D&AD, there wasn't any way for them to get credit.

So, D&AD was established for creatives, by creatives.

That was what made it different.

D&AD wasn't part of the traditional fat-cat advertising establishment.

Title Razor Blade
Client The Economist
Agency Ogilvy & Mather Singapore

John Webster: 1934–2006

Title Stella Artois – Classic Films
Client InBev UK
Agency Lowe London

You could tell because all the other awards looked the same.

Silly, pompous, imitation gold trophies.

D&AD wasn't just another one of those.

D&AD was a pencil stub.

Symbolising the work.

D&AD was the irreverent outsider.

It wasn't just about a piss-up on Awards night, like all the rest.

It was about the work, first, second and third.

Which is why D&AD was the only awards scheme that published a complete Annual of all the work.

That's why, for us, just getting into the D&AD Annual was more important than winning an award at Cannes.

When I was young at BMP, we used to wait for the new D&AD Annual like children waiting for Christmas.

Then we'd pore over every word of every ad.

Then turn to the index at the back, to see who had most numbers after their name.

Those D&AD Annuals were all saved, and gone through time after time.

Year after year.

For me, what made D&AD different to other awards was its motto:

STIMULATION NOT CONGRATULATION.

Like John Webster, D&AD understood it wasn't advertising's job to sell stuff.

It was marketing's job to sell stuff.

Advertising was just the noisy, visible part of marketing.

Other awards, like the Institute of Practitioners in Advertising Awards, are solely about marketing.

They are effectiveness awards, measured by sales.

"D&AD was the irreverent outsider. It wasn't just about a piss-up on Awards night, like all the rest. It was about the work, first, second and third.

But you can't measure creativity.

It is advertising's job to amplify marketing's strategy.

To be provocative, outrageous, stimulating.

To create word of mouth, to "go viral" and generate free media.

That's what D&AD understood.

And that's what John Webster was superb at.

Which is why they fitted so brilliantly together.

Year after year.

One year, BMP won six D&AD Awards.

More than any other agency, including CDP.

I remember that night sitting next to Stanley Pollitt, he was so proud.

Not because we'd won so many Awards.

But because, for once, John Webster had only won half of them.

The entire rest of the creative department, put together, had finally

managed to win as many Awards as John had on his own.

Stanley saw that as a sign of his agency's creative maturity.

When John died, I asked D&AD to change the name of the 30" TV Award to the John Webster Award.

After all, John had virtually made that category his own.

It would be a tribute.

Like retiring a great player's number when they stopped playing.

But the D&AD Executive Committee refused.

They said it might create a precedent. (If we listened to people like that, we wouldn't have Nelson's Column, in case it created a precedent.)

In the D&AD Annual 2006 they gave John's work just a double-page spread at the front of the book.

But what a DPS.

In my humble opinion, John's DPS is better than the rest of the Annual put together.

Not just the 2006 Annual, any Annual.

Title Balls
Client Sony Europe
Agency Fallon London

March

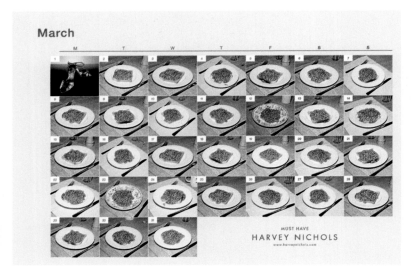

May

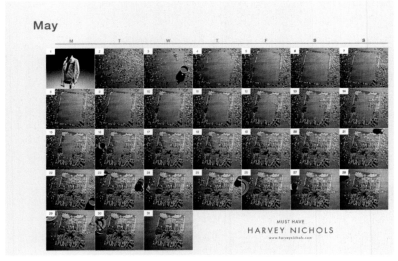

June

April

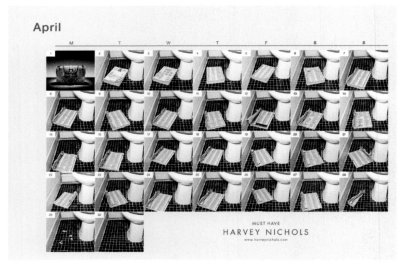

Title Must Have
Client Harvey Nichols
Agency DDB London

"

It is advertising's job
to amplify marketing's
strategy. To be provocative,
outrageous, stimulating.

VW – 'Singin' in the Rain'

The advert opens on the iconic scene from the film 'Singin' in the Rain' as Gene Kelly dances down a rainy city street. As the song builds, his dance routine becomes more energetic and exciting, reflecting the song lyrics: "What a glorious feeling, I'm happy again". The dance routine then moves to another level. Kelly begins to seamlessly incorporate highly impressive and acrobatic steps. At the scene's climax our hero arrives at a new Golf GTI, another updated original.

Campaigns for Smash (the Martians), The Guardian ('Points of View'), Sugar Puffs (the Honey Monster), Sony (John Cleese), John Smith's (Arkwright), Pepsi ('Lipsmackin''), John Smith's (Jack Dee), Hofmeister ('Follow the Bear'), Cresta (the Cresta Bear), Kia-Ora, Courage Best ('Gertcha'), Walkers crisps (Gary Lineker).

John's DPS was better than the entire 500-page Annual that followed.

And 2006 wasn't a bad year.

There was a really nice ad for Sony, coloured balls bouncing down a hill.

There was an ad that John would have loved, 'Singin' in the Rain', for Volkswagen.

There were a couple of terrific Economist posters.

One was just a huge red razor blade.

The other had the headline "Someone mentions Jordan. You think of a Middle Eastern country with a 3.3% growth rate."

There were some very nice press ads for Stella Artois Classic Films.

A combination of lots of different visual clues for you to guess the names of the films.

So there was some very nice work in the D&AD Annual 2006.

Just as there were probably some very nice records made in the year Buddy Holly died. ⬡

Title Singin' in the Rain
Client Volkswagen
Agency DDB London

2007
Tony Davidson

Tony Davidson puts much of his creativity down to his late father, who was an inventor in the "Heath Robinson" mould. He joined Boase Massimi Pollitt as a junior art director in 1985, where he teamed up with Kim Papworth, his long-term creative partner. It was here that he won his first Black Pencil, for Volkswagen.

In 1995 Davidson moved on to Leagas Delaney, where he created the Adidas Euro 96 'Nickname' campaign, before switching to Bartle Bogle Hegarty and finding fame with Levi's 'Flat Eric'.

In 2000, he set about building the then-flagging ship of Wieden+Kennedy London. Today it is one of the most admired agencies in the world, having won plaudits across the globe for its provocative and highly effective work across a broad range of clients and projects, including Nike's 'Run London' event and Honda's 'The Power of Dreams' campaign.

Davidson was President of D&AD in 2007 and was made a Global Partner of Wieden+Kennedy in 2009.

2004 Annual

Annual Design **Fabrica**

Alan Fletcher: 1931–2006

Reflection is a wonderful thing and not something we get time to do enough of in this constantly updating world.

Looking back, I would say that 2007 was a year of big change for D&AD. As a result it was an exciting time to be President, albeit a very time-consuming one. A year in the role is not a long time to make a difference. For this reason I will always be indebted to the previous President, Dick Powell, and to Simon Waterfall, who followed me. Together we made a concerted effort to align our years and set more of a long-term vision for D&AD.

The organisation faced many challenges. It felt like the old establishment was still wary of globalisation and thought that D&AD should remain uniquely British. But it was clear to us that the organisation had gone beyond the tipping point and that to be taken as a serious player it had to push forwards, not look back. There is a diverse wealth of incredible creative talent outside the UK and we need to stand for the very

finest creative excellence globally. I am the first to put my hand up and say this transition isn't easy. There will always be teething problems, but you have to believe that by attracting the very best global talent to judge alongside our best UK talent, D&AD's high standards can be maintained. Great ideas that are well executed are able to transcend cultural and geographical boundaries.

In line with the global theme, I awarded the design of the Annual for the first time to a design group outside the UK. The Fabrica team, led by Renzo Di Renzo and Paolo Palma, delivered the 'Flag Project', which asked fans of D&AD to participate for the first time. The end result was a collection of global images about personal creativity and cultural differences that were used at the beginning of each section of the Annual. It also utilised a new hexagonal D&AD kitemark, a symbol that should be championed more in order to be recognised beyond just our own industry as a mark of creative excellence.

Title Freitag shop, Zurich
Client Freitag
Designers Harald Echsle, Annette Spillmann

Title Nike+
Client Nike
Agency R/GA

"With experiences like Nike+, advertising as a narrative is left behind in favour of a new form of storytelling, in which ideas are presented in an engaging way that is novel and surprising.

The President's Lectures are one of the highlights of the role. Attracting great talent to educate and inspire the next generation is a core part of D&AD's reason to exist. With global being a key theme, I pushed hard to secure major talent from outside as well as inside the UK. Vince Frost, recently emigrated to Australia, started the series that included such luminaries as Wim Crouwel, Lance Wyman, the Global Pentagram Partners, Dan Wieden and David Kennedy. As an added bonus, I also spent an evening with Frank Gehry following a collaboration between the Royal Institute of British Architects and D&AD.

When it came to the Awards, with our first Digital President-Elect waiting in the wings, the traditional model of "paid-for media" and "interruption" continued to be challenged by new models. While you could argue that Pencils were awarded too easily in some of the newer categories – a pattern that runs through D&AD's history and something that settles once initial standards have been set – the year saw excellent digital work come to the fore as the Nike+ website became a worthy recipient of the prestigious Black Pencil. Weave Toshi's beautifully designed 'Daydream' website is also worthy of a mention.

Traditional media felt a little more laboured alongside this, especially Print and Radio, which didn't feel that fresh. While it was arguably not a classic year for Broadcast, there were some notable highlights, like the leftfield US campaign for Skittles that won Yellow Pencils. (Whoever sold that work deserves a Pencil in my mind.)

Environmental Design was one of my favourite categories. Noteworthy mentions go to Freitag's store in Zurich, aptly built of recycled objects just like its signature bags, Virgin Atlantic's Upper Class Clubhouse at London Heathrow and Longchamp's contemporary flagship store in New York, La Maison Unique.

In the Digital Installations category, United Visual Artists came out on top with a piece entitled 'Volume' that consisted of a field of 48 luminous sound-emitting columns that respond to movement. Anyone who visited the piece when it was at the Victoria & Albert Museum will have enjoyed creating their own unique journey in light and sound. It is a great example of technology being used in an emotionally engaging way.

Title Volume
Client Victoria & Albert Museum
Design Group United Visual Artists

Skittles – 'Beard'

An office. A woman is interviewing a man with a long beard. The beard can operate like a trunk.

WOMAN (reading the man's CV): Good. Good. You're in Nansfield?

The man uses his beard to feed himself a Skittle.

MAN: Mm-hmm.

WOMAN: I have a cousin from Nansfield.

MAN: That's nice.

The man eats another Skittle.

WOMAN: Your résumé looks good, but we're looking for someone with more experience.

The man uses his beard to feed the woman a Skittle and strokes the side of her face.

MAN: Experience. (laughs) Ohhh, funny. (throws a Skittle into his mouth)

MVO (macho): Share the rainbow. Taste the rainbow.

> "It felt like the old establishment was still wary of globalisation and thought that D&AD should remain uniquely British.

Gaming saw Yellow Pencils for the Nintendo Wii Sports games. In a move made possible by innovation in controller hardware, Shigeru Miyamoto challenged how we play games by using actions similar to those in live sports, and in doing so changed perception and made gameplay accessible to those who might have been wary of "hardcore" consoles.

When it came to the President's Award, I chose as recipient Sir Tim Berners-Lee, creator of the worldwide web. He has changed our industry and given the world one of the most democratic creative tools.

Sadly, the year saw the passing away of one of D&AD's founders, the hugely talented designer Alan Fletcher. We are all indebted to him, as without his vision this whole organisation may never have happened.

Summing up, I would say 2007 was the year traditional media got a kick up the arse. While engaging work – whatever the format – is still about smart ideas, with experiences like Nike+, advertising as a narrative is left behind in favour of a new form of storytelling in which ideas are presented in an engaging way that is novel and surprising. Staying relevant to consumers who have moved on in their media lives is clearly something that parts of our industry were struggling to embrace, and still are to this day.

The message is loud and clear: change or die, my friends. ●

Title Skittles – Beard
Client Masterfoods
Advertising Agency TBWA/Chiat/Day New York

2008
Simon Waterfall

Photo **Christine Donnier-Valentin**

Creative Director Simon Waterfall was
an engineer first, before going to Brunel
University to study "the big stuff". He
was awarded a scholarship to study
stone carving with a Japanese master in
Germany, and rounded off his education
with a Master's in Industrial Design at the
Royal College of Art. Waterfall has been
a self-starter since the age of 16, when
he started his first company programming
games for Commodore 64s. He went on
to co-found Deepend in 1994 and Poke
in 2000, and more recently set up his
new collaborative venture Fray, which
aims to "defend creativity" above all else.

2008 Annual

Annual Design **Research Studios**

Paul Arden: 1940–2008

As the first D&AD Digital President, I am used to "the new" being held up as the ultimate social currency. But the lustre of the new fades as fast as a haircut in Hoxton, and only the few ever make it to iconic status. These are the ideas that plainly reveal, "This is new to our planet."

In 2008 we had three clear jaw-dropping pieces, and the reason I can write about them now, five years later, is that they are still being talked about, still held up as works of art against anything new launched today.

The first is 'Uniqlock' from Uniqlo. It's hard to remember a time before this piece. It came from nowhere, or rather, it was so surprising and so perfectly formed that it appeared to come from another planet. A planet where people have been dancing, spinning and perfecting abstract time in movement that couldn't exist in any other place than on my screen. I still can't believe how fundamentally different it was to anything else happening in the rest of the industry. God of small details, it's flawless.

The next came to us in a haze of purple. No introduction, no set-up, nothing leaked to the press to spoil the first time you tasted it: Cadbury's 'Gorilla' by Fallon. It was captivating in its art direction, and suspended disbelief in this perfect, powerful animal sitting and sneering at us. But more shocking than the natural talent of this drumming ape was the music choice. The use of Phil Collins was a stroke of genius, and I can't think of another advert since that has matched it musically. The track itself, held in the vaults of the kingdom of guilty pleasures just like the confection it soundtracked, was ravaged and celebrated in a sweet chocolate-y rush of pleasure that left us all asking what had happened to our old Phil Collins LPs.

And then there was the seismic shift that destroyed markets, changed an industry and brought the world that much closer together: the iPhone was launched. I need a certain pause here, because phones up to this point had been placed solely in one category: Communications. You made calls on them; sent a few messages. It was in

> " And then there was the seismic shift that destroyed markets, changed an industry and brought the world that much closer together: the iPhone was launched.

your pocket but not even close to being in your life. Brands and manufacturers thought they knew you, and knew what you wanted. So confident were they in their assumptions that they gave you everything they thought you needed already locked into the phone. Not only is that a risky strategy, but had they actually got everything completely right, rather freaky. The iPhone smashed all of this. It combined Apple's iPod and elements of its laptop for the first time in a believable device. You remember the first time you used it – the moment when listening to all of your voice messages suddenly became unnecessary, when email genuinely became mobile, when a product truly converged its content with you and your life.

The final part of my year held joy and sadness in equal measure, with the disappearance of one legend and the celebration of another. We lost Paul Arden that year. I only knew him through his work, which included the now strangely illicit Silk Cut campaign and the magical InterCity advert he made with director Tony Kaye. Roger Kennedy's foreword to the Annual summed up what I had long suspected was deep in many creative people's subconscious: "My working with Paul was probably quite typical – a rollercoaster ride swinging wildly between profound admiration and dark thoughts of homicide. To be complacent was the reddest rag ever shown to a bull." Never was there a more fitting epitaph for a man of such energy, proving, like many

Title **Uniqlock**
Client **Uniqlo**
Agency **Paragraph**

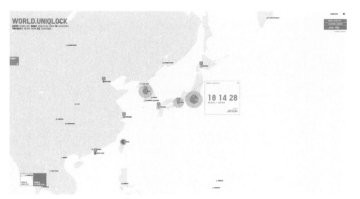

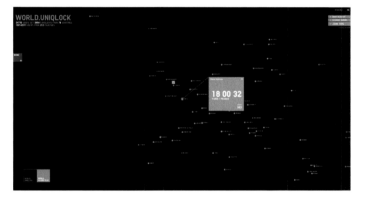

" No introduction, no set-up, nothing leaked to the press to spoil the first time you tasted it: Cadbury's 'Gorilla' by Fallon... Phil Collins was a stroke of genius; I can't think of another advert since that has matched it musically.

Title Dairy Milk – Gorilla
Client Cadbury
Agency Fallon London

people on this small island, that you can get away with being eccentric only if you are truly exceptional.

Immense personal joy and enormous gratitude completed the year when living legend Neville Brody agreed to design and direct the 2008 D&AD Annual. Having been at the head of the collision of graphic design and the digital landscape, he was the perfect ambassador, along with his fantastic crew at the Research Studios, to examine how the industry was coming to terms with its changing structure. Running through the whole book were larger-than-life URLs leading straight to the work in its natural environment and, through the movement of the pages, a question that I struggle with today: digital versus anti-digital. We used to be driven forward because technology enabled us to do new things. As the industry grew up and the truth of what we were talking about became more important than the medium, our focus turned into: should we drive this message, and what authenticity can we put behind our intention? Surely, the recipe for future icons. ⬡

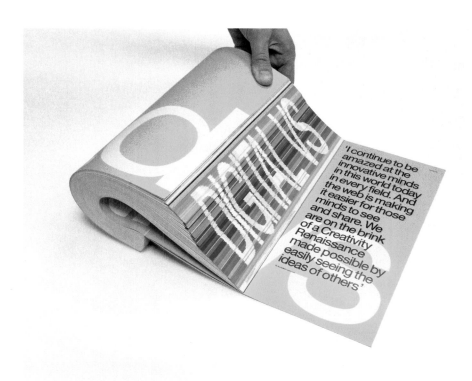

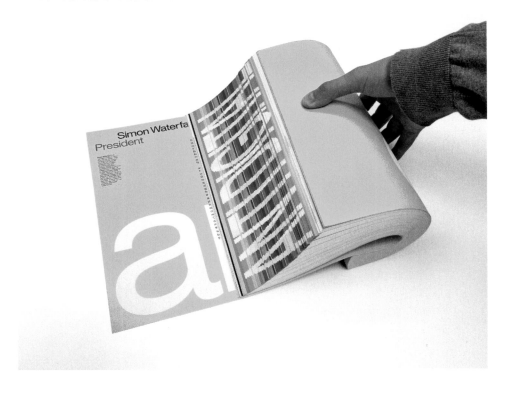

Title **D&AD Annual 2008**
Client **D&AD**
Design Group **Research Studios**

2009
Garrick Hamm

Garrick joined Michael Peters & Partners after graduating from Somerset College of Art in 1989. Four years later he joined Tutssels Lambie-Nairn, where he worked across a variety of different design disciplines and fell in love with moving image. He joined London-based brand design consultancy Williams & Murray in 1999 and is now Creative Partner at Williams Murray Hamm. Garrick was D&AD President in 2009 and is a Fellow of the Royal Society of Arts. An avid filmmaker, his most recent short, 'The Man Who Married Himself', won Best Comedy Award at the Los Angeles International Short Film Festival 2010.

2009 Annual

Art Direction Peter Saville
Design Luke Sanders

Title Million
Client New York City Department of Education
Advertising Agency Droga5
Digital Agency POKE New York

It was the year that Barack Obama took office in the White House and won the Nobel Peace Prize. We lost Patrick Swayze and Michael Jackson and the downturn in the world economy continued to put fear into the hearts and minds of clients everywhere. At D&AD HQ we were concerned that creativity might suffer. Fortunately, we were in for a few surprises.

The breadth of creative work awarded in 2009 was pretty exceptional. Although we were in the midst of a very challenging time, the industry proved it was capable of not only surviving these challenges, but surmounting them. Each of the four winners demonstrated the power and all-encompassing nature of creativity – in education, in politics, even down to the loose change in our pockets. The winners were more than just great pieces of communication; they touched our lives and changed our behaviour.

Four Black Pencils were awarded across multiple categories. Droga5 set a new standard by winning two Black Pencils for separate entries: 'Million', the mobile-technology-driven solution that tackled the problem of student apathy in New York, and 'The Great Schlep', which mobilised young Jewish voters to engage with their grandparents in Florida. Graphic designer Matt Dent became the youngest Black Pencil winner with his redesign of the reverse side of UK coins, and ART+COM was awarded for its kinetic sculpture installed in the BMW Museum.

“
Great creatives share a spark of something: nerve, ambition, a point to prove.

Title Bigger Storage Ideas
Client IKEA Germany
Agency Ogilvy Frankfurt

"
We lost Patrick Swayze and Michael Jackson
and the downturn in the world economy
continued to put fear into the hearts and
minds of clients everywhere.

The D&AD Awards ceremony was held "in the round" at Camden's legendary Roundhouse, and was hosted by Richard E Grant. It was a memorable evening – presenting in this style in front of around 900 people is not for the faint of heart.

My single-minded proposition during the four years I spent as D&AD Education Chairman was, without doubt, education. It was a no-brainer, then, that education provided the central theme for the Annual of my tenure, with a focus on all the great things D&AD does to develop new talent and bring fresh thinking to the industry.

For the 2009 Annual, design master Peter Saville took on the brief of demonstrating how D&AD uses your money for its education programme. We decided that Saville would use this opportunity to mentor graduate designer Luke Sanders, ensuring that the process itself was educational. The end result – a stunning series of graphic statistics – was a lesson in design for us all.

During the evening of the ceremony, I continued my crusade for education by mounting 'Everyone Starts Somewhere', an exhibition demonstrating that not all successful creatives are born "geniuses". On paper it sounded good. Everyone I had asked insisted that they had loads of "rubbish" early work. When I began to collect these early examples, however, I found that none of these modest creatives had sent through any truly bad work – probably because they had never produced any. What the collection does illustrate is that great creatives share a spark of something: nerve, ambition, a point to prove. That little bit of something special. I hope that it encourages people to nurture their own spark, the one that makes them unique, and to never, never give up.

More4 – 'Stanley Kubrick Season'

The campaign was designed to promote a season of Stanley Kubrick films and a bespoke Channel 4 documentary about Kubrick on More4. It was important to us that the technique of shooting was faithful to Kubrick's – there could be no post-production work, special effects or invisible edits. It needed to be shot entirely in camera with a Steadicam, a technique Kubrick pioneered in 'The Shining'. Kubrick possessed a fearsome presence on set, and an obsessive-compulsive attention to detail. The objective of the trail was to convey those idiosyncrasies, while at the same time revering his genius.

Camera takes Stanley Kubrick's journey through various sets all in one take.

WOMAN: Your script, Mr Kubrick.

Kubrick emerges and places a tricycle in the corridor (from 'The Shining'), not forgetting a final polish.

MVO: See the world through the eyes of a master. The Stanley Kubrick Season begins Tuesday at ten on More4.

Title More4 – Stanley Kubrick season
Client Channel 4
Agency 4Creative

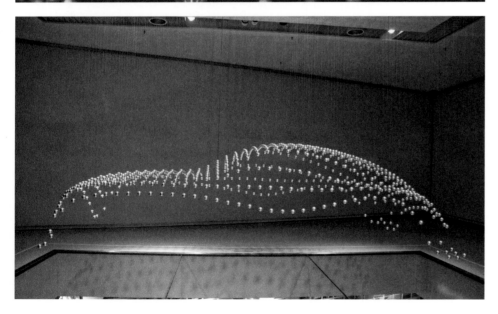

"Although we were in the midst of a very challenging time, the industry proved it was capable of not only surviving these challenges, but surmounting them.

Title Kinetic Sculpture for BMW Design
Client BMW
Design Group ART+COM

Title The Great Schlep
Client Jewish Council for Education and Research
Agency Droga5

The President's Lectures presented an incredibly diverse collection of speakers: firstly, Kyle Cooper, creator of some of the tidiest film title sequences ever made, including those of 'Se7en' and 'Gattaca'. As part of the Liverpool Design Symposium, we presented Matt Pyke (Universal Everything); back in London, another speaker was Michael Peters, founder of Identica, who has bridged the two disciplines of design and business so effortlessly for more than 35 years.

One of the main cries I heard during this time was that D&AD had lost the younger generation of creatives due to its lack of digital presence and poor daily interaction. There was no denying it was still the benchmark of awards, but as an inspiring tool, it was losing out to Ffffound and online creative Flickr books. To catch up, we introduced a new website with a blog and back copies of the Annual. 2009 was also the year in which we welcomed Dick Powell as the new Chairman of D&AD, taking over from the wonderful Anthony Simonds-Gooding after a marvellous innings of 17 years.

On reflection, not having a CEO made my Presidency fairly hard going at times, but it is one of the proudest things I've achieved, and I hold my Annual very dear to my heart. ⬢

2010
Paul Brazier

Paul Brazier started his career in advertising with four years at Cogents before moving to WCRS to work on BMW and Carling Black Label. Then, in 1991, he was lured by David Abbott to join Abbott Mead Vickers.

Over the years he has won countless awards, including a dozen One Shows and the top prize at Cannes, but is particularly proud of his six D&AD Pencils.

However, Brazier considers becoming Executive Creative Director of AMV BBDO and being President of D&AD in 2010 the highlights of his career.

2010 Annual

Art Direction and Original Artwork Bob and Roberta Smith
Design Keith Sargent

Title High Line
Client Friends of the High Line
Urban Design James Corner Field Operations

It's nice to look back at my Presidential year in relative calm. At the time, it felt full-on. Fitting this task into the day job, or fitting the day job into the task, was a challenge.

It's funny looking back at the judging itself. At the time it felt as if I was in a fast-paced documentary, bombarded with flash cuts and whip pans where there should have been an edit.

Somehow, though, I remember it in a totally different light – more like a 35mm film with slow tracking shots and high production values, ruthlessly edited for the best highlights.

It was an honour to choose Spike Jonze for my President's Award. And it was even more special when he showed up in person on Awards night to pick it up. I loved collaborating with Bob and Roberta Smith on the Book. I admire the skill and patience it took to create something so playful and spontaneous-looking.

There were disruptions, even eruptions. The Icelandic volcano Mount Whatamouthful decided to cause chaos with the travel plans of our international jurors, as it left ash floating across flight paths everywhere. But the show, as they say, must go on.

One judge, Mori Harano, took a flight from Japan to Lyon, got in a taxi and drove through the night, caught a ferry at Calais, got to see the white cliffs of Dover for the first time and managed to arrive at the judging by the skin of his teeth.

Title **Treehouse**
Client **Yellow Pages**
Agency **Colenso BBDO**

"

The work filled the immense space. It felt like the warehouse scene in 'Raiders of the Lost Ark'. Row after row of possibilities... and somewhere in there, the Ark.

My trip was simpler – all the way from Islington in a black cab.

The first day's judging began at Olympia on a clear April morning. I admit I had a sense of pride in being the D&AD President, but I still wasn't prepared for the sight that hit me early that morning.

The Grand Hall was empty of people, but full of entries. The work, regimentally ordered, easily filled the immense space. It felt like the warehouse scene in 'Raiders of the Lost Ark'. Row after row of possibilities... and somewhere in there, the Ark. (As it turned out, there was more than one Ark; we handed out five Black Pencils.)

I remember wondering how many millions must have been spent on the business hours that had produced all this work. And, of course, these entries only represented a tiny fraction of the creative work done around the world over the course of the year. Billions must be spent on the craft of creativity.

One of my most vivid memories was seeing how the graphic designers were getting on. I paused at a simple trestle table, full of work. It was another fine April day and the sun shone through the 85 tons of solar reflective glass, softly touching the layer of varnish that had been applied to a beautifully crafted typographic poster. I was lost in wonderment and respect for the craftspeople behind the work. I was practically stroking them. (The posters, not the craftspeople.) Then Michael Johnson patted me on the back and said: "That's the rejected table, mate." I couldn't believe it. The standard is so impossibly high.

If there was plenty of light in the main hall, there was very little in the rooms where Digital and TV Crafts were judged. They spent four days in the dark, but there were glimmers of light from the work.

The online idea of remaking the moon landing in real time was an adventurous and innovative way to mark the 40th anniversary of the landing for the John F Kennedy Presidential Library and Museum. The 3D animation alongside some spectacular imagery made the experience even more realistic.

Title We Choose the Moon
Client John F Kennedy Presidential Library and Museum
Agency The Martin Agency

Title Closet
Client Canal+
Agency BETC Euro RSCG

Title Thomas Meyerhoffer surfboards
Client Global Surf Industries

" The D&AD machine moved on through the week, one piece after the other, revealing the very best of the work – like a sculptor chipping away at a marble stone until finally a masterpiece is revealed.

Title Trillion Dollar Campaign
Client The Zimbabwean
Advertising Agency TBWA\Hunt\Lascaris Johannesburg

The D&AD machine moved on through the week, one piece after the other, revealing the very best of the work – like a sculptor chipping away at a marble stone until finally a masterpiece is revealed.

I would have to pick out The Zimbabwean newspaper's 'Trillion Dollar Campaign'. In fact, I hired the team responsible: Nicholas Hulley and Nadja Lossgott. Their brilliant idea was to print messages on trillion-dollar notes, to raise awareness of the now unaffordable newspaper. These notes achieved huge coverage overnight.

The much talked about and awarded Yellow Pages 'Treehouse' was created by some friends of mine in New Zealand (no, I wasn't allowed to vote). It really did demonstrate that with the aid of Yellow Pages, anyone can get any job done. Three months and 65 listed companies later, the treehouse restaurant was complete – a unique structure.

The 'Closet' TV ad for Canal+ was beautifully told, and an inventive, humorous way of portraying a strong message.

Finally, New York's High Line – one and a half miles of urban beauty, located in the streets of western Manhattan. The park, built on an abandoned elevated railroad, is an extraordinary structure, open to the public and offering breathtaking views of the buzzing city and its uneven skyline. It is a classic case of turning a negative into a positive.

I also remember, at the end of the week, watching D&AD staff unwrap a beautiful set of surfboards by Thomas Meyerhoffer. I'm by no means an expert, but these sleek and slender sculptures stood out and made me want to take up surfing. Industrial design experts were soon gathering, and eventually awarded the surfboards a Pencil.

So much quality and diversity. It was like being a kid in a sweet shop. I could have eaten it all.

20,000 pieces of work judged.
552 made it into the Book.
133 of these were Pencil-nominated.
37 Yellow Pencils.
Five Black Pencils. ●

2011
Simon Sankarayya

Sanky is a founding partner of interactive agency AllofUs.

He studied information design at Nottingham, then joined Digit at its inception as an art director. He has spoken at Design Indaba, IdN conferences in Sydney and Singapore, Flashforward, The Typographic Circle and Designyatra in Goa.

He also teaches at the London College of Communication, Hyper Island in Sweden and Space Invaders in Copenhagen.

2011 Annual

Design Pentagram London

Five key moments from 2011:

1. Wieden+Kennedy Portland for Old Spice – 'The Man Your Man Could Smell Like'

This was an example of using social content to amplify different people's interest in the brand in appropriate ways. There are three points to make here – it was brave, experimental and traditional in its use of great writing and casting. Part of its charm comes from Isaiah Mustafa, who is about to burst into laughter and lose it completely. This was all intelligently kept in the edit… real "realness" for once. The last ad Old Spice put out was a kind of self-referential 'Seinfeld'-esque quip at the whole process.

Title Old Spice – The Man Your Man Could Smell Like
Client Proctor & Gamble
Agency Wieden+Kennedy Portland

2. FedEx posters

When walking around judging at Olympia, you find a lot of dark nooks and crannies hiding people who are rigorously looking over the work, so sometimes you have no real idea what's going to surface from the entries. I love it when you can see the idea from way across the room and it keeps getting better as you draw closer. This was a truly wonderful idea for FedEx, which had no language barrier – it didn't even need words. A perfectly delivered idea (no pun intended).

Title **FedEx**
Client **FedEx**
Agency **DDB Brasil**

"

Taking Alan Fletcher's work and attempting to not only remain true to it but to extend its value is not a task that every designer would relish.

3. Troika for the Victoria & Albert Museum – 'Palindrome'

Taking Alan Fletcher's work and attempting to not only remain true to it but extend its value is not a task that every designer would relish. Thankfully, Troika managed to take a cultural icon, the V&A Museum logo, and reappropriate it into a new form of which Alan would be proud. It's a captivating piece of work that amplifies the beauty of what Alan did all those years ago. Wonderful.

Title Palindrome
Client Victoria & Albert Museum
Design Group Troika

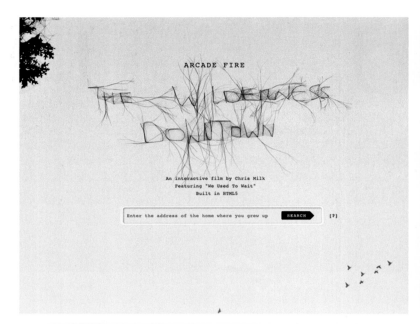

Title The Wilderness Downtown
Client Arcade Fire
Agency B-Reel

4. Arcade Fire's 'The Wilderness Downtown' and Sour's 'Mirror'

The music industry has always been the perfect platform on which to challenge formats – there have been lots of great examples in the past (the Pet Shop Boys' 'Integral', for example) that illustrate ways in which technology can personalise fans' experience of music. 'Mirror' and 'The Wilderness Downtown' are charming, surprising and lo-fi – dialogues, not broadcasts. Yes, both films are maybe a bit of a geek-out, but they are celebrations of types of play that are sensitive to their audience. Without projects like these, we would keep living in a predictable future.

"Chris Doyle's 'Guidelines' is a witty, tongue-in-cheek look at what he thinks we shouldn't be doing to promote ourselves – while promoting himself.

Title Guidelines
Clients & Designers Christopher Doyle, Elliott Scott

5. Chris Doyle – 'Guidelines'

The world is full to the brim of self-initiated nonsense. Our drive to create the things we don't get a chance to do in our working lives sometimes seems worrying, but Mr Doyle's work is curiously different in a way that's hard to pinpoint (usually the sign of greatness). After the overnight success of his identity guidelines for himself in 2008, his follow-up in 2009 was a witty, tongue-in-cheek look at what he thinks we shouldn't be doing to promote ourselves – while promoting himself. The charm and knowing irony makes this one keepworthy, and after meeting Chris it became clear that 'Guidelines' is a refreshingly real extension of who he is and the talent he possesses. ●

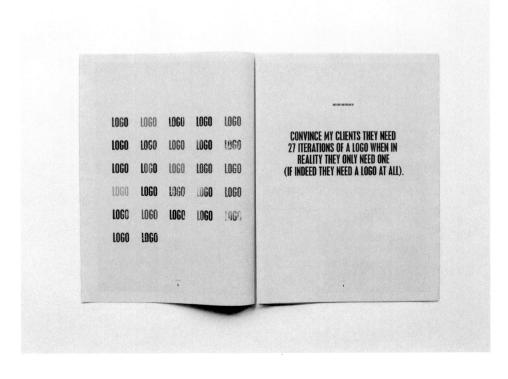

2012
Rosie Arnold

Rosie started moonlighting at a tiny
creative hotshop called Bartle Bogle
Hegarty (BBH) in 1983 while studying at
Central Saint Martins. She has been there
ever since. She has been responsible for
some of the agency's most iconic work:
Pretty Polly, Levi's, The Independent, Tag,
Robinson's, Axe (Lynx) and Yeo Valley.

Her work has amassed many awards,
including six Cannes Gold Lions, six D&AD
Pencils and three Campaign Golds.

In September 2007 Rosie took a three-
month sabbatical and went back to art
school at the Royal College of Art to
pursue a personal project.

On her return to BBH, she was one of
the three Creative Directors appointed to
the UK management board, and in 2008
was appointed Deputy Executive Creative
Director. She is, sadly, one of just a few
women running creative departments in
advertising agencies in the UK. She is
President of D&AD in 2012.

2012 Annual

Design johnson banks

Title **Heaven & Hell**
Client **Samsonite**
Agency **JWT**

I first came into contact with D&AD at Central Saint Martins College of Art and Design, when my then boyfriend (now husband) suggested I looked at "the Book" to learn about advertising. I opened the pages and instantly fell in love.

The Annual was bursting with the most inspiring, beautifully crafted work I'd seen – and not just in advertising. I loved that Typography, Illustration and Film Crafts rubbed shoulders with each other. I have always been passionate about visual communication, so I thought I'd died and gone to heaven. I wanted desperately to get my work in the Annual or even win a Pencil, which at the time seemed way out of my reach. If someone had told me then that one day I would be President, but more than that, President in D&AD's 50th year, I would have died from pride.

Before I took on the role, I asked former Presidents what I should expect – so

I had a pretty good idea of how much work and (gulp) public speaking I would be letting myself in for. What I hadn't realised was what extraordinary people work at D&AD.

Passionate, committed individuals who know their stuff. The sad thing was that they were all stuck in a dreary office in the back end of Vauxhall with not even a local coffee shop to lift their spirits. Sanky (Simon Sankarayya), the President before me, had started the process, but it is with great pride I can say that a team including CEO Tim Lindsay and COO Dara Lynch moved heaven and earth to bring about a much-needed office relocation, which finally happened at the very, very end of 2011. So, I am the proud President of a fabulous office in Shoreditch with everyone on one floor, with groovy Plumen lightbulbs and decent coffee a stone's throw away. It is the perfect start for D&AD's next 50 years.

Title Johnnie Walker 1910 Commemorative Edition bottles
Client Diageo
Agency LOVE

> **It is my belief that the answers to the world's problems lie in creative solutions.**

Reflecting on the changes that have taken place over the last 50 years led to a revolutionary idea: to introduce a new Pencil. A White Pencil. This will be awarded to a piece of creative thinking – non-discipline-specific – that changes the world for the better. To kick off the Award, we felt we needed to choose a cause that had universal relevance, and that organisation is Peace One Day. It was set up in 2001 by an inspirational individual, Jeremy Gilley, who has made it his life's work to bring about a day of peace, when humanitarian aid can help people affected by conflict – whether war or gang violence or simply bullying. It is my belief that the answers to the world's problems

lie in creative solutions, and it is my fervent hope that we will be stunned by the innovation of thinking, and that the White Pencil will continue to inspire and help different organisations and causes every year.

Another major innovation this year has been the restructuring of D&AD to introduce a Foundation. This is distinct from the general day-to-day running of the organisation, which can now be more focused on commercial issues. It will enable us to fundraise directly into the Foundation with numerous benefits. It is an incredibly important development because it means real clarity of intent,

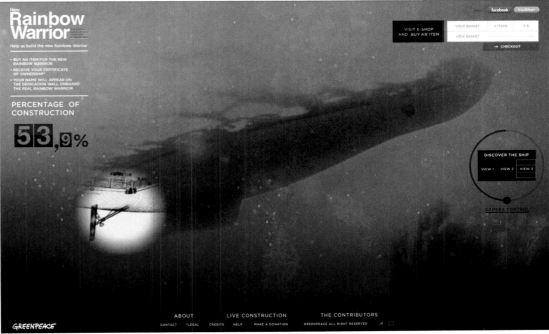

Title A New Warrior
Client Greenpeace
Agency DDB Paris

Military Base of FUDRA (Fast Deployment Force). La Macarena, Meta.
Main Location for the Operation Christmas.

Jungles of Colombia.
Soldiers decorating a 25ft. tree with Christmas lights.

All the Team.
Soldiers, Producers and Agency staff.

> "To kick off the White Pencil Award, we felt we needed to choose a cause that had universal relevance, and that organisation is Peace One Day. It was set up in 2001 by an inspirational individual, Jeremy Gilley, who has made it his life's work to bring about a day of peace, when humanitarian aid can help people affected by conflict.

Title Operation Christmas
Client Ministry of Defence; Colombia
Agency Lowe/SSP3

and of course now, if you fancy leaving a bequest to D&AD, you can do so with real confidence that it is all going towards education.

I write this at the close of the Black Pencil judging for 2012, so it is difficult to have a clear perspective on the work, but my initial observation is that a D&AD Award remains as tough to win as ever. The Awarded work this year is truly global, with pieces from Colombia, China and Malaysia, as well as the many other countries we have seen appearing in previous years. My overwhelming feeling is that the industry and clients have adopted a more socially responsible and sustainable approach to the world, and to work.

It seems that all the new technology and communication channels are being used for good. This gladdens my heart. The work for Colombia to convince guerrillas to lay down their weapons, or for Greenpeace to buy a new Rainbow Warrior boat bit by bit, are beautifully crafted, extraordinary ideas that make real differences.

D&AD has always cultivated and promoted excellence in design and advertising, and our organisation continues to be an important force in attracting real talent into the industry and setting the benchmark of what constitutes an outstanding piece of work. It seems, going into the future, that not only is D&AD stronger than ever, but it is setting new standards of behavioural excellence too.

Title Rivers of Light
Client Ministry of Defence; Colombia
Agency Lowe/SSP3

344

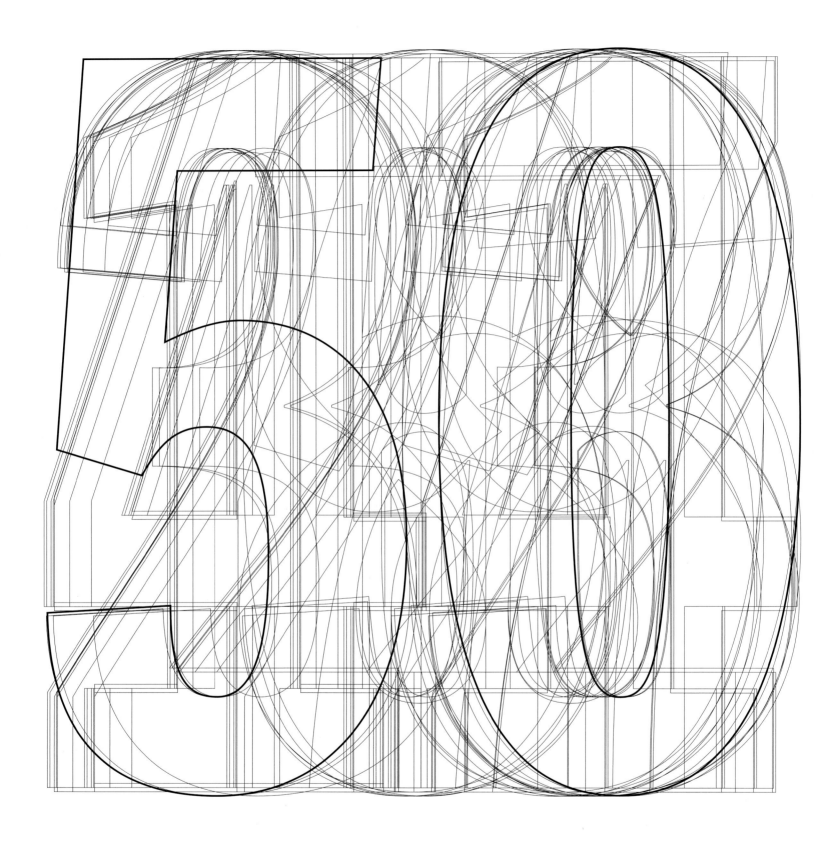

> "Moving image, coding and processing, writing, sound design, layout, typography, architecture, physical design, music, interactivity... All of these things are interconnected now – you cannot separate any of them out.

The Next 50 Years?

Neville Brody

D&AD President 2013

The 50th anniversary of D&AD arrives at a critical moment, as the next generation confronts a number of political, social and economic challenges. So, what should the organisation's response be? Internationally renowned designer Neville Brody, the first President of the next half-century, tells editor Rod Stanley why a commitment to creative education must be a priority, and that excellence is not enough in itself. "Design and art direction are no longer protected from their context," Brody says. "If they are not aware of their political consequences, then there is no future for them."

Rod Stanley As a designer, your work has focused on the future. Sometimes, though, is it important to look back?

Neville Brody D&AD is now at a juncture where it can celebrate its past – its 50 years give it authority, and it has been authenticated through that history. It's been a big part of the boom period in British communications.

—

RS It covers a period from one revolution up to another – from the changes of the 60s to the digital revolution of today.

NB This book celebrates that period, although certain times are not as well represented. With a lot of the work that was happening in the 80s, 90s and even the late 70s, it was more the small agencies doing the exciting stuff, but of course they didn't have the budgets or interest in entering the Awards, so are not reflected directly in this history.

—

RS Do you feel that the D&AD history of British design does not tell the full story?

NB Yes, but how does one address that? Going forward is the most important thing for me. When they asked me to put my name forward for the Executive Committee, I said I would do it if we could work towards a remit that said: 'D&AD exists to celebrate excellence and to help make money to put into education.' Two years later, this has been agreed as a core remit, which is extraordinary!

—

RS D&AD has previously stated its commitment to education, though?

NB Yes, but there's been a need for a strong framework, particularly for assessing the criteria: What should we do? Why should we do it? Could it be done better? I'm not criticising – we have done some really amazing things in education, from New Blood to the university network to the Student Awards.

RS But do you think this now needs to go further?

NB I think it is about the clarity of intent. I've been Chairman of the educational sub-committee, and we came up with the phrase: 'With a Pencil Comes Responsibility.' We are floating ideas like: if you win a Pencil, should you do educational community service? Should a Black Pencil be 12 hours and a Yellow Pencil eight? It's just a reminder that it's really important to nurture the next generation. It's critical – without excellence in creative education, we couldn't award such high standards.

—

RS How will the D&AD Foundation make a difference in this respect?

NB D&AD is launching this Foundation to directly raise money through endowments and the profits from D&AD to pay for student grants and bursaries, a fantastic thing to achieve! It clarifies D&AD's commitment to education, and represents the biggest step for D&AD for years and years.

—

RS This 50th anniversary provides a convenient narrative point – do you see it as a chance to not just celebrate what has been achieved, but reinvigorate?

NB I think the most important thing for an association to remain relevant is for it to be socially conscious. D&AD has always had the ability to do that in some form. Look at when Rosie Arnold brought in the White Pencil (awarded to a creative idea that changes the world for the better). It was already a real statement of intent about where D&AD should be relevant.

It's never been hugely political in the past, but design, advertising and particularly education have become highly politicised. What does it mean if you're coming out of an underprivileged area and you're denied the opportunity to go into creative education – why should it be based on your financial background, when it's to do with creativity? It makes no sense – it should be a meritocracy, not a moneytocracy.

–

RS These changing times are perhaps felt most acutely by young people at the moment – how should D&AD respond?

NB It's easy to object and oppose, but not so easy to propose an alternative. You can say that this is wrong, this government is making the wrong decisions, and that it's not protecting the very future it's going to have to rely on. It's destroying the creative infrastructure in a country where the creative economy is generally understood to be around six to eight per cent of GDP.

–

RS Which is about the same size as financial services, which the government protects and champions. Why do you think the creative industries have not achieved a similar kind of status in this country?

NB It's based on a lack of proper consultation. They make decisions ideologically without doing the proper background research. What happens if we stop supporting creative education? Where's the knock-on effect on the economy? Where's the knock-on effect on our culture? And how much is that culture worth in terms of tourism?

–

RS There are these social, political and economic challenges that face the next generation, but do you agree that it's also a tremendously exciting time, in terms of opportunity and change?

NB D&AD within its remit has managed to develop a groundbreaking response by developing the Foundation, and I think it is a model that needs to be taken up by other organisations as well, especially within the creative industries. Studios and agencies need designers and creative directors and photographers and writers. No matter what opportunities are coming up, if you are not educating people into that space then you have no industry. I'm saying this to tie into your second point.

I want within a few years for us to be supporting hundreds of students a year. And if that's replicated by other organisations, then I think we will have an alternative education base free of government decisions. But the revolutionary side of it all is coming from other areas – let's start with the apparent expansion of opportunity, but the actual reduction of creative risk. That's what I call 25 years of 'success culture' – part of the legacy of the 80s is that everything is measurable in numbers. The whole economy is set up so that ideas are not deemed relevant unless they support success culture. If an idea is judged uncommercial, it no longer gets developed and real innovation is stifled.

Let me talk about the other side of it. There are so many graduates from creative universities that were being supported by a growing industry, but are now likely to leave college and not get a job. What do they do? Either they become more polished, more professional...

–

RS And more employable?

NB Yes, but that doesn't seem to be happening. What is happening instead is that people are saying, 'Well, I probably won't get a job, so fuck it – I'm going to take a risk with my work.' There's this bubbling up of risk-taking and fearlessness. I'm hoping support will come for the idea that failure is relevant.

I think the British core industry has always been invention and innovation. What we've never been very good at is trading that. We have exceptions, the Paul Smiths and Dysons... but we are fundamentally crap at selling ideas. Jony Ive is at Apple, not a UK company.

> "Design and art direction are no longer protected from their context. If they are not aware of their political consequences, then there is no future for them.

RS Are you suggesting that we are at our best creatively when our backs are against the wall – when we are forced to innovate to survive?

NB Well, punk didn't happen anywhere else, really.

–

RS So, do you think there's any parallel between that time of punk, when you were starting out, and today?

NB If you look at it romantically, yes.

–

RS And practically?

NB Practically, times have changed. The way that social networks operate is radically different to the way street culture worked in the 70s and 80s. Then, it was possible to have a culture that could nurture itself underground before exploding onto the streets, and that is what happened with punk. It was a cult; in the 70s, culture and especially youth culture was far more tribal. Now, that tribal thing has largely gone online.

–

RS It's atomised into a thousand micro-tribes. It's become this omnipresent pick'n'mix hipster culture, where each person can take a bit of what they fancy.

NB Yes, so there's very little cultural commitment, if you like... Don't get me wrong – I am actually really optimistic.

–

RS What gives you particular cause for optimism at the moment?

NB I think Britain still produces the most amazing minds, and those minds are starting to understand that design isn't a small, comfortable luxury. Everything is about design – you might design policy, that's just as valid. You might design social spaces, behaviour, or a tip of a pen, or an RFID chip that sits in your clothes and logs its history.

There has been a real shift in the purpose, definition and relevance of design. In the 80s, design became the support mechanism for industry. It was part of a big sales boom, and a lot of people started to reject that and develop their own 'design land'. You had Zwemmer, the design bookstore in Charing Cross Road, which obviously led to Magma – and much as I love Magma, there is a bit of a Magmatisation in which designers design for designers' sake.

–

RS Do you worry that it has become a bit fetishistic?

NB Yes, which is fine – you can publish a book and sell to other designers, that's sort of okay, but that then puts you in a craft space. Meanwhile, I think design is becoming part of a post-disciplinary area. Moving image, coding and processing, writing, sound design, layout, typography, architecture, physical design, music, interactivity... All of these things are interconnected now – you cannot separate any of them out. You might have a specialist in one area in terms of skills, but they will work in the other areas with all the other skilled individuals. You have to become what I call horizontally active or horizontally aware... vertically specialised but horizontally active.

–

RS You can see the results of that already in DIY culture, in which young artists and technologists are coming together to make really interesting things. There is an electronic music duo who are working with a programmer to create an audiovisual environment with console-standard graphics; a playable first-person game in which a track becomes, say, a radioactive swamp you can explore. These experiences have been designed together. It's partly the accessibility to that technology, but also the thinking: 'I am not just a musician – I am going to create an entire world to experience.' In terms of ambition, it's pretty incredible.

NB That's what I call the post-discipline era! It's extraordinary. At the Royal College of Art (RCA), part of the vision that I encourage is mixed studios. It's a Bauhaus model – in the middle, you have this 'making space', and then there's this 'tracking space' around the edge, so everyone is making together. So, we have illustrators sitting next to programmers sitting next to visual designers, sitting next to moving image, animation, information designers, sound designers, and they are cross-fertilising. They are collaborating on projects, and that for me is the future.

And the question then is: if that's the future of the next 50 years, how does D&AD respond? What will happen is that digital will simultaneously have its areas within the existing broad churches. We should celebrate this now and promote it heavily; get behind it as D&AD, and see the opportunities for it to become fresher and more exciting. Or maybe digital will integrate design and art direction into itself. Print might as well be vase-making or crochet – in a few years time, print will be a luxury.

When I came to the RCA, all that some students wanted to do was produce a single book – not a book in many editions, just one! Handbound... a precious thing that would only ever exist alone. On one level, it was a cry for intimacy and tactility in this depersonalised social-industrial network. We are now heavily involved in what I think is the fourth revolutionary space, which is the Digital Public Space. It's an extraordinary thing: 'All knowledge ever recorded by mankind will be available to anyone, anywhere, any time and on any platform.'

—

RS What are the implications of that?

NB I've been calling it '4A' – Anyone, Anytime, Anywhere, Anything. That will be the reality, and that will be a revolution as important to our knowledge space as the Gutenberg printing press. In terms of its effect on society, our industrial models, our work, how we interact, how we behave, how we understand our existence – all of that will change radically. It's the BBC, BFI, British Museum, Tate, National Archives and then the universities. All these knowledge pools will be digitised using the same compression and storage algorithms, so they are interchangeable, and use the same taxonomy – the tagging system – throughout everything.

Once you've got that, you have this extraordinarily amazing cross-searchable, cross-referenceable space. And then what you have to develop is the engines that help you navigate that. In the long term, imagine the ability for this information to self-cluster like cells in the body. A cell only knows what it should be by understanding what the cell next to it is. So, that signal says, 'I'm going to be a cell in the nail,' or whatever. Because the cells contain the same DNA – they decide what they are going to be simply by proximity, in the same way the brain clusters and grows areas of knowledge. Now, if you imagine that applied to this Digital Public Space, it's self-regulating, self-clustering...

—

RS Perhaps we are at the beginning of this journey, but when you think about it, and the kind of work you've been doing on it, what do you think is possible?

NB I cannot believe we are here at this point in human history! I can't even imagine what our response should be at this point. How absolutely amazing that we are there! It will revolutionise everything. The Gutenberg printing press changed governments, changed social classes, changed religion. I'm obsessed with what the consequences of all this will be...

And what happens when the centre of gravity of the economy moves permanently east and south; at least

> "The Digital Public Space will be a revolution as important to our knowledge space as the Gutenberg printing press... I cannot believe we are here at this point in human history!

within our lifetime, where is the response? Do we become a cultural space, and celebrate that? It's all of this, and I'm not sure what all this is doing within the D&AD 50-year book. But it's about contextualisation. What will the D&AD response be?

—

RS I think these are fundamental questions to think about. Why is it important, why is it relevant? Because it's not just 50 years of celebrating making things look good, or selling things. Isn't there a more fundamental role that has importance to the way we lived, and the way we will live in the future?

NB D&AD must become more political and start lobbying. I think that for 50 years it's been possible for it to live in a hermetically sealed balloon. And it's great – it has celebrated excellence and some of the most amazing pieces of work, and is part of our legacy as a nation. It now shifts – that's the point. This 50-year anniversary has come right in the middle of a huge juncture of change, and D&AD now needs to ask itself questions about what its function should be. Instead of being a channel for celebration, should it shift to being a much more supportive, empowering and enabling association? My feeling is that yes, it should. As a community, it should also be a forum for asking some of those critical questions.

Design and art direction are no longer protected from their context. If they are not aware of their political consequences, then there is no future for them. You'll find art directors have never been more political than they are now, maybe not since the 60s when D&AD was first formed. It's interesting that they have put me in as President for the 51st year.

As I said, knowledge is revolution. Nothing is invisible, and the students we have now are so informed, much more than we were. You can find stuff out, and so they do. We had passion and a desire for change, but that's now been matched by this knowledge. It's all very exciting.

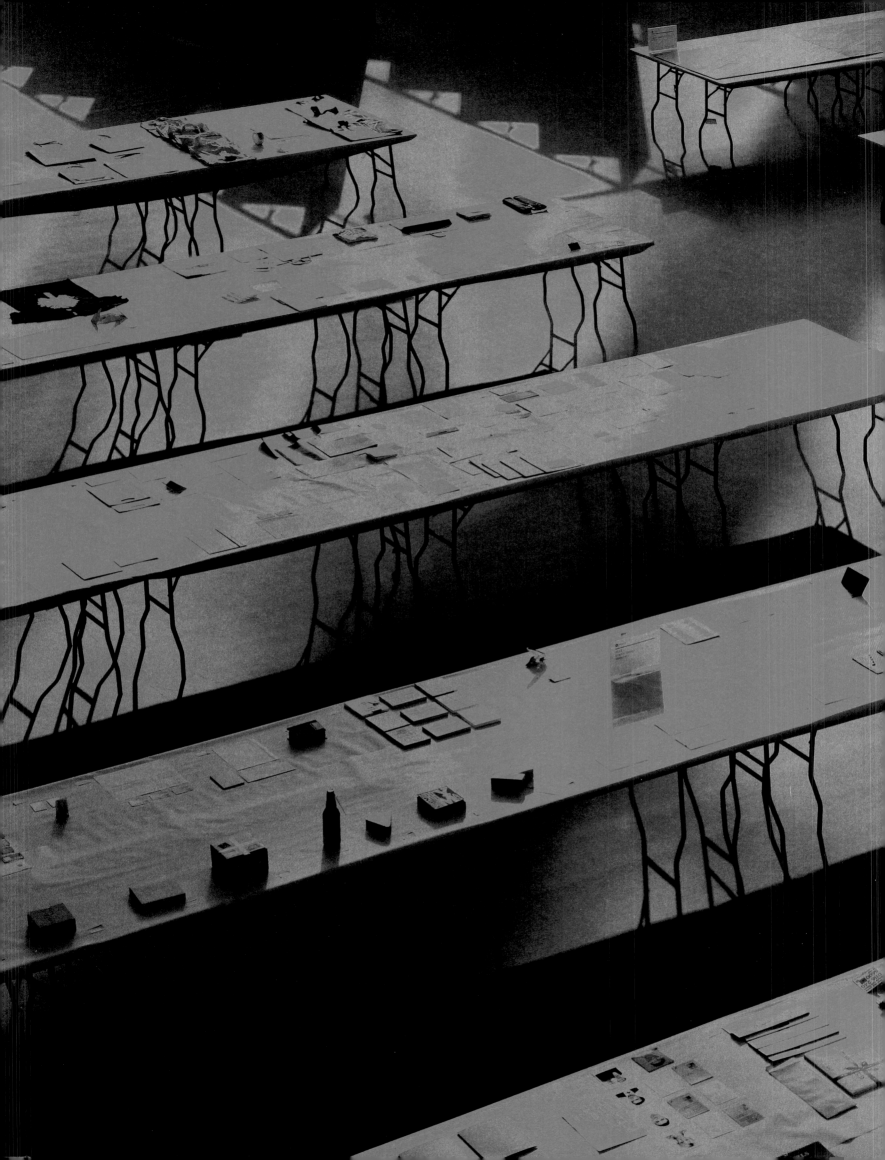

Acknowledgements

Awards Director
Holly Hall

Editorial Manager
Jana Labaki

Editorial Assistants
Charlie Dickinson
Zosia Gibbs
Xanthia Hallissey
Edmund Mills

Special Thanks

D&AD would like to extend its gratitude to all the past Presidents and contributors who made this book possible; to the History of Advertising Trust for generously providing images from their archive; and to Sarah Copplestone for her invaluable input.

–

D&AD50

Editor
Rod Stanley

Assistant Editor
Sarah Fakray

Sub-Editor
Rory Lewarne

–

TASCHEN

Editor in Charge
Julius Wiedemann

Editorial Coordination
Daniel Siciliano Bretas

Editorial Assistant
Nora Dohrmann

German Translation
Jürgen Dubau

French Translation
Aurélie Daniel

Lithography Manager
Tina Ciborowius

–

planning unit

Design by PlanningUnit.co.uk
Jeff Knowles, Nick Hard

Planning Unit Re:Est 2011

Planning Unit was launched in 2011, and is a reincarnation of co-founder Nick Hard's grandfather's design studio of the same name. They are proud and delighted that some of the original studio's work, for the furniture company Meredew, has been selected by Derek Birdsall from the 1965 D&AD Annual for inclusion in his chapter.

–

From page 55

Title Bo Peep
Client D Meredew, Bo Peep
Agency Planning Unit

TASCHEN

50...